CLIMBEC.

195 World Bank Discussion Papers

Towards A Sustainable Urban Environment

The Rio de Janeiro Study

edited by
Alcira Kreimer
Thereza Lobo
Braz Menezes
Mohan Munasinghe
Ronald Parker

The World Bank
Washington, D.C.

one of more than 2,000,000
information products
available from

microinfo ltd
publisher and distributor
of specialist information

Microinfo Ltd
P.O. Box 3
Omega Park
Alton
Hampshire
GU34 2PG
England
Tel: 0420 86848 Fax: 0420 89889
Telex: 858431 MINFO G

Copyright © 1993
The International Bank for Reconstruction
and Development/THE WORLD BANK
1818 H Street, N.W.
Washington, D.C. 20433, U.S.A.

All rights reserved
Manufactured in the United States of America
First printing March 1993

Discussion Papers present results of country analysis or research that is circulated to encourage discussion and comment within the development community. To present these results with the least possible delay, the typescript of this paper has not been prepared in accordance with the procedures appropriate to formal printed texts, and the World Bank accepts no responsibility for errors.

The findings, interpretations, and conclusions expressed in this paper are entirely those of the author(s) and should not be attributed in any manner to the World Bank, to its affiliated organizations, or to members of its Board of Executive Directors or the countries they represent. The World Bank does not guarantee the accuracy of the data included in this publication and accepts no responsibility whatsoever for any consequence of their use. Any maps that accompany the text have been prepared solely for the convenience of readers; the designations and presentation of material in them do not imply the expression of any opinion whatsoever on the part of the World Bank, its affiliates, or its Board or member countries concerning the legal status of any country, territory, city, or area or of the authorities thereof or concerning the delimitation of its boundaries or its national affiliation.

The material in this publication is copyrighted. Requests for permission to reproduce portions of it should be sent to the Office of the Publisher at the address shown in the copyright notice above. The World Bank encourages dissemination of its work and will normally give permission promptly and, when the reproduction is for noncommercial purposes, without asking a fee. Permission to copy portions for classroom use is granted through the Copyright Clearance Center, 27 Congress Street, Salem, Massachusetts 01970, U.S.A.

The complete backlist of publications from the World Bank is shown in the annual *Index of Publications,* which contains an alphabetical title list (with full ordering information) and indexes of subjects, authors, and countries and regions. The latest edition is available free of charge from the Distribution Unit, Office of the Publisher, Department F, The World Bank, 1818 H Street, N.W., Washington, D.C. 20433, U.S.A., or from Publications, The World Bank, 66, avenue d'Iéna, 75116 Paris, France.

ISSN: 0259-210X

Alcira Kreimer is senior environmental specialist in, and Mohan Munasinghe is division chief of, the Policy and Research Division of the World Bank's Environment Department. Braz Menezes is principal urban planner for Brazil, Peru, and Venezuela, in the Infrastructure Sector Operations Division of the Bank's Latin America and the Caribbean Regional Office. Thereza Lobo and Ronald Parker are consultants in the Policy and Research Division of the Environment Department.

Library of Congress Cataloging-in-Publication Data

Towards a sustainable urban environment : the Rio de Janeiro study /
    edited by Alcira Kreimer ... [et al.].
        p.   cm. — (World Bank discussion papers, ISSN 0259-210X ;
195)
        Papers presented at a seminar organized by the Brazilian Institute
for Metropolitan Administration, Rio de Janeiro, Nov. 16-17, 1992.
        Includes bibliographical references.
        ISBN 0-8213-2388-1
        1. Urban ecology—Brazil—Rio de Janeiro—Congresses.
    2. Environmental policy—Brazil—Rio de Janeiro—Congresses.
    3. Sustainable development—Brazil—Rio de Janeiro—Congresses.
    I. Kreimer, Alcira.   II. Series.
    HT243.B62R568   1993
    307.76'0981'53—dc20

93-6969
CIP

LIVERPOOL INSTITUTE
OF HIGHER EDUCATION

Order No. ￡13.72
L3118/143288

Accession
171392

Class No.
0914.202/CRE

Contro
ISBN.

Catal.
LJ194

Contents

Boxes

This work was conducted in collaboration with the United Nations Development Programme and the United Nations Centre for Human Settlements under Project INT-90-701. It also received support from the Norwegian Environmental Fund and Pan American Health Organization.

Foreword

This case study is intended to provide an overview of the main linkages between sustainable development, environmental degradation and disaster vulnerability. This case study follows after the Rio meeting as a contribution to improve the welfare and environmental conditions in developing countries. It is the Bank's hope to build on this analysis to promote better coordination among all the parties working on these topics to arrive at shared policy recommendations aimed at overcoming key constraints governing the management of a sustainable development. An additional purpose of this research effort has been to contribute to the dialogue on the environmentally sustainable development for the world's major metropolitan areas.

Uncontrolled population growth, chronic poverty and environmental degradation have increased urban vulnerability to what are often called "natural" and "technological" disasters. The cumulative impact of day-to-day environmental deterioration in large cities amount to severe extreme events. Both the impacts and responses to all types of disaster are growing more similar and inter-related. At least partly as a result of severe environmental degradation, the natural/technological distinction is beginning to blur. The uncertainty about global warming underscores the relationship between the environment and disaster. A flood caused by rising sea levels swelled by a melting of the poles would be both a natural and a technological disaster. The disaster in Chernobyl that seriously disrupted the economic development process and caused unparalleled social upheaval, was clearly a technological disaster, but dealing with its impact on crops, agricultural soil, and livestock is an environmental problem. Every disaster, no matter what the cause, has an environmental impact.

The study of Rio de Janeiro is part of an effort being conducted in collaboration with the United Nations Development Programme (UNDP) and the United Nations Centre for Human Settlements (Habitat) in metropolitan areas in three countries: Brazil, Turkey, and the Philippines. The main objectives of the Rio de Janeiro case study are (a) to improve understanding of environmental degradation in the metropolitan area of Rio de Janeiro, (b) devise appropriate guidelines and strategies to reduce environmental degradation and disaster vulnerability, (c) develop city-specific policy instruments for environmental degradation and disaster prevention and mitigation, and (d) prepare dissemination materials for applying environmental protection in metropolitan areas.

To further the aims of this case study, the Brazilian Institute for Metropolitan Administration (IBAM) organized a seminar held November 16-17, 1992, on the case study of Rio de Janeiro. The seminar provided a productive forum for discussing contributions to the study, reaching consensus on the main environmental issues, defining priorities for further study and for action, and examining follow-up activities needed to complete the case study.

This World Bank Discussion Paper is being published with the following aims: to improve understanding of the issue of sustainable development in the context of the urban environment in Rio, to disseminate the results of the rapid diagnostic explored in the case study, to help researchers of urban environmental issues in Brazil consolidate their work, to improve the mechanisms for transferring the findings from research into urban environmental management, and to define better ways of disseminating research results. This work is expected to contribute to the environmentally sustainable development of cities in developing countries.

Mohamed T. El-Ashry
Director
Environment Department

Contributors, Discussants, and Registered Participants

[Agriculture Secretariat] Secretaria de Estado da Agricultura e Abastecimento
    Luiz Rogerio M. Gonçalves
CEF [Federal Development Bank] Caixa Economica Federal
    Marcio Miller Santos (speaker)
COPPE/UFRJ [Coordination of Programs in Post-Graduate Engineering] Coordenação de
    Programas de Pos-graduação em Engenharia; [Federal University of Rio de Janeiro]
    Universidade Federal do Rio de Janeiro
    Claudio Dreitas Neves, Adjunct Professor
    Aquilino Senra Martinez (speaker)
CPRM [Mineral Research Company] Companhia de Pesquisas de Recursos Minerais
    Jane Codedilla
Consultores Nucleares Associados
    Ronald Araujo da Silva (discussant)
DCBS [Biological Sciences Department] Departamento de Ciencias Biologicas e da Saude
    Coordenação de Meio Ambiente
    Jose Ricardo de Morais Lopes
[Executive Group for the De-Pollution of Guanabara Bay] Grupo Executivo de
    Despoluição da Baia de Guanabara
    Amarilio Pereira de Souza
    Marcia Marques Gomes
    Mihai Constantin Cauli
    Carolina P. D. Bolubeux
    Monica P. C. Serraz
FBCN [Brazilian Foundation for the Conservation of Nature] Fundação Brasileira para a
    Conservação da Natureza
    Jairo Costa, President
    Leila Lavinia
    Alfredo Brito (speaker)
    Pedro Braile
    Patricia Amazonas
FEEMA [State Foundation for the Environment] Fundação Estadual de Engenharia do
    Meio Ambiente
    Vitoria Valle Braile
    Elizabeth do Nascimento Brito (discussant)
FIPERJ [Fishing Institute, State of Rio de Janeiro] Fundação Instituto de Pesca do
    Estado do Rio de Janeiro
    Marcia Bezerra, Director
GEROE [Executive Group for the Recovery and Special Works] Grupo Executivo para a
    Recuperação e Obras Especiais
    Victor Novicki
    Maria Augusta Bittencourt

GERSA [Division of Sanitation and Urban Development] Gerencia de Saneamento e
    Desenvolvimento Urbano
    Azer Cortines Peixoto Filho, Manager
    Marcio Seroa de Araujo Coriolano (speaker)
IBAMA [Brazilian Institute for the Environment] Instituto Brasileiro do Meio Ambiente e
    Recursos Naturais e Renovaveis
    Vicente M. Conti
IEF [State Institute and Foundation for Forests] Fundação Instituto Estadual de Florestas
    Axel Schmidt Grael, President
INEP [Study and Project Financing] Financiadora de Estudos e Projetos
IPEA [Institute for Applied Economic Research] Instituto de Pesquisa Economica
Aplicada
    Renato Villela (discussant)
[Ministry of Regional Integration] Ministerio da Integração Regional
    Rosana Bazzo
Municipality of Rio de Janeiro
    Fernando Walcacer (discussant)
NDES [Social and Economic Development Bank] Banco Nacional de Desenvolvimento
    Economico e Social
    Jose Roberto Afonso (speaker)
OPAS [Pan American Health Organization] Organização Pan-americana da Saude
    Luis Jorge Perez (speaker)
[Office of the Municipal Budget] Coordenatoria de Captação de Recursos Externos da
    Subchefia de Orcamento do Gabinete do Prefeito
    Antonio Jofre Z. de Andrade, Coordinator
PNUD [United Nations Development Programme] Programa das Nacoes Unidas para o
    Desenvolvimento
    Flora Cerqueira
PUC/RJ [Catholic University] Pontificia Universidade Catolica
    Luiz Roberto A. Cunha (speaker)
PRO-VITA
    Augusto Sergio Pinto Guimarães, Director (discussant)
[Public Works Secretariat] Secretaria Municipal de Obras e Serviços Publicos
    Luiz Paulo Correa da Rocha, Secretary
Representatives of IBAM
    Lino Ferreira Netto
    Mara D. Biasi Ferrari Pinto (speaker)
    Alexandre Santos
    Carlos Alberto Trindade (discussant)
    Helia Nacif Xavier (speaker)
    Maria Lais Pereira da Silva (discussant)
    Marlene Fernandes (discussant)
    Tereza Cristina Baratta
    Victor Zular Zveibil
    Romay Conde Garcia

Representatives of the World Bank
  Alcira Kreimer
  Braz Menezes
  Ronald Parker
  Martha Preece
  Thereza Lobo
SEAIN [International Secretariat, Planning] Secretaria de Assuntos Internacionais da
    Secretaria de Planejamento
  Carlos Eduardo Lampert Costa, Chief, Coordination and Planning
  Regina Gourgel de Saboya (discussant)
SEMAM [Secretariat of State for the Environment and Special Projects] Secretaria de
    Estado de Meio Ambiente e Projetos Especiais
  Roberto Ferrareto D'Avila, Secretary of State
SERLA [State Secretary for Rivers and Lakes] Superintendencia Estadual de Rios e
    Lagoas
  Paulo Canedo Megalhães, Vice President
  Jerson Kelman, Director of Studies and Projects
SIMBIO [Biological and Environmental Monitoring] Sistemas para Monitoramento
    Biologico e Ambiental Ltda.
  Sandra Harris, Director
  Patricia Mousinho Paredes, Director
SMDS [Municipal Secretariat of Social Development] Secretaria Municipal de
    Desenvolvimento Social
  Bruno Fernandes
[Sciences Academy] Academia Brasileira de Ciencias
  Paulo de Gões Filho (speaker)
Secretaria Nacional de Politicas de Saneamento; [Ministry of Welfare] Ministerio de Bem-
    estar Social
  Tobias Jerozolimski
[State Secretariat for Agriculture] Secretaria de Estado da Agricultura e Abastecimento
  Maria Alice Maximo, Technical Specialist
UFF [Federal Fluminense University] Universidade Federal Fluminense
  Marlice Nazareth S. de Azevedo
  Hildete Pereira de Melo (discussant)
UFRJ [Federal University of Rio de Janeiro] Universidade Federal do Rio de Janeiro
  Mauro Sergio Fernandes Argento (speaker)
UFRJ [Federal University of Rio de Janeiro] Universidade Federal do Rio de Janeiro
  Luiz Edmundo H. B. Costa Leite (consultant
  Dalia Maimon (speaker)
  Luiz Henrique Aguiar de Azevedo (discussant)

Editors' Note

The purpose of this volume is to report findings from meetings held November 16-17, 1992, at the Brazilian Institute for Municipal Administration to explore mechanisms that are needed to attain an environmentally sustainable development in Rio de Janeiro.

On July 1992, immediately after UNCED, the Environmental Policy and Research Division, Environment Department, in collaboration with the Infrastructure Division of the Latin America and the Caribbean Country Department I of the World Bank launched a study on environmental management and urban vulnerability in Rio de Janeiro. The study's objectives were to (a) improve understanding of the relationship between socioeconomic and physical activities, environmental degradation and vulnerability in large cities; (b) devise appropriate strategies to reduce environmental degradation; (c) provide central and local governments with background to assess environmental degradation and disaster risk in large cities; (d) promote the exchange of experience to foster actions that can be replicated in other cities and countries that face similar vulnerability problems; (e) help identify appropriate incentives for public participation including private enterprises, nongovernmental organizations (NGOs) and community organizations; and (f) provide the basis for developing policy guidelines for Bank member countries concerning strategic and economic investments for managing the environment and increasing resilience in metropolitan areas.

During the launching of the study in July, consultations were held between the coordinators of the study and agencies at the Federal, State and Municipal level, involved in Rio's development to seek their input, concurrence and suggestions on the study. There was consensus among the agencies met that Rio provides an excellent situation to analyze vulnerability in a metropolitan area with a significant potential for developing strategies and replicating findings in other areas. Of special interest to the agencies consulted in Rio and Brasilia was the fact that the study of Rio is part of an effort that includes also the analysis of cases in Turkey and the Philippines.

As a further step into this effort, on November 16-17, 1992, the World Bank sponsored a conference in Rio de Janeiro to discuss findings from the study and to promote the exchange of experiences and ideas regarding the environmental sustainability of Rio de Janeiro. The conference was organized by the Brazilian Institute for Municipal Administration (IBAM).

The study was part of an effort currently being conducted by the World Bank, Habitat, and the United Nations Development Programme (UNDP) on "Disaster Prevention and Mitigation in Metropolitan Areas," INT/90/701. It also received support from the Norwegian Environmental Fund and the Pan American Health Organization.

The conference at IBAM was attended by about 60 people from a variety of organizations and government dependencies, including federal, state, and municipal agencies, NGOs, and universities. The papers gathered in this volume represent the concerns expressed at the conference and some of the lessons shared there about how to improve our management of environmental degradation in urban areas.

The following fundamental issues were highlighted at the seminar:

• The importance of understanding Rio de Janeiro's natural attractiveness as a public good, and to develop policies to preserve its sustainability. The concept of Rio as a public good induces two types of behaviors on those who consume it (a) incentives to behave as "free riders", and (b) a tendency to overutilize the public good.

• The need to contemplate future development in Rio within an integrated coastal management framework. Although there is legislation addressing coastal zone management at the national level, an efficient management system of Rio as a coastal city is not in place. The establishment of such a system will require further efforts at the macro and micro levels.

• The importance of considering urban development from a perspective integrating diverse technologies, that is, from a pluralistic technological view. This notion entails the simultaneous development and application (e.g., transport, communications, recycling, infrastructure) of cutting edge technologies as well as low-cost technologies.

• The importance of strengthening local institutions which are fragile, particularly those institutions in the public sector that deal with urban environmental issues. Several speakers noted that institutional capacity to analyze, develop and implement policies to mitigate the continued deterioration of the urban environment and its surrounding ecosystem is limited.

• The need to deal with the inadequate transparency of public expenditures for environmental activities. Authors and discussants noted that for some Rio institutions determining what has actually been spent on environmental measures is problematic.

• The importance of broadening the current emphasis in public expenditure programs on curative approaches. The programmatic structure of federal and state expenditures on the environment, particularly in health and sanitation, reveals a lack of attention to preventative mechanisms.

• The importance of supporting community participation and dialogue in establishing investment priorities. It was noted that currently nongovernmental groups are divided into two broad sets which represent a dichotomy based on each group's access to resources and funding: on the one hand there are those groups defined at the meeting as NGOs with capital letters, and on the other there are those that were described as "ngo's." Participants emphasized the need to redress this situation, through improving the access to resources by all NGOs.

• The need to deal with the intellectual vacuum resulting from a shortage of funds for research and a lack of specific studies aimed at strengthening urban environmental management policies. Of particular concern were (a) the lack of strategies and action-oriented knowledge in the state and municipal governments and (b) the lack of institutionalized knowledge-sharing mechanisms among the members of the research community.

At the opening of the November 1992 Rio conference, Roberto D'Avila, the State Secretary of the Environment, represented Governor Brizola and pointed out that 1992 was an important year, not only for UNCED, but also because of this World Bank Conference. He stressed that important environmental improvements are being carried out by the state and municipal governments with the World Bank's and with the Inter-American Development Bank's (IDB's) assistance. According to the Secretary, the environment is no longer considered a frivolous subject, and sustainability is now clearly recognized as pivotal to the survival of the human species.

The representative of the mayor, Fernando Walcacer, highlighted the institutional effort that is being made by the Municipality, both through the creation of the Secretariat of Environment and the formation of a special *Procuradoria*. Walcacer emphasized the fact that local governments are now much more important because of their Constitutional role. Rio's situation is improving due to the new possibilities created by new responsibilities.

For IBAM's superintendent, Lino Ferreira Netto, the conference theme was especially relevant because environmental degradation is a problem in all major cities. He noted that urban expansion has led to environmental problems over an extensive urban geography, and that reversing this trend will eliminate important constraints to a sustainable urban development in Brazil.

The organization of this volume

The editors begin this volume with a summary paper that discusses the vulnerability of Rio de Janeiro to environmental degradation and explores several historical antecedents. The papers which have been contributed to this volume have been grouped around seven main topics: conceptual issues, institutional issues, financial issues, operational experience and technological issues, and training, and the view from the NGOs.

The chapter in the first section of this book provides a background to the physical characteristics of the city and examines the historical framework for the centralized urban development pattern, both in the country and in the State of Rio de Janeiro. The chapter discusses the impact of human interventions on environmental issues, the severity of environmental threats, including land, deforestation, beach erosion, water and sanitation systems, sewage and industrial pollution, air quality issues, and the impact of the environment on the fishing industry. The evolution of environmental policies through the regulatory system and legislation is explored. The chapter summarizes recommendations and policy options discussed at the conference, including Rio's comparative advantage, the use of incentives to reduce negative externalities, environmentally-friendly investments, coastal zone management, land management instruments, institutional and technical capacity building, and future research needs.

Chapters in the second section of the book explore the conceptual framework within which to analyze the case of Rio. A provocative idea raised in the chapter by Jose Marcio Camargo is that although the Rio region has very few natural and manmade resources in the conventional sense, it has overwhelming natural beauty. This attractiveness has an important economic value, and its intelligent exploitation could contribute to jump-starting the local economy. According to Camargo, the aesthetic attributes of Rio, which tend to be dismissed as trivial by most policymakers, are in fact among the unique factors which differentiate the city from any number of other large urban areas in the country and in the world. Camargo argues that the attributes of Rio as a public good induce two sorts of behaviors on those who consume it: (a) incentives to behave as "free riders" and (b) a tendency to overutilize the public good. Overutilization, in turn, generates externalities, the costs of which are borne by all users and the general public. Treating Rio as a public good would entail a drastic change in the city's development strategies, including the development of policies to limit the overutilization of public spaces, the implementation of especially targeted fiscal policies, a modification of current infrastructure priorities and public sector investments, the provision of incentives to attract qualified labor, the adoption of technological innovations (water, sanitation, recycling, energy use) that help a sustainable development, and the promotion of Rio's comparative advantage to attract productive activities that are nonpolluting, intensive in their use of technology and to utilize qualified labor (e.g., informatics, electronics, telecommunications, biotechnology, services to support external trade and commerce, specialized insurance industries, etc.). In the same section, the urban environmental problems in Rio are discussed by Mauro Sergio F. Argento within a coastal zone management framework. Argento underlines the holistic view needed in coastal zone management in order to take into account the needs of cities and the requirements of the environment.

Chapters in the third section of the book explore the institutional framework of environmental policy in Brazil and the financing of public expenditures on the environment. Paulo de Gões Filho describes the history of the Brazilian system efforts to monitor the environment, including its three milestones: the creation of the Special Environmental Secretariat, the National Environmental System, and the Brazilian Institute of the Environment and Renewable Resources. He discusses the need to unify and to make compatible the decision-making levels and instruments required for formulating a strategy for urban development with a view toward environmental sustainability. Braz Menezes provides a snapshot of the evolution and subsequent deterioration of the institutional framework for urban policy in Brazil, and highlights the state of confusion that now exists, along with the extremely high costs on the national economy that such a situation must represent. Jose Roberto Afonso discusses the patterns of public finance, with a special emphasis on their relationship to the environment, including health and sanitation. He emphasizes the unreliability of public accounts in Brazil. Mara D. Biasi Ferrari Pinto identifies the need for strengthening municipal administrations, and describes training programs implemented by IBAM between 1977 and 1991. Luis Jorge Perez argues for improved health and sanitation programs, with an emphasis on health prevention. Marcio Seroa de Araujo Coriolano discusses research topics concerning the urban environment in Rio. He identifies the chronology of research, outlines the organization of research institutions and topics, and identifies the critical issues that hamper progress in research, particularly the insufficient interchange of experiences, sparse sources of regular financing, and the inadequate integration between research centers and their main users—government agencies and organized communities. Pedro Braile examines the contributions to the environment from NGOs, and he establishes a contrast between the approaches of NGOs and of traditional political organizations to environmental sustainability.

Operational experience and technological issues are the theme of the fourth section of this book. Improvements on a sustainable basis can only be done within the context of a broader political, socioeconomic, and institutional framework. The chapter by Luiz Robert Cunha and Marcio Miller Santos describes the arrival of the World Bank in Rio de Janeiro in 1988 after an absence of nearly 20 years, discusses the Bank's catalytic role in initiating activities and actions on a broad front of urban environmental concerns, and makes some recommendations for such operations in the future. The chapter by Braz Menezes and Thereza Lobo was written soon *after* the conference to fill in the gap in the institutional memory from a different perspective. The authors reflect on the "doing by learning" experience, some tangible results under the project to date, and the broadening of the relationship between the municipality of Rio and the Bank, leading up to the negotiation of follow-up projects by both the Bank (rehabilitation and transfer of the Brazilian Urban Train System (CBTU-RJ)), and by the Inter-American Development Bank (IDB) (depollution of the Bay of Guanabara). The chapter by Dalia Maimon and Claudison Rodriguez argues in favor of technological pluralism aimed at eco-development and stresses that appropriate technologies need not be confused with low-cost implementation technologies. Aquilino Senra Martinez provides an overview of potential accidents in industrial installations, and discusses the use of probability analyses in risk assessment.

Throughout the book, contributions by Helia Nacif Xavier analyze different efforts being undertaken in Rio, including the Megacities Project, the Basic Sanitation Program for Guanabara Bay, Training Programs for Developing Human Resources in the Field of the Environment, and the Transfer of the Urban Train Program from the federal government to the state and municipality.

Acknowledgments

The Brazilian Institute of Municipal Administration (IBAM) did an exceptional job putting together the Rio seminar. We would like to recognize the unstinting efforts of Mara D. Biasi Ferrari Pinto in all the organizational aspects. Session coordinators Tereza Cristina Baratta, Alexandre Santos, and Victor Zular did a wonderful job identifying key issues, developing areas of agreement and highlighting the participants' conclusions and recommendations. The thoughtful contributions of the discussants were also much appreciated. IBAM will be publishing the conference proceedings in Portuguese in the near future.

We are grateful to the authors of the papers in this volume not only for preparing the papers but for submitting to the whittling and other editorial changes needed to convert conference papers written originally in Portuguese for an audience highly familiar with the local situation into a book that would be useful for English-speaking readers who could not attend the conference and who may never have been to Brazil. We have endeavored in all our editorial efforts to ensure that this publication remains a coherent reflection of the main conference themes.

We gratefully acknowledge institutional support provided by Claude de Ville, and the Pan American Health Organization, noting particularly the participation of the PAHO regional coordinator Dr. Luis Jorge Perez and consultant Paulo Cesar Pinto in the study commencement mission. We would like to express our appreciation for the contributions to the study of Ignacio Armillas, Habitat; Flora Cerqueira, UNDP, Brasilia; and Frank Harvelt, UNDP, New York. The following Brazilian institutions provided guidance, information, and logistical support during the formative stages of the project: Acompanhamento Projectos Prefeitura, Agricultura, CEDAE, CEHAB, COMLURB, DEAIN, Civil Defense, Drenages/Prefeitura, CPRH, FBCN, FEEMA, FIPERJ, Geotecnica, GEROE, IBAM, IBAMA, IEF, PPE/COPPE/UFRJ, Provita, PUC/RJ, Health Secretariat, SMDS, SECPLAN, SEICCT, SERLA, and UFF.

We want to highlight the contribution to the introduction in this volume by Luis Jorge Perez, Paulo Cesar Pinto, and Louise Fallon Scura.

Significant support at different phases in the project was provided by Robin Bates, Armeane Choksi, Michael Cohen, Al Duda, Mohamed El-Ashry, Antonio Estache, Asif Faiz, Kenneth King, Maritta Koch-Weser, Josef Leitmann, George Papadopoulos, Demetr:s Papageorgiou, John Redwood, Iona Sebastian, Ismael Serageldin, Rainer Steckhan, and Andrew Steer.

Rebecca Kary provided invaluable help in shaping the conference materials into this volume.

Felicia Quarcoo and Marietta Visaya provided invaluable administrative support, for which we are also grateful.

Carolyn Brissett and Ana Maria Lyra in Rio provided important assistance in summarizing the conference papers for the English version.

L   E.
THE   LIBRARY
WOOLTON   L, L16 8ND

Summary of Opening Statements

Remarks by Alcira Kreimer

It is a pleasure to welcome you to the Conference "Environmental Degradation in Urban Areas: The Case of Rio de Janeiro" on behalf of the Environment Department at the World Bank. We are delighted to count on the sponsorship of IBAM [the Brazilian Institute for Metropolitan Administration] and the collaboration of many important agencies and distinguished individuals and consultants on this effort. This conference is part of an effort the Environment Department is undertaking to understand the problems on the environment brought about by urban development. We are currently working on three countries: Brazil, Turkey, and the Philippines. These countries were selected because they have a strong institutional base in urban management that will help disseminate the findings to other countries that have weaker institutional frameworks.

Rio was selected because it provided an opportunity to build on work already done here and to help promote an exchange of experiences internationally to foster actions that can be replicated in other countries and in other cities that face similar environmental and vulnerability problems. We think that the study's timing after ECO92 is appropriate in which we are attempting to build on the important efforts already done in this city concerning the environment. Our current effort on the issue of urban vulnerability provides also a basis for the Bank's long term involvement in reducing environmental degradation and promoting the resilience of urban areas.

Since 1950, the world's urban population has been increasing at the rate of 4 percent a year, compared with a 1.7 percent rate of increase for the world's overall population. A pattern of rapid urbanization has emerged in many countries over the last 50 years.

Typically cities have developed with opposite characteristics: one a developed city, which is modern, well serviced and well equipped, and the other an undeveloped city, without adequate housing and services and poorly equipped. In other words, in the past decades we have witnessed the development of highly polarized urban structures.

The rapid increase in urban population has had environmental implications. Along with such an increase in population there is (a) more transport and its related problems (such as more carbon dioxide in the atmosphere), (b) more waste to deal with; (c) worse living conditions for the poor; (d) more basic services (water, sewerage) to provide; (e) a higher level of technology and fewer jobs for unskilled labor; and (f) worse economic conditions in general.

The characteristics of cities can both contribute to and reduce risks to environmental degradation and their vulnerability to extreme events. They can contribute to environmental degradation because of the concentration of population in a limited space, the large number of people that require services, and the inevitable proximity in many cases of densely populated areas to natural and man-made hazards. Just to mention a few cases, in the past decade we have witnessed major destruction in Mexico City, Manila, Cairo, in cities in Armenia, in Bangladesh, in Pakistan, in Nepal, and in Turkey. On the other hand cities provide greater wealth and access to services, and higher levels of education and professional skills, which may be factors in reducing vulnerability.

Given the trends of growth of urban areas and their very high exposure to environmental degradation, a proactive stance vis-a-vis environmental conditions in cities is required. The consequences of inaction will be severe. We are beyond the discussion of whether more urbanization is good or bad. Rather, we are confronted by a number of questions that require answers: (a) Is there something we can do that will make urbanization environmental more sustainable? (b) Can we make urban populations less vulnerable? (c) What are viable approaches for preventing and mitigating environmental degradation and potential natural and technological hazards? In short, the question of dealing with environmental risks in urban areas is *when*, not *if*.

We have in front of us a set of challenging papers and contributions from professionals in different disciplines. I hope our discussions will be of assistance in maximizing the efficiency of reducing environmental degradation and working together in achieving a productive and successful follow-up to the challenges posed by ECO 92.

Thank you.

Remarks by Lino Ferreira Netto

I have the great pleasure of welcoming you on behalf of IBAM. We at the Institute are very honored to receive our colleagues in these institutions for a debate on such a relevant theme: Environmental Degradation and Urban Vulnerability: The Case of Rio de Janeiro.

We know that the impact of human activities on the environment tend to be especially strong in big cities. The concentration of people and the consequent urban expansion have been accompanied by environmental problems such as the degradation of natural resources and the increase of social problems. These factors present obstacles to substantial development.

The gravity and complexity of the environmental question are unequaled. Studies being carried out indicate many causes:

- Economic activities that are carried out in inappropriate ways.
- The inadequacy or fragility of institutional mechanisms for environmental control.
- Insufficient consciousness of the social risks of environmental degradation.
- Depletion of (or limited) resources for building and maintaining infrastructures.
- Organizational and managerial limitations.
- And, in many cases, insufficient political mobilization to address the questions.

Because of their complexity, because of the interests involved, and because of the implications of changing well-entrenched practices, implementing solutions to the problem of environmental degradation presupposes, without doubt, firmness and persistence—not only on the part of the public sector, but also from organized society.

Appropriate measures are available to the government: for example, laws can be legislated and executed, and infrastructures can be built. Other measures that can be carried out in organized society are worth mentioning:

- Strengthening of the collective consciousness of individuals and organizations toward environmental problems.
- Promotion of dialogue, cooperation, and understanding in the sense of favoring solutions to these problems.
- The introduction of governmental measures toward solving problems of environmental degradation, as well as

the offer of support and stimulation in these initiatives.

In the area of Brazilian institutions, IBAM plays the role of helping local governments and municipalities grapple with solutions to the environmental problems in their realm of responsibility and competence. For example, they are responsible for the following:

• Physical planning of cities, with delimitation of urban areas and establishment of norms for parceling urban land.
• Regulation and control of occupation and use of urban land.
• Regulation and control of construction.
• Construction of urban infrastructures.
• Provision of transportation services, directly or by third parties, as well as basic sanitation.
• The opening and maintenance of pedestrian areas.

These examples add dimension to the role that the local governments can potentially play in alleviating environmental problems. Other responsibilities include the following:

• Protecting the environment and combatting pollution in its various forms.
• Preserving the forests, flora, and fauna.

Conscious of the importance of municipal participation in dealing with environmental matters, IBAM has for many years been developing a series of activities for support to local government in this area. The Institute has made this a priority in the following ways:

• An editorial program, which includes publication of articles on the theme in the *Revista de Administração [Journal of Administration]* and in other works, such as "City, Development, and the Environment," which has been distributed to all prefectures and city chambers.

• Participation in seminars and other events on the environment.
• Introduction of the environmental variable in technical assistance that the Institute provides municipalities in different areas: urban planning, municipal development, reorganization of services, and managerial development, among others.
• Inclusion of the environmental theme in training courses that the Institute gives.

The environmental question cannot be treated without taking into account the city with its variety of functions and possibilities. The city must be supported so that it can develop all its potential.

I congratulate the World Bank for initiating this seminar and am grateful for having been chosen to hold it at IBAM. I wish you all success in your work that develops today and tomorrow.

Remarks by Braz Menezes

The selection of Rio de Janeiro as the host city for the United nations Conference on the Environment and Development (UNCED) in June 1992, was both ironic and appropriate. It is difficult to name another city that combines such incredible natural beauty, with such a blatant abuse of the ecosystem; a city that brings thousands instantly together to celebrate any occasion, but struggles daily to get its many institutions to work collectively towards a common purpose; a city where conspicuous opulence and desperate poverty co-exist; and where, like many cities around the world, it is mainly the law-abiding that live in seclusion behind security bars and high protective walls.

There is reason for some modest optimism, however. There have been discernable improvements recently. Every major project intervention, conference, seminar or other similar event, generates preparatory studies, discussions, and valuable exchanges of ideas. In Rio de Janeiro we are heartened to see an emerging dialogue between the community and its leaders—one which is producing a new way of thinking about a sustainable urban environment that will lead to a better future. For the World Bank, the complexity of the task becomes somewhat more clear with hindsight.

Nearly five years before UNCED, the Bank was invited to Rio de Janeiro to deal with the devastating results of severe and prolonged rains in the metropolitan region of Rio. The nature of the damage (landslides, flooding, collapsed structures, a breakdown of basic services), and the wide geographical disaster-affected area required more than directly-targeted reconstruction. In the event, it demanded a broader view of urban environmental management, one focused on prevention—and hence the implementation of a program which targeted institutional strengthening (improved coordination, instruments, policies and plans) that would in time lead to an increased and sustainable capacity for dealing with Rio's serious environmental problems.

Because of that emergency, the Bank had to make a rapid appraisal, take some calculable risks, but move quickly. It was expected that the three levels of government would continue to regard the project as a high priority after loan approval. This was not to be so.

Three crucial and inter-related groups of problems can be readily identified as having had a serious impact on project performance (and I mention them here because their impact is continuous): (a) the fragility of the institutional framework; (b) the impact of very rapidly changing economic and financial reforms by the federal government; and (c) the intermittent conflict between the different levels of government, exacerbated by the cyclic rhythm of alternate state and

municipal elections every 24 months; elections that are generally followed by a total replacement of technical and administrative staff.

The complex political tensions that fluctuated alternatively between the State and Municipality, and that characterize Rio de Janeiro to this day, were temporarily swept under the carpet, stimulated no doubt by the common objective of dealing with the emergency or perhaps, of obtaining money from the World Bank. More important perhaps, the widespread national public sympathy for Rio's plight following the floods provided an opportunity for the State and Municipality to extract concessions and financial support from the federal government, which was at the time introducing tight fiscal controls on state and municipal spending, focused initially on Rio.

During the history of the Rio Flood Reconstruction Project these tensions were to erupt often into confrontations by one or the other party directed at each other, or at the federal government. The message that I want to leave with you today as we begin thinking about policies that will help to build a better and more sustainable tomorrow, is that unless we take careful stock of where we are, the route which we map out into the future will not take us where we want to go. Four years later, one may say that the Project had achieved its objectives, urban vulnerability has been reduced through a series of interventions designed to improve and to control the urban environment. Medium- and long-term objectives for the recovery and prevention of disasters has particularly led the municipality down the path of conservation. Perhaps more importantly, the mitigation of natural hazards and environmental degradation is now a priority.

These works have been for long now, object of attention of the agencies responsible for civil defense in the city.

The main result may be seen in the fact that, after 1988 many heavy rains have fallen in the city and no major disaster has occurred. It should be also underlined that the works executed under the project generated new technologies that improved the technical capacity of the municipal agencies.

In brief, many favorable impacts arose from the experience gained during Project implementation. Among others:

• Rehabilitation of the affected areas.
• Recovery of the economic activities and of the urban infrastructure.
• Some improvement in the prevention of natural disasters; much remains to be done.
• Strengthening of municipal institutions.
• Definition of policies directed to longer-term urban environment protection.

The financing crisis of the Brazilian public sector demonstrates that the environment sector cannot walk with its own legs, unless it is helped by joint action with the private sector. The impact of the Rio case may be particularly interesting if we are able to craft policies building on the idea that its natural beauty is a public good, as explored by Jose Marcio Camargo's document. In addition, however, we will need to discover new institutional and financial arrangements between the public and the private sector if we are going to make long-term improvements in urban resilience to environmental degradation. Either profit or social oriented, private entities have much to say and to do. Building up the institutional capacity at the public sector is of utmost importance. A comprehensive institutional development program should be launched at the state level, and would cover agencies belonging to the three levels of government working in the Rio metropolitan area. Adopting a strategy based on the demand for services and a supply of private and public institutions that could serve their demand, the sector could advance towards a more rational and adequate performance, avoiding further environment degradation and urban vulnerability.

I. Introduction

1. Rio de Janeiro—In Search of Sustainability

Alcira Kreimer, Thereza Lobo, Braz Menezes,
Mohan Munasinghe, Ronald Parker, and Martha Preece

In danger of losing its spell

Rio de Janeiro is an extended and chaotic city, of an overwhelming natural beauty. According to Camargo, Rio's attractiveness has an important economic value (see Camargo, this volume). The city has a population of 9.6 million—estimated by the preliminary results of the 1991 census—counting only 13 municipalities. The size of the metropolitan area, however, defies easy definition. Currently there is no state legislation to demarcate the confines of the urban agglomeration, which is variously described by different government agencies as consisting of between 12 and 17 municipalities. Increasing income gaps, significant social differences, growing crime rates, and pervasive unemployment seem to be among the key issues that will be greeting the end of the 20th century. In recent years, the increasing dualism between the poor and the rich in the city has increased, with the well-to-do becoming more and more confined behind high fences (e.g., in high income areas like Ipanema, Copacabana, and Leblon), while the poor become more and more socially peripheral. In Camargo's words, there is an "official" and a "non-official" city. The growing degradation of Rio's urban environment has been defined by an observer as the "northeastization" of the city (Hildete Pereira de Melo, discussant at the meetings held November 16-17, 1992, at IBAM in Rio de Janeiro). According to Coriolano (this volume), environmental degradation is reaching a point in which it is more expensive *not* to study what is going on in the city than to do so.

A major asset of the city is its coastal area. The city has 80 kilometers just of recreational beach, while the State of Rio de Janeiro has a coastline of approximately 800 kilometers. The growing prospects of widespread coastal pollution are alarming. The coastal area has been for many years the subject of a number of predatory activities, carried out by both public and private agents. Among the most severe problems in the coastal area are the many waste disposal, commercial and industrial activities that are heavy polluters. Those activities concentrate around two major ocean inlets, Guanabara and Sepetiba Bays. An interesting comparison can be made between the types and degrees of pollution in the two bays. Guanabara Bay is definitely the more polluted, and also the more heavily studied of the two bays. The land surrounding Guanabara Bay is for the most part privately owned and land uses tend to be extremely diversified and mixed. As a result, the sources and types of pollution are also diverse. In the Bay area are found approximately 10,000 industries including oil refining and storage, ship transport and repair, chemical manufacturing, and metallurgy. In addition there are military and recreational facilities, including seaside resorts and water-sports. The dangers from pollution affect both the local and the tourist population. Tourists are particularly at risk since they are not always aware of the

L. I. H. E.
THE BECK LIBRARY
WOOLTON RD., LIVERPOOL, L16 8ND

potential for trouble. For example, announcements concerning the degree of pollution in the beaches on any given day are issued by FEEMA and published in the local newspaper. Tourists are not particularly well placed to read those warnings in Portuguese. Belatedly, pollution issues in the coastal area are beginning to be addressed now. Efforts to control pollution are currently being undertaken, for example a pollution control project in Guanabara Bay is currently being appraised by the Inter-American Development Bank (see Box 9.2).

Could things really improve? It certainly would take a major and coordinated effort. According to Camargo, to treat Rio as a public good would entail a drastic change in the city's management and location policies, including attracting productive activities that are non polluting, intensive in technology use and utilizing qualified labor (e.g., informatics, electronics, telecommunications, biotechnology, insurance and trade services, etc.). The consistent and coordinated administration of power by a consortium of municipal and state agencies to ensure that the necessary institutional leverage, grouping and cooperation are in place is another key factor in the process of establishing an efficient pollution control system. Market mechanisms should go hand-in-hand with regulatory instruments.

Other crucial phenomena that contribute to the physical, environmental, and urban vulnerability of the Metropolitan Region of Rio de Janeiro are the following: (a) A rapid and uncontrolled expansion of urban settlements over peripheral land, a vulnerable situation exacerbated by the inability of local governments to supply basic services; (b) The peculiar topography of the region containing three large mountain ranges (Pedra Branca, Tijuca and Gerincino),

which has driven urban expansion towards environmentally vulnerable areas: Baixada de Jacarepagua, Baixada de Sepetiba, Baixada Fluminense, and Baixada de Guanabara; (c) The shortage of housing compounded by the absence of an efficient institutional framework for urban development planning; (d) The widespread land speculation which has led to an accelerated growth of illegal settlements in highly vulnerable areas; (e) The concentration of services in the city of Rio de Janeiro added to the inadequacy of the transportation infrastructure which has created a distorted pattern of provision and use of social services.

Institutional policy meanwhile has been drifting. Municipal authorities do not have total control over development decisions at the local level, much less at the metropolitan level. Furthermore, even with the best of intentions, most local governments are too poorly endowed to effectively administer urban and environmental planning in their own jurisdictions. Despite the fact that responsibilities over land use and zoning regulations rest almost entirely with the municipal governments, there are many coordination problems among the various public agencies that are involved in urban matters. For example, environmental zoning can be used at the three levels of government and in most cases, the laws have not been implemented efficiently. In that sense, the metropolitan region has become an illustrative case of uncontrolled expansion resulting from ineffective zoning and land-use regulations. As Estache (1991) argues, at the state level, zoning laws are used to control the location of polluting firms; and at the federal level, they are focused on the protection of forests and ecological reserves; whereas, local governments have the authority to regulate commercial and residential use as long as their regulations do not conflict with federal and state laws. These overlapping competencies often discourage coordination between different bodies of authorities and restrict effective actions on questions of urban development while limiting the land management powers of municipal governments. To compound the problem, with the exception of Rio de Janeiro, the rest of the municipalities suffer from outdated property and other cadastre information, thus making it extremely difficult to reach efficiency in the implementation of projects and in the enforcement of the law.

The beginnings

Following the discovery of Brazil by the Portuguese at the beginning of the sixteenth century, São Paulo and Recife were the earliest coastal cities. Only after a French expeditionary force established itself in what is now the metropolitan Rio de Janeiro area in 1555 did the Portuguese take a serious interest in monitoring what was happening in the Rio area. When the Portuguese finally did establish a settlement in Rio in 1567, the colonial government's interest was defense of colonial territory from Portugal's European enemies. The city remained small until a gold rush in inland Minas Gerais required the facilities of the city's excellent port. Rio was the nation's capital from 1763 until 1961 when it was moved to Brasilia.

During the first centuries of Rio de Janeiro's history urban vulnerability to disaster was slight. The bays produced a plentiful supply of wholesome fish and shellfish, the rivers ran clear and clean with potable water, and the first inhabitants eschewed those habitats which were at risk of landslide, flashflooding and tidal inundation. The intervening years have greatly increased the dangers for the area's inhabitants. By the time of Independence in 1822 environmental degradation was already widespread. In 1990s' Rio, seafood is contaminated, rivers

are anaerobic, and landslides and floods place urban dwellers in continuous peril. Worse yet, technology has added a component to urban vulnerability which is not yet fully understood: the world is only beginning to come to realize the dangers posed by toxic and hazardous wastes, heavy metals, chemical spills, industrial air pollution and even the threat of nuclear accidents. As the urban population has grown, so has urban vulnerability.

Infrastructure and urbanization

In the 1960s and 1970s, the Brazilian government lashed out on massive scale infrastructure investments to accompany its industrialization strategies, as well as its colonization policies in the Amazonia. These policies were key contributors to the emergence of major cities, such as São Paulo and Rio de Janeiro in the southeast; Belo Horizonte in the central west; Curitiba and Porto Alegre in the south; Fortaleza, Recife, and Salvador in the northeast; and Belem in the north. The industrialization process took over virtually all states, with a predominance in the south-central states, including São Paulo, Minas Gerais, Rio de Janeiro and Parana. As a result, large contingents of migrants from rural areas moved to major cities, primarily to Greater São Paulo and Rio.

By the early 1970s, when the government began to move towards a more balanced development of the national territory, the seemingly intractable poverty in the North generated growing concerns over unbalanced rates of urban growth favoring the south. It prompted governmental development strategies aimed at creating economic opportunities for the densely populated drought-prone rural areas in the Northeast. Plans for the expansion of the frontier into the Amazônia were seen as the most plausible instrument to control the increasing size and density of the urban population in the industrialized regions (e.g., São Paulo, Rio de Janeiro, and Belo Horizonte). However, far from alleviating the problem of uncontrolled expansion, the program stimulated additional migration to cities and towns, fueling the process of unrestrained growth of rural and urban settlement in areas that are ecologically fragile and stirring fundamental changes in the rate and distribution of population increase. For example, the Program for National Integration, announced in 1970, called for the construction of the Transamazon and Cuibá-Santarén Highways, and gave impetus to the large infrastructure investments in transport, infrastructure and mining that accompanied the POLONOROESTE Development Program launched in 1981. The program's principal objective was to absorb population influx by raising agricultural productivity and by expanding road infrastructure. The project coincided with one of the country's most severe economic crises which fueled migration to already vulnerable areas bringing increasing pressures on natural resources. According to the World Bank, the rapid expansion of gold prospecting, cassiterite mining and commercial timber extraction became major attractions to migrants whose activities were further encouraged and supported by extension of feeder roads. Mining activities and urban sewage have increased pollution in various of the region's main rivers, while forest clearing has caused the loss of soil fertility and increased erosion. Despite what had been designed on paper, the completion of the Transamazon not only exacerbated problems that already existed but created a new set of difficulties that undermined the stated objectives of mobilizing investment in other parts of the country and ensuring regional balance in the distribution of population and economic activities in the country. In sum, efforts to balance development in the Northeast through the Transamazon project are an example of how environmental damage may be worsened by failure to consider the potential environmental impacts of large development programs.

Little seemed to be going right for urban development in the 1970s and 1980s. Neither the industrialization program of the south, nor the colonization projects of the Amazônia accomplished much in terms of generating a comprehensive urban development strategy to help the regions absorb the massive impact of the incoming populations. Despite the government's efforts to expand the economic frontier in the North, profound regional disparities still persisted in the late 1980s. Ever since the decline in sugar prices in the eighteenth century, which left the once wealthy northeastern plantation economy in ruins, development has favored central and southern Brazil. Institutions were unable to cope. Increasing economic problems further affected the ability of public institutions at the federal and local levels to deal with complex management and policy problems in land, housing, infrastructure and public services (see Box 1.1).

Population and urbanization in Brazil

As Brazil evolved, the growth of urban areas struggled amid a dearth of urban development policies. The country's two most populous metropolitan areas—São Paulo with approximately 15 million and Rio de Janeiro with approximately 10 million inhabitants—contributed to Brazil's transition from being 68 to 77 percent urban. Currently, of the total population of about 150 million, 77 percent reside in urban centers. However, rural migration to the cities is diminishing considerably. Problems concerning urbanization in the Metropolitan Region of Rio de Janeiro

Box 1.1: Megacities Project
Hélia Nacif Xavier

Of the 23 megacities of the United Nations, only two—Rio de Janeiro and São Paulo—are in the south of Brazil. However, they all feature similar problems. U.S. sociologist Janice Perlman noted that these cities have more in common with each other than with other towns in their own countries. One reason is that each has a Third World city within it, where subnutrition, infant mortality, homelessness, and joblessness are rife. On the other hand, every Third World nation has small pockets of high technology, modern development, and high finance. Janice Perlman noted that problems demanded lengthy solutions, while a total lack of communication between urban researchers prevented successful, innovative solutions from being used in other countries with similar problems.

Based at New York University, the Megacities Project operates in 16 cities: Bangkok, Bombay, Buenos Aires, Cairo, Calcutta, Mexico City, Jakarta, Karachi, London, Los Angeles, Moscow, New Delhi, New York, Rio de Janeiro, São Paulo, and Tokyo. Still not incorporated are Lagos, Seoul, Beijing, Tianjin, Shanghai, Daccar, and Manila. Smaller towns with interesting solutions—like that of Curitiba—are also welcome. The Rio de Janeiro Coordination Office was taken over in March 1990 by IBAM; in São Paulo it is coordinated by architect Jorge Wilhelm, chairman of the Greater São Paulo Planning Authority.

The Megacities Project emphasizes the particular environment, generation of income and the informal economy, with democratic city management and the well-being of women and children. Accepted innovations must be socially fair; economically feasible; ecologically sustainable; culturally transferable; and involve the community.

Of the 82 experiments on file for Rio de Janeiro, some 26 are potential sources for the World Bank study on environmental degradation and urban vulnerability. They include the following:
- Rio de Janeiro Metropolitan Region Urban Context.
- Paid Mutual-Help Project.
- The Private Sector Role in Sustainable Development in Megacities—Rio de Janeiro.
- Projeto Rio—An Innovative Experimental Laboratory.

The Urban Context of the Rio de Janeiro Metropolitan Region
Produced in April 1992 with backing from the McArthur Foundation, it involves Rio de Janeiro, Mexico and New York in a comparative and conceptual study of the historical background of land use, institutional structure, final responsibilities, demographic shifts, the economy and the informal sector, and social indicators and the environmental situation.

Paid Mutual-Help Project
This study was initially prepared by the Rio de Janeiro Municipal Social Development Bureau—SMOS with backing from the MONTREAL City Council for presentation of the Second Meeting of Megacity Mayors held in Montreal in October 1991. It covers the agency's background since it was founded in 1980, fostering self-help projects in *favelas* (slums), incorporating environmental education and increased community participation through paid advisers from each community, offering advice of urban improvements and sanitation, reforestation, and environmental education to low-income sectors.

Box 1.1 (continued)

The Role of the Private Sector in Sustainable Development in Megacities—Rio de Janeiro

This study is part of a study comparing Latin America's megacities (Rio de Janeiro, São Paulo, Mexico City, and Buenos Aires) with those of Asia (Tokyo, New Delhi, Bombay, Calcutta and Karachi). The Latin American side was financed by the Business Council for Sustainable Development and the Asian side by the Sumitomo Trust Bank Research Institute, and they were presented at the Sixth Meeting of Megacities Project Coordinators (Rio de Janeiro, May 1992).

This emphasized that the performance of grassroots movements, nongovernmental organizations (NGOs), and the government sector in striving for sustainable development is well known, while the private sector is often accused of degrading the environment. Four cases were analyzed: Shell, White Martins, Inga Zinc, and Microferramentaria, all of which implemented environmental policies independent of legislation, using alternative technologies to handle and reuse industrial wastes and spills.

Projeto Rio—An Innovative Experimental Laboratory

This report resulted from an IBAM study carried out in January 1991 that was sponsored by CEDAE. Part of the PROMORAR housing program, it was a benchmark in changing official policy on low-cost housing by abolishing subhousing without transferring the population to other areas.

are no longer related to rapid growth, but rather to uncontrolled urban expansion and dualism. Over the last decade neighboring concentrations of affluence and poverty have co-evolved in urban area centers.

The urban crisis worsened in the last decades. Far from providing a respite for rural migrants, the outcome of the government's development policies has been a high concentration of urban poverty and environmental degradation in metropolitan centers. The São Paulo metropolitan region is an example of the environmental disruption caused by an inefficient management of urban land coupled with socioeconomic constraints. According to a World Bank report, during the economic crisis of the 1980s, low-income population occupied ecologically fragile land around watersheds leading to the progressive degradation of related reservoirs. At the same time, encroachment has occurred on steep hillsides and floodplains increasing the

vulnerability of these areas to natural disasters. The combined effects of buildings, streets and parking lots have altered the natural drainage characteristics and decreased the permeability of soils. Large areas are at a high risk of devastation from landslides. More than 400 areas in the city have been identified as being in danger, and approximately 75,000 people—mostly poor slum-dwellers—are periodically affected by flooding. According to a World Bank report, the three most important rivers serving the São Paulo metropolitan area as well as their associated reservoirs are seriously affected by urban sewage and industrial wastewater. Only 40 percent of the sewage covering 65 percent of the metropolitan region is treated, and deficient collection and disposal of the 4000 tons of solid waste produced per day has resulted in groundwater contamination and surface water pollution.

Population and urbanization in Rio

Although the northeast continues to be the most rural of Brazil's five macro-regions, a rural exodus of major proportions took place during the 1970s creating pronounced urban growth in every northeastern state. By 1991, more than half of its population lived in urban areas, including three of its largest cities: Recife (2.9 million), Salvador (2.5 million) and Fortaleza (2.3 million) which serve as important ports for the country's foreign trade. Fiscal incentives and subsidies to encourage private investments for industrial development are among the major reasons for the concentration of people and economic activities in these cities. Also, the extreme vulnerability of the region to severe droughts combined with insecure land tenure situations have caused massive rural exodus towards urban centers, particularly Fortaleza, Recife and Salvador and to the metropolitan areas of São Paulo and Rio de Janeiro. As in the case of Rio and São Paulo, low-income squatters have settled in make-shift dwellings on ill-suited land, such as flood plains along major rivers. The vulnerability of urban centers to flooding is often exacerbated by the constraints imposed by recurrent droughts on municipal spending for infrastructure development. Drought-hit areas often become a priority in terms of resource allocation for disaster mitigation. This often leaves little leeway when rains come again, as happened during the devastating floods of 1985 which affected 458 of the total 1,386 municipalities in the region. More than 700,000 urban dwellers had to be evacuated, many towns had to be abandoned, and 414 municipalities were declared in a state of emergency. Some poor neighborhoods, settled on low-lying areas, were deluged by meters of water

and completely isolated from emergency relief and rescue operations (Preece 1992).

Population centralization in the State of Rio de Janeiro is prevalent. This is not only a local phenomenon but a national trend. Between 1960 and 1991, while the country's total population grew 2.1 times—from 60 million in 1960 to 150 million in 1991—the metropolitan regions grew faster—2.6 times—from 15.0 million in 1960, to 42.2 million in 1991. Data provided by the three last censuses show that from 1960, large cities had been increasing their share of the total population up until 1980. In the last decade, both the country and the metropolitan regions have slowed the growth of their population. In 1960, the metropolitan regions accounted for 21.4 percent of the country's total population; in 1970, this percentage increased to 25.3 percent, and to 28.9 percent in 1980, a percentage share that remained almost the same through 1991. This trend is mostly explained by the low rate of growth of São Paulo and Rio de Janeiro which grew at 1.73 percent and 0.82 percent per year respectively. The highest rate of population growth in the country occurred in peripheral municipalities which grew 2.95 percent a year as compared to 1.26 percent in the cores. According to Braile in this volume, the metropolitan region of Rio accounts for 76.3 percent of the total population of the state while occupying only 14.6 percent of its area. However, the population's assault on the municipal area has been less volatile recently. During the period 1980-91, the Metropolitan Region of Rio de Janeiro grew at 0.82 percent per year, and the municipality of Rio at 0.43 percent per year. This compares with the national average of 1.89 percent per year during the same period.

The reversing trend in population growth in Rio de Janeiro began in 1980. With 8.8 million inhabitants in 1980, it presented the lowest growth annual rate—2.44 percent—among the cities with an accentuated pattern of peripheral development. While in 1960, a mere 32 percent of its total population was located in the peripheral municipalities, by 1991 this share had increased to almost 50 percent. This pattern of urban expansion was connected to acute problems in city management. Administrative capacity was not able to cope with the demands of rapid urbanization.

Government policies that influenced industrial location essentially promoted concentration to take advantage of such benefits as efficiencies in labor markets and services. Land constraints in urban areas caused externalities—such as crowding and degradation—through rent increases in prime locations. The growth of a large population that falls beneath the poverty line and land-use shifts to accommodate soaring densities in urban populations have had three major effects, first, the multiplication of slums, second the occupation of high risk, hazard-prone areas, and third the proliferation of drugs, prostitution and crime, particularly in the favelas.

"Favelization" is one of the most visible features of urban metropolitan expansion in Rio. The "official" urban development process proceeded through the subdivision of land for industrial use and for mainly upper- and middle-income group housing. Further migration from the northeast of Brazil and from the depressed rural areas of the states of Rio de Janeiro, Minas Gerais, and Espirito Santo, accounted for the emergence of squatter settlements on marginal land. The *favelas* became the housing solution for the poor, in the absence of plans and legislation to regulate expansion, disorganized physical growth took over unsuitable land. Simultaneously there was an outburst of speculative land subdivision in Rio de Janeiro. According to Gondim (1992), the peripheral munici-

palities became a major location for the very poor, giving way to the clandestine subdivision of rural properties. The result of this speculative practice has been that large spaces remain empty within and between settlements, and more people become segregated to the farthest and most vulnerable areas increasing their exposure to hazardous conditions.

Sustainable environmental development in Rio

The nature of the urbanization process in Brazil illustrates how human interventions can impact the spatial equilibrium of metropolitan systems and generate chains of events that lead to critical alterations of environmental structures. In some instances, skewed development strategies, or inadequate or non-existent urban environmental policies have forced the concentration of people in vulnerable locations; in others, failure to evaluate environmental costs of major public programs have triggered uncontrolled expansion heightening the depletion of natural resources and straining the ability of public institutions to efficiently manage urban growth.

During the 1940s and due to increasing migration, lowlands areas around the Guanabara Bay began to develop. It was during this period that Baixada Fluminense—comprising the municipalities of Duque de Caxias, Nilópolis, Nova Iguacu and São João de Meriti—became the attraction pole of new settlers as well as of industries. A few large landlords controlled the greatest proportion of the available land creating a genuine monopoly over real estate operations and restricting the access to land by the urban poor. With the only exception of Nilópolis, by 1930 most land had been subdivided. The following two decades showed tremendous increase in population growth rates.

With the growing importance of the city as a commercial center first, and later as the Capital of the country, pressures on land grew steadily. Lowlands, that had been mostly devoted to agriculture became the attraction pole of new settlers. However, conflicts of interests among landowners and the state limited the power of the public sector to take control over the land under its jurisdiction and thus limited the alternatives for urban development. Between 1950 and 1960, population in the municipalities of the Baixada grew at 140 percent—with the exception of São Gonçalo and Nilópolis which grew 95 and 105 percent respectively (Governo do Estado do Rio de Janeiro 1991). Between 1940 and 1970s the Baixada Fluminense led the direction of urban expansion. Seventy percent of the municipal resources of the last three years have been allocated in drainage, roads, recuperation of degraded land, housing, education and health, in Campo Grande, Jacarepagua and Madureira, designated as "expansion areas" in the 1992 master plan.

Land and living

A number of landholders in the periphery of Rio hold land for speculative purposes. Thus, large tracts of land are left idle. Most of these areas do not have basic infrastructure and in most cases, land-use regulations do not require improvements other than the opening of unpaved access roads. Further, lawful acquisition of a plot of land is a long, costly and burdensome process, requiring land access, registration, and permission to develop. Informal transactions, on the other hand, offer not only low-costs but a very simplified form of purchase. As Gondim (1992) points out, while from 1975 to the end of 1980, the National Housing Bank's PROFILURB program financed less than 43,000 urbanized lots in the entire country,

private developers (*loteadores*) dealing with the informal market made available 230,000 lots in the peripheral municipalities of Rio.

There is a process of peripheral land speculation. Due to lack of facilities and poor accessibility of these developments, the first lots are sold at very low prices. Subsequently, dwellers obtain basic infrastructure, through lobbying the service companies or paying with their own money. As a result of the improvements, land values escalate, forcing newcomers to settle farther away, where land costs are cheaper. Thus, large spaces within settlements remain empty, while urban development stretches farther away. The vicious circle of low densities and increasing infrastructure and transport costs can be daunting.

The first *favela* appeared in Rio at the end of the 1880s in the Morro de Providência, followed by a second low-income settlement on de San Antonio Hill. By the middle of the 1940s, the total number of *favelas* in Rio reached 105, containing 138,837 inhabitants—7 percent of the total population of the Federal District (Governo do Estado do Rio de Janeiro 1991). The process of *favelization* coincided with the implementation of eradication measures to evict low-income population from the center of the city. Between 1962 and 1974, relocation programs moved around 140,000 persons from *favelas* to low-income housing projects in the suburbs of Rio. Despite continuous government efforts to eradicate them, population in the *favelas* increased at 5.4 percent annually in the 1960s (Gondim 1992). One major reason for that trend was the relatively high cost of the low-income housing alternatives offered by the government through the then National Housing Bank (BNH). Deprived of housing and with limited alternatives to settle close to labor markets, the poor resorted to their only "affordable" option, that is the occupation of degraded land subject to massive damage, flooding and collapse. While in 1980, the population living in *favelas* represented 14.2 percent of Rio's total population, in 1987 it reached 18 percent. Presently, there are 545 *favelas* in the municipality of Rio, and 926 irregular settlements—30 percent of the total number of housing in the municipality, or around 400,000 units sheltering almost 17 percent of the metropolitan region's total population—on public and private land. A typical feature of the land and housing markets in the *favelas* is that although all transactions are held in the informal market, real estate values follow the values of the official market. Today 76 percent of the real estate market for low-income people is located in *favelas* (IPLANRIO 1988).

In 1983, the government initiated a squatter upgrading program in an attempt to incorporate illegal land into the formal market. Paradoxically, far from achieving the government's objective, these efforts accelerated the process of land speculation and further displaced low-income population towards marginal lands, often highly vulnerable. Illegal occupations in the region can be explained by several multifarious factors, among them are: (a) the large number of urban plots without legal titles and the overlap of land ownership among different individuals; (b) insecure or nonexistent property rights; (c) rapidly increasing urban land prices; (d) low incomes and weak purchasing power of most families living in slums and squatter settlements; (e) ambiguity on the part of policymakers concerning potential alternatives, since they often see illegal settlements as a solution to the problem of rapid urban growth; (f) large amounts of idle land left for speculation purposes, particularly in the periphery; and (g) weak enforcement capacity for the implementa-

tion of both environmental and urban development laws.

Environmental threats

Land

The development of the physical configuration of Rio de Janeiro is an example of land occupation leading to the widespread alteration of natural habitats. In its early years the city was a strategic anchorage for some of the Colony's most important commercial activities. Its particular physiography—mostly lowlands, mangroves, swamps and hills—was a key factor influencing the location patterns of the new communities. Thus, since the very beginning, the process of "conquering nature" was central to the expansion of the city. In addition to the very specific constraints imposed by its physical geography, strategic as well as economic reasons were key in the location of the first colonists.

The earliest settlements were located on environmentally sensitive areas, particularly on hillsides which provided better building sites than the marshes, lagoons and the water-logged lands of the plains. The increasing disturbance of surficial deposits created major slope-stability problems as well as the severe flooding that has recurrently plagued the region. The Castelo hill, for example, settled in 1550, has been subject to severe landslides due to the artificial transformation of the natural relief of the land. In 1759 and 1811, the recurrence of landslides led to the eventual removal of the hill, and the subsequent filling of swampy sections of the city. A number of other hills in the city have been removed since due to stability problems. Historically, most landslides and erosion have occurred at cuts and fills in slopes where the natural relief of the land has been severely altered by man. Today, as in the past, the destruction of trees and natural groundcover alter the water retention characteristics of the soil. Flashflooding and landslides are an inevitable outcome.

One of the current areas affected by slope-stability problems is the Tijuca range (Prefeitura da Cidade do Rio de Janeiro, 1992). Major hazard-risks are confronted also by the *favelas* located at Grajaú-Jacarepagua, Morro Dois Irmâos and Estrada da Gávea, in the Tijuca range, and in flood plains, particularly Baixada Fluminense which contains 44 percent of the total population of the *favelas* in the municipality of Rio. Marcio Coriolano's article in this volume describes the development of the Landslide Susceptibility Map which establishes an instability rating for all Rio de Janeiro hillsides, on a scale of 1:25,000 by examining geology, steepness, surface deposits and land use. The Map assesses relative landslide potential, defines four classes of landslide susceptibility: very low, low, moderate, high. Coriolano also describes the Hillside Monitoring System that allows long-distance monitoring of difficult-access slopes through electric sensors that measure soil-shift, rainfall, pressure, load, flow, and other parameters.

At high risk are also *favelas* located in coastal areas, tidal estuaries and along rivers. Changes in relative land and water levels and riverine flows following heavy rains have resulted in vulnerability to high tides and storms. Development along the rivers has been the result of people's need to be close to water resources even in the face of repeated disasters. However, this pattern has led to a conflict between natural and human habitats. Flood-plains are transformed into flood hazard areas,in which the destruction of life and property, and the disruption of commerce and services are commonplace. Measures to reduce flood hazards in the country have

concentrated mostly on engineering works which have had numerous benefits. Increased control of river flows have often reduced inundation during times of heavy runoff. Paradoxically, these flood control measures have provided a false sense of safety, and encouraged new illegal developments, increasing the risks of damage in vulnerable locations.

Mudslides and floods destroyed the homes of several thousand families in 1988. While this number was high because of heavier than usual rains, it is not uncommon for several hundred homes to be lost occasionally. The primary causes can be traced to two problems: poor maintenance of drainage systems and the silting-over of rivers and streams that provide a natural drainage outlet for the city. The municipal government's capacity to handle the vast quantity of solid and dissolved wastes (about 5,000 tons a day) is woefully inadequate. Much of this waste goes uncollected, especially in poor neighborhoods. From there it finds its way into the water system, silting up the rivers and clogging drains. When it rains there are few outlets for excess water. As the rivers overflow and drains back up, water levels rise destroying entire neighborhoods—primarily poor ones located in vulnerable areas. Moreover, these conditions destabilize the huge embankments upon which many of these neighborhoods are built, resulting in massive mudslides (*The Urban Edge* 1991).

Deforestation

The region-wide deterioration of the natural environment is shown in the fast pace of deforestation which has led to severe erosion and degradation of water sources. Different assessments of the rate of deforestation have been made in the last few years. For example, in 1972, the deforested areas above 100m sea level was 9,265 ha; in 1978, it reached 10,624 ha; and in 1984, 19,874 ha. Presently, only 40 percent of the original vegetation remains (Prefeitura da Cidade do Rio de Janeiro, 1992). The growing problem of deforestation in the hills has affected the retention capacity of the soil and as a consequence, downstream river systems have water-flows that are excessively high during the rainy season. Furthermore, soil and other debris from erosion have caused sedimentation of riverbeds, aggravating the risk of flooding in low-lying areas. Quarries have dramatically reduced slope stability and caused disintegration and stress of the slope which ultimately results in rock fall and avalanches.

Beach erosion

Beach erosion has long been a major problem in the state of Rio. Atafona Beach has been so severely eroded that a section of beach 400 meters wide has disappeared altogether (Valentini and Neves 1989). Engineering projects to prevent erosion do not contribute significantly to alleviating the vulnerability of urban inhabitants, yet these operations have an extremely high cost. Money spent maintaining the beaches in wealthy areas is not available to deal with more life-threatening aspects of environmental degradation elsewhere in the city.

Leblon beach illustrates a pattern which is typical of many of Rio's most popular beaches. In hope of attracting more tourists to the seashore, roads are constructed directly on or near the beaches. However, these roads are often built in total disregard for the beaches' natural dynamics, and in interfering with their restorative processes they cause extensive erosion. While these roads are built to increase the commercial value of the beaches, in effect they bring about their extinction.

Waterways and drainage systems

By the middle of 1870s, the filling of mangroves, marshes and lagoons were part of an extensive process of land recovery begun in the south of the city. In 1926, this process extended to seashore areas. The Piratininga and Itaipu lagoons, considered major causes of health problems, were artificially connected to the ocean to "facilitate drainage." This induced an accelerated process of salinization and resilience with a substantial loss in the total volume of water. The Marajendi lagoon suffered a similar procedure, and the destruction of mangroves in Guanabara Bay resulted in sedimentation with a subsequent reduction of its navigability. By the end of the 19th century all the midtown lagoons had been filled in except Sentinela. Also, since very early times, the slopes of the Guanabara watershed were denuded to obtain trees for lumber and fuel and to clear space for agriculture. More recently, as the city has continued to expand up the slopes, the vegetative cover has been further removed for the construction of roads and buildings, and squatter settlements have been taking over higher levels on the hills.

Explosive population growth—a key feature of Rio's urban development up to the early 1980s—in combination with the city's uneven topography, created a shortage of suitable land for urban expansion. As a result, the process of land reclamation accelerated. Meanwhile, the occupation of lowland areas for agriculture purposes around the lagoons created additional vulnerability problems as rainwater runoff from the hills could find no outlet to the sea. The difficulty was compounded by the very poor natural drainage of these newly created areas which became subject to frequent flooding and landslides. Moreover, the amount of earth brought down from the hillsides compounded the difficulties as the eroded soil was added to the water and channels became plugged and runoff became insurmountable.

Flooding along the low-lying plains has had disastrous consequences for as long as people have been living on the lands around lagoons, near rivers and on river-beds (i.e., Baixada Fluminense). Rainwater and earth—resulting from eroded soil—pouring down from the mountains during the summer rains often overflow stream channels and inundate the floodplain. The most frequent type of flooding in the area is flash flooding resulting from the combination of intense precipitation, steep slopes and impervious ground surfaces. The inadequacies of the water-disposal system add to the problem. This became obvious during the rainy season of 1988. Mud blocked the drainage system as unusual amounts of rainfall softened the hillsides and the eroded soil was added to the water plugging channels and turning the streets into rivers.

The first measures to alleviate the problem concentrated on channeling run-off waters around the houses; later, conduits were dug to drain the lagoons. The first one was built in 1641 to carry off the waters of Santo Antônio Hill. But plans that have been put into effect for water disposal have not responded to an overall integrated strategy, and the master plan for the laying of rainwater drains is still in the preparation phase.

In another highly visible case, in São Conrado the filling of five rivers for the construction of a tunnel created a critical alteration of the region's hydrological system. Although an artificial channel was built in order to restore the natural drainage, the presence of the *favela* of Rocinha, has practically annihilated the benefits of the channel by disrupting the system and increasing the risk of flooding in low-lying areas. The construction of the railroad system produced a further transformation of land-use patterns, and in doing so created hazardous conditions for most of the population concentrated along the railway and in the surroundings of industrial complexes.

The flat land adjacent to the Santa Ursulina channel is subject to periodic inundation. The population settled in the Paciência neighborhood is dangerously exposed to the extreme contamination of the tributaries of the river Cação Vermelho. Similarly, the Campinho river, in the Campo Grande region, receives untreated sewage from households as well as industrial discharges, and so does the Mendanha river which crosses the industrial district of Campo Grande. The latter is one the most seriously polluted rivers of the Sepetiba Basin's system.

Water pollution

The main types of water pollutants found in Rio de Janeiro are suspended and dissolved solids, both organic and inorganic, including nutrients; pathogenic organisms; and various toxic wastes, such as oil and grease, heavy metals and pesticides. These pollutants originate from both point and non-point sources. The major point sources are collected but inadequately treated domestic sewage and industrial effluent from chemicals, petrochemicals and petroleum refining; and iron and steel production and other metal refining industries. The main non-point sources are uncollected and untreated domestic wastes, agricultural run-off, storm water run-off, and improperly disposed solid waste.

Water contaminated by untreated human excreta plays a major role in the transmission of enteric and diarrheal diseases. Inadequate collection, treatment and disposal of human sewage, inadequate access to safe drinking water and use of contaminated water for irrigation are the primary factors which encourage the spread of diseases with fecal-oral transmission routes. In addition, disrepair of systems can lead to the possibility for cross-contamination.

Aquatic flora and fauna are harmed directly by toxic substances, pollutants with high biological oxygen demands which reduce the dissolved oxygen concentration in the water and accelerate eutrophication, and through deposition of solids. Bioaccumulation of sublethal levels of toxic substances reduces the value of these plants and animals as a source of human food. Similarly, food crops from agriculture and aquaculture operations can be contaminated by a polluted water source, water delivery and irrigation systems can become clogged, and productivity decreased. Particularly sensitive industrial processes depending on polluted water sources may require expensive pre-treatment or switching to an alternative source to avoid contamination.

Sewage pollution

Per capita water consumption in the metropolitan area currently runs at 446.8 cubic meters per year (Maimon and Rodrigues 1992). The contamination of water sources has become a major issue facing the region, in particular, its coastal area. The main source of water supply is the Paraiba River, the head waters of the which run through heavily industrialized areas of the states of São Paulo and Rio de Janeiro. This creates considerable risk with contamination of the only drinking water source for Rio de Janeiro. A spill of coolant from a storage area for electrical transformers spilled a large amount of PCBs into the Paraiba-Guandu system,

effectively cutting off the city's water supply, and causing the production of drinking water to be suspended for three days.

Suspended particles have been found to be the primary means by which metals such as Cu and Zn are carried by the rivers. Scientists believe that the rivers's extremely high level of organic pollution — fecal and coli concentrations—serves to transport the metals, since organic matter is known to have a "high metal-binding capacity in natural waters" (Malm et al. 1989).

Treatment of collected sewage is virtually non-existent; most collected sewage is directly discharged into surface waters—rivers, bays and nearshore oceanic waters—without treatment. An exception is sewage collected from approximately 2 million people in the Ipanema area which is disposed of through the Ipanema outfall located approximately 3.5 km offshore of Ipanema Beach. The sewage collected from the remaining 3.5 million people served by the system is disposed of in surface water, including rivers, bays and nearshore waters, without treatment. Pollution from domestic and industrial sources results from both the amount of discharges and the lack of sufficient treatment.

The rainwater drainage system is separated from the sewage system, and it drains directly into surface waters. However, the State Water and Sewage Company (CEDAE) estimates that several hundred clandestine household sewage connections have been made into the rainwater system. Clandestine connections can seriously harm the integrity of the drainage system. Nevertheless, direct disposal of collected sewage is as polluting as the clandestine connections. In fact, lack of sewage treatment after collection largely defeats the purpose of separate systems in the respect that the potential benefits of a separate collection system are related to ease of treatment as a result of reduction of extreme flows. These benefits are not able to be captured in the absence of sewage treatment. It is estimated that the total amount of sewage from CEDAE, combined with the illegal connections into the rainwater drainage system, amount to 470 tons per day of sanitary sewage disposed directly into the rivers, bays and nearshore waters.

Industrial pollution

The coastline of the State of Rio de Janeiro has a remarkable diversity of environments which support several industries vital to the state's economy. Wood harvested from the state's extensive mangrove forests, fishing and tourism represent several of the key activities that support a sizable portion of the region's inhabitants. However, the growing industrialization and urbanization of the coastline and adjacent inland areas have put increasing pressure on these important resources and threaten to undermine their viability. Oil, heavy metals, and urban waste are the three most common forms of pollution that threaten the coastline. Scientists have paid particularly close attention to the build-up of heavy metal deposits within bays and estuaries. Of the kinds of pollutants produced by industry, heavy metals are of particular concern because they can be incorporated into ecosystems and thus find their way into food consumed by human beings.

Sepetiba Bay. The total area of the Sepetiba Bay is approximately 486 sq km and around its periphery dwells a population of 730,467—11 percent of the total population of the municipality of Rio (Prefeitura da Cidade do Rio de Janeiro, 1992). For more than three centuries the area was devoted to agriculture, until the nineteenth century when most of the land

was subdivided, concentrating on the production of citrus and vegetables. Presently, the eastern shore is still devoted to vegetable production for the metropolitan region. Industrialization and continuous urbanization have led to increasing environmental degradation in the area, particularly along the Piraquê River bank and the Serra do Cantagalo and Maciço de Pedra Branca slopes, which have been occupied by squatter settlements. Encroachments in this fragile area have led to deforestation with the subsequent silting of riverbeds, while uncollected solid waste, dumped indiscriminately in low-lying land areas and in streambeds, have contributed to the pollution of surface water through runoff and direct contamination of streams.

The Bay, located 60 km to the south of Rio de Janeiro, is receiving increasing attention from Brazilian and foreign scientists. The Bay, a semi-closed lagoon, is one of the most important fishing spots in the state. It has an astonishing level of metal contamination, similar to heavily industrialized areas in Europe and the United States, despite the fact that industry was only introduced to the area 15-20 years ago. The Bay's metallurgical industries release contaminated water containing high levels of heavy metals which give the Bay a metal concentration in excess of the Brazilian Standards of the Environment. An analysis of the sediments and biota revealed that Cd, Cr, Pb, and Zn are the primary metal pollutants. The source of Zn and Cd pollution is suspected to be the milling and smelting plants located in the area. It is also believed that an immense tailing disposal site (600,000 tons) has been the primary route for other trace metals entering the environment.

It has been noted that in Sepetiba Bay, there are several characteristics of mangrove sediments which favor the accumulation of heavy metals. Although the concentrations can reach very high levels, the mangroves themselves appear to be relatively unaffected. In acting as a biogeochemical physical barrier, mangroves prevent solid waste materials from moving out into the open sea, and thus play a key role as a "sink" for contaminates such as Pb, Fe, and Cr. But it has been noted that with increasing industrial activity, these ecosystems can contribute to cycling certain pollutants in the local environment, either as sinks or as conveyors of pollutants to marine food chains.

Guanabara Bay. Guanabara Bay has 10,000 industries, 10 oil terminals, 12 shipyards and two oil refineries, making it the second largest industrialized zone in the country. The discharge of organic matter into the bay reaches 465 ton per day, out of which 68 ton per day receive adequate treatment. Industrial liquid wastes are responsible for 25 percent of the organic material contribution and almost 100 percent of the pollution caused by toxic substances and heavy metals. Oil pollution is estimated to be 9.5 ton per day. About 7,000 ton per day of garbage is thrown out at the city dumps, some of them located at the margins of the bay. Man's actions have caused serious hazards, both in the ecological sense and in the socioeconomic sense: the water of the bay is inappropriate for bathing, the area which was originally covered by mangroves has been reduced by 90 percent in the past 20 years, and the intense sedimentation has forced an increase of the dredging costs of circulation, affecting the ecological balance of the area in an irreversible way.

Because of the current low oxygen concentrations in some portions of Guanabara Bay, much of the trace metal pollutants are sequestered in the sediment. Should the nutrient input into the Bay be substantially decreased and, as a result, the dissolved oxygen concentrations increased, the trace metals will be released from the sediment and will again be actively cycled in the food web.

The Iguacu and Estrela Rivers which drain the Guanabara Bay watershed are the most polluted rivers in the state. The two rivers are often anoxic and produce a strong hydrogen sulfide smell. These rivers drain an immense industrial park, home to a wide array of industries, which produce contaminants such as Cu, Cr, Cd, Zn, Mn, Pb (Lacerda et al. 1987). Of the 37 rivers which drain the Bay's watershed that are monitored by FEEMA, 7 are considered to be the principal polluters: Bacia do Sarapui, São João do Miriti, Caceribu, Iguacu, Iraja, Guapimirim, and the canals of Cunha and Mangue (Maimon and Rodrigues 1992). Taken together these 7 account for 80 percent of the Bay's pollution. Unlike Sepetiba Bay, which suffers mostly from the impacts of an industrial park, it has been noted that Guanabara Bay's situation is different in that high eutrophication from untreated urban wastes interacts with heavy metals from industrial origin.

In Rio de Janeiro, industrial water use is a relatively minor part of total water withdrawals. Nevertheless, many areas of the metropolitan region have a high degree of industrial development. Increasingly, industrial wastewater is adding the health risks associated with exposure to toxic chemical pollutants to the persistent traditional health risks associated with water polluted by sewage. In fact, the nature of economic growth in Rio de Janeiro has worked to increase health risks in the short-run; many are now exposed to the worst of both developing and developed worlds—the so-called "risk-transition."

Impacts of environmental degradation on the fishing industry

In the State of Rio de Janeiro, it is estimated that there are 70,000 registered fishermen, the majority of which are small-scale fishermen. Unregistered artisan fishermen are common in many areas, for example Sepetiba Bay, because of the underground economy created by the high unemployment in the State economy.

A combination of loss of habitat and pollution in the Guanabara and Sepetiba Bays are thought to create a major problem for fisheries production. Because Guanabara Bay is considered a very important nursery ground for the fisheries of the whole State of Rio de Janeiro, both estuarine and oceanic, local problems in the Bay have regional impact.

While there has been no closure of the fishery in Sepetiba Bay due to contamination, high trace metals are routinely found in oysters and fish near the bottom of the food web which are typically of low market value. This has serious health implications for the small-scale fishing communities surrounding the Bay, since they sell the more valuable components of their catch and keep the lower value fish for their own consumption.

Recreation and tourism have also been affected through the reduction of the aesthetic qualities of the water, and decline in use for fishing, boating and swimming. Navigation is impaired by floating and submerged solid wastes, nutrient-induced blooms of aquatic weeds, and sedimentation.

Air quality issues

Air pollution contributes to respiratory and pulmonary disease, shortens the life spans of urban residents, and threatens the planet's protective ozone layer.

Additionally, it can produce acid rain which corrodes urban infrastructure, decimates forests, kills lakes and dissolves important cultural patrimony. Air pollution damage has been noted in Rio in both modern and historic buildings:

Elevated levels of vehicle emissions are reflected in the physical appearance of many buildings within the city center where high densities of private and commercial traffic are frequently channelled along streets flanked by high-rise buildings. Pollution tends to concentrate and persist within these "corridors" and its most obvious long-term effect is the black staining of many buildings near to street level (Smith and Magee 1990, p. 143).

Rio experiences relatively high levels of sulfur emissions. As a result of the prevailing wind patterns and the surrounding hills, atmospheric sulfur pollution is greater in intensity than that found in the industrial centers of São Paulo and Belo Horizonte (Smith and Magee 1990, p. 143). Acidic rain with an average pH of 4.6 was measured in the Tijuca Forest Preserve, located within the city. Rainfall chemistry ranged between pH 4.16 and pH 6.05 during the period monitored (Moreira-Nordemann quoted in Smith and Magee 1990). Other acidic pollutants regularly found in Rio's atmosphere are sodium and chlorine. One 1985 FEEMA study (quoted in Moreira Nordemann) suggested than nitrogenous compounds in the atmosphere were approximately 20 percent of sulfur levels, and attributed 35 percent of anthropogenic emissions to the exhaust emissions of motor vehicles. Topographic features and air inversions sometimes trap industrial and automotive gas and particulate emissions causing periods when air quality presents a significant health risk to urban populations.

Rio's most abundant air pollutant is formaldehyde followed by acetaldehyde.

Acetaldehyde has been measured at levels which are much higher than in other urban centers in the world, whereas atmospheric levels of formaldehyde in Rio and other Brazilian cities are as high, but not significantly higher than those found in other urban areas. It has been concluded that the most likely cause of these high levels of acetaldehyde stems from the large-scale use of ethanol as a vehicle fuel.

Air pollution in the neighborhoods of Copacabana and São Cristovão is significantly higher than in other areas of the city. Copacabana is a residential area near the seashore that receives considerable winds from the sea and is highly affected by garbage incineration. São Cristovão is situated behind several tall hills and is highly industrialized. Both of these areas receive considerable motor vehicle traffic. Scientists studying these areas in the aftermath of the 1977 law forbidding apartment and house garbage incineration did not find that the air quality had significantly improved.

As noted earlier, heavy metals reach the coast primarily via the state's rivers and bays. However, there is a second important source: atmospheric pollution. Rio's rugged topography restricts the movement of air, and in doing so prevents the release of harmful contaminants into the atmosphere. It has been suggested that this dramatically increases the amount of heavy metals that are found along Rio's coastal regions. Moreover, it has also been found that winds regularly transport pollution from industrial sites over many miles and deposit it in lakes and other water systems. For example, in Guarpina Lagoon (90 miles east of Rio) they measured significant amounts of lead which they determined came from the atmospheric precipitation of automobile emissions originating from Rio.

Environmental policies

Responsibilities

The evolution of environmental policies at the federal, state and local level are analyzed in detail in de Góes Filho (this volume). Although environmental policy is essentially enforced through the use of the zoning and licensing instruments, local governments tend to be unwilling to share the responsibility for the implementation of the federal and state laws because of the high costs involved. The municipalities are responsible for designing comprehensive land-use zoning and regulations to ensure orderly use of land within their own jurisdictions. They also have control over building and subdivision ordinances and thus they have the power to prohibit development of any house or building on land deemed inappropriate for human habitation. However, even assuming that every municipality in the metropolitan region enforces its own regulations (which they often do not), governance of the entire region is a patchwork quilt of federal, state and local governments. In Gondim's (1992) words:

"In the state of Rio, the federal government operates the railroad system and the state government operates marine transportation in Guanabara Bay, the subway, bus transportation between municipalities, and one bus company in Rio. Up until very recently, electricity and water supply, sewage systems, telephones and even transit operations were under the responsibility of the state government. State and federal governments controlled the supply of public health services and elementary education, and local governments were left with garbage collection, street and road paving and land use control."

Public authority over watersheds and flood plains is divided between local, state and federal governments, whereas public power is functionally divided among operating agencies within each unit of government. The result of this fragmentation is the impairment of the efficient execution of the specific responsibilities of individual public agencies (see Box 1.2).

With the promulgation of the new Constitution on October 5, 1988, local governments have gained considerable new powers and responsibilities. Under Article 30 of the Constitution, municipalities are now required to prepare master plans, provide local services such as basic sanitation, water supply, education, and health care; all this in addition to statutory responsibilities for administration, land use control, taxation and some aspects of local law and order. Municipalities thus find themselves shouldering a constitutional responsibility for the delivery of such diverse services. However, the size of increase in total municipal revenue available will vary from municipality to municipality according to the size and type of its economic activity. In general, the total increase in municipal current revenues from the fiscal reform is inversely proportional to population size. Smaller municipalities with industrial bases will benefit the most, whereas large dormitory suburbs such as the municipality of São João de Meriti, and the municipality of Nilopolis—where many of the MR's poor live, will probably not gain as much as others under the reform, due to their large populations and limited economic bases. In addition, on the operational side, municipalities have the option of either handling these services themselves or delegating them to a higher level of government. Under the terms of the fiscal reform, municipalities now have increased taxing powers (including the receipt of transfer payments from what were previously federal taxes). Thus, municipalities will be provided with revenues derived

from user charg
and subsidized
Notwithst?
these reform
bilities of lo
the institut
ities to c
and to f
sources, st...
is today, municipa...
administrations and secto...
the state government for guidan...
assistance. For example, the State Water and Sewerage Company (CEDAE) is in charge of the provision of water supply and sanitation; the State Secretariat of the Environment (SEMA) for environmental policy; the State Low-income Housing Company (CEHAB) for technical assistance and financing of low-income residential development; the State Secretariat of Planning (SECPLAN) for overall planning and coordination of development programs; the State Roads Department (DER-RJ) for highway construction and maintenance; and the State Superintendency of Rivers and Lakes (SERLA) for overall conservation of water bodies within the State's territory. Other secretariats are responsible for policy and program implementation for education, health, etc.

Regulatory system and legislation

From the above examples it could be gathered that enforcement of land-use regulations and ordinances are critical problems for the metropolitan region. This situation is exacerbated by the fact that most local governments are poorly equipped to deal with the environmental and managerial problems associated with peripheral growth. To compound the difficulty, the complexity of social and spatial conflicts in the region has intensified the magnitude and problems of

Impact of Environmental Degradation on Public Health in Rio de Janeiro
Jorge Perez

Rio de Janeiro—capital of the State of Rio de Janeiro and second most important city in Brazil—is the most densely populated of all cities in the state. Rio de Janeiro is bordered on the north by the four municipalities of *Baixada Fluminense*—Duque de Caxias, Nilopolis, Nova Iguacu, and São João de Meriti—on the west by Itaguai and Sepetiba Bay, on the east by the Bay of Guanabara, and on the south by the Atlantic Ocean. The United Nations projects a population growth—to more than 10 million by the year 2,000—putting Rio in the category of "megacity". In part because of its history as the country's capital, Rio has the largest network of health services in the country. The hospital system includes about 57 units that range in complexity from national facilities (e.g., the National Cancer Institute) to specialized institutes. On the other hand, Rio presents an extreme dichotomy; in health it is both a modern and an underdeveloped city. Sanitation problems are severe, there is a lack of access to water, and important impacts from rains. In terms of basic sanitation, the status of Rio as the capital meant that there was practically no community participation; all the decisions were centralized. The entire health system in Rio, based on health policies defined in the 1930s, is geared to deal with health as an emergency. In 1991 there were two major health events, a dengue epidemic, which peaked in January with about 20,000 cases, and the entry of cholera to South America through Peru, which also reached Rio. The incidence of leptospirosis, usually related to rain levels, has affected Rio throughout the year. Climate is not the only factor in the disease; it has been noted that precarious housing and sanitation conditions also have an impact.

The main areas that need to be addressed in health are training of human resources, increased resources for basic health units, improved access to communications and data processing systems, along with structural reforms. Community activities geared to improving environmental sanitation could include education and community information programs, improved systems for water provision and solid waste removal.

urban management. Many protracted conflicts have become serious obstacles to the implementation of zoning regulations and building standards. In some cases this issue has turned into a potential disaster when authorities have overlooked unsafe buildings in sites where hazards are likely to occur. This is particularly the case in sites where the surficial deposits on the slopes have been disturbed. Slope failures have been associated with building on the hills. Roads and excavations that have been placed at successively higher altitudes in combination with cuts caused by building at the toes of the slopes have severed the surface soil mantle at its most critical points. This undercutting of the toe, in conjunction with higher cuts in the slopes and the removal of the vegetative cover for streets, trials, highways and buildings, has served to accelerate the process of creep in the soil mantle and to set the stage for slope failures and slides all the way from the bottom to the top. Further, the stabilization works constructed on some of the slopes have become counterproductive as they have stimulated expansion of the built environment to the verge of what are still very dangerous cliffs. This situation is well illustrated by a case in front of the State Environmental Agency (FEEMA) where works initiated to stabilize a potentially unstable ridge have induced further occupation of the land up to the edge of the cliff, thereby increasing total risk.

The process of land speculation coupled with the scarcity of updated property and cadastre information have seriously curtailed the ability of the government to formulate urban policy, and to devise and finance development programs. Superimposition of federal, state and local jurisdictions compounds the problem by making almost impossible the allocation of responsibilities for implementing overall urban policies. The absence of readily identifiable political surrogates has made it very difficult to design and maintain a coherent and sustainable integrated approach to contain environmental damage. Successive laws and decrees have been enacted in an effort to control the effects of natural hazards. Slope stability, drainage, and land use restrictions have become prime factors—at least on paper—in engineering planning and urban management. For example:

• Law No. 13 of 1991, establishes a protection program for flood-prone areas and provides for the control of urban expansion over areas that might be affected by sliding and flood-plains. Its provisions cover the implementation of drainage and sewerage systems in *favelas* as well as condemn any hillside-construction plan that might create slope-stability problems. For safety and development purposes, the law places strong emphasis on the implementation of macro-drainage works in lowlands and permanent monitoring of risk areas.

• Decree No 6.787 of July 2, 1987, provides for the reforestation and preservation of the vegetative cover in denuded areas prone to slope failures, erosion, and landslides. Its provisions cover educational campaigns, and technical assistance.

• Decree No 8.066 of August 29, 1988, provides regulations governing the selection of sites and operations of quarries. For safety and slope-stability purposes, it places a large part of the control of quarries under the Diretoria

de Geotécnica of the Municipal Secretariat of Public Works.

• Decree No 9.767 of November 8, 1990, establishes regulations and specifications for construction on slopes. It provides for official review and approval of all plans, and outlines drainage works required before a license or permit to construct buildings on hills can be issued. It provides for the use of retaining walls and stabilization measures to avert possible slope failures.

In an attempt to ease the legal requirements for subdivision approval and to facilitate the integration of formal and informal land markets, the central government enacted law 6766 of 1979. Its provisions focus on simplifying the procedures and requirements for land development.

The Municipality of Rio de Janeiro Environmental Master Plan

The Rio de Janeiro Environmental Master Plan (Plan Director de Ordenamiento Ambiental de Rio de Janeiro) was created to deal with a complex situation involving a number of factors: (a) the high population concentration in the City of Rio de Janeiro; (b) the absence of a clear definition of municipal borders (c) the majority of peripheral municipalities that are considered *cidades dormitorias* (bedroom communities) of Rio de Janeiro; (d) the uncontrolled expansion of urban growth in all the municipalities of the metropolitan region where a large number of urban plots do not have legal titles; (e) the rapid increase in the price of urban land with the consequent expansion of marginal areas (there are 545 *favelas* in the Municipality and 926 irregular plots lacking infrastructure and services on public and private land); (f) a housing deficit of the city of Rio de Janeiro that amounts to about 300,000 units (compared with a national housing deficit estimated at about 3,000,000 units); and (g) serious financial and planning deficits in the urban transport system: the operational deficit of the transport sector is about US$50 million per year; commuting travel between Rio and the Baixada Fluminense takes about four hours.

The new master plan focuses on the environmental management of the city and emphasizes the rational use of urban land by introducing the concept of *suelo creado* (built-up land). This concept is based on building codes and ordinances which establish the index of building occupancy on which the building taxes are based. It also aims at reducing land speculation and stimulating urban deconcentration. The plan identifies three actions concerning land use: (a) restricted areas; (b) expansion areas—Jacarepagua, Campo Grande and Madureira—which will operate as regional poles; and (c) occupation areas.

In the last three years, the number of illegal lands has grown threefold. The problem of solid waste disposal has achieved dramatic characteristics, and there have been several attempts to encourage collection at the household level, without much success. Final disposal is done in three main landfills: (a) Duque de Caxias, already described above, is a main source of water contamination in the Guanabara Bay; (b) Cayu—in the Municipality of Rio de Janeiro; and (c) Jacarepagua. Among the main depollution projects in pipeline are (a) the recuperation of the Guanabara Bay (IDB and Japanese funds); (b) micro-drainage works (World Bank); (c) macro-drainage and canalization of the Jacarepagua River System in Barra da Tijuca (World Bank); and (d) cleaning up of the Sepetiba Bay (Caixa Economica Federal—US$6 million).

US$70 million have been allocated for landslide prevention works.

Among the central environmental problems identified by the master plan are the following:

- Deforestation which reaches 4m^2 per day in the city (Today, only 40 percent of the original vegetation—the "Mata Atlantica"—remains. In 1972, the deforested areas above 100m sea level spread over 9,265 ha; in 1978, it reached 10,624 ha; in 1984, 19,874 ha.).
- Flooding.
- Contamination of water sources—household discharges, and industrial waste.

With respect to household discharges, both state—CEDAE—and local institutions—Secretariat of Planning—place strong emphasis on the clandestine connections of household sewers to the drainage system mentioned previously in this chapter. Although the implication of this process in terms of water contamination is meaningless (to the extent that the majority of sewerage discharge does not receive adequate treatment), from the point of view of health hazards it has enormous significance. Lack of solid waste collection has severely altered the drainage system as well as become a major source of contamination of rivers and channels; (d) toxic pollution from industrial sources in 25 rivers of the municipality of Rio; (e) air pollution from fixed points—industries—and from motor vehicle emission; (and f) noise pollution: According to data from the Secretariat of Planning of the Municipality of Rio de Janeiro, in 1980, more than 50 percent of the city's population lived in areas where noise intensity reached critical levels.

The plan divides the region according to its main hydrographic basins namely, Guanabara, Sepetiba and Coastal Lagoons, which in turn are subdivided according to the existent river basins. The plan also contains an environmental matrix to (a) identify four major environmental programs which are grouped as follows: (i) Erosion; (ii) Deforestation; (iii) Flood; (iv) Pollution: air, water, soil, noise; and (b) identify public interventions to alleviate those problems. The plan has several study maps dealing with (a) deforestation, which shows that policy intervention has focused on the Guanabara Bay and on hill slopes which were differentiated by ongoing, finished, and proposed interventions; (b) watershed areas, which shows that natural resources are in danger of depletion, with an emphasis on surface water. The maps identify four types of industrial zones: (i) ZEI, strictly industrial zone; (ii) ZUPI, predominantly industrial zone; (iii) ZUDI, diversified use zone; and (iv) ZP, harbor zone; (v) infrastructure; (vi) air pollution—based on air basins-considering only TSP and SO_x emissions. As legally defined, the Municipality of Rio de Janeiro consists of 1,356 square kilometers of which 64 percent are lowlands. The evolution of its population shows an expansionary pattern over ecologically fragile areas, and towards the periphery in areas such as Bangu, Anchieta, Campo Grande, Santa Cruz, and Jacarepagua, in the western part of the city.

Building and subdivision regulations in restricted areas are used as a tool to insure safe development patterns in hazardous lands. Major emphasis has been placed in the plan on command and control mechanisms to regulate urban growth and explicit devises have been formulated to prevent further degradation and encroachment in hazard-prone areas. With respect to government intervention in land development, the plan envisions public participation for allocation decisions on: (a) land identified as of "historical interest"; (b) land subject to environmental degradation (c) disaster-prone areas; and (d) densely populated areas lacking access to adequate infrastructure and services. The group of policy instruments proposed relates to allocation of public land,

optimization of the provision of basic infrastructure and services, regulation and control of urban expansion in floodplains and coastal areas. In every case the plan deals with both preventive as well as curative actions.

In its attempt to organize and systematize the growth of the city, the plan defines several construction and license requisites related to projects that might alter the urban environmental system, increase vulnerability to natural hazards, or intensify the depletion of natural resources. They include housing projects and other construction works which imply opening or diversion of waterways and channels, interception of flood waters, mining activities, slope stabilization problems, and removal of the vegetative cover. Article 97 provides for official review and approval of all projects and establishes penalties in the case of violations. Regarding matters of zoning and land-use regulations, the plan delineates five operational areas according to their principal use: industrial, residential, commercial and services, mixed, and environmental preservation. For each case, the plan defines ordinances and regulations to govern the use of the zoned areas. It includes general rules about building codes, height limitations, land subdivision, and densities. The plan is vague in referring to regularization of land tenure in the *favelas* and of land subdivisions in low-income neighborhoods. Although articles 147-155 attempt to delineate the criteria applicable to the urbanization and regularization of slums including: access to land, registration of land, elaboration of cadastral maps, and provision of basic infrastructure and services, the strategy does not address the issue of how to solve the conflict between the parallel unofficial land market system and how to avoid conflict and confusion in land management. Changes in traditional approaches towards land are key to the success of a more market-oriented scheme.

In sum, the plan offers a pragmatic land-use strategy to control urban environmental degradation with emphasis on command and control instruments. Some problems remain as the plan fails to broaden its approach to deal with the fundamental constrains to integrated land-use management in the city, namely (a) the existence of severe distortions in land markets that have hampered the efficiency of investments; (b) critical coordination problems among the various public agencies involved in urban matters; and (c) separation of formal and informal land markets. Further, the plan does not consider the financial feasibility of proposed policies and programs, nor does it estimate the necessary resource allocation or the viability of implementation of its proposed recommendations and programs. In that respect, implementation issues are virtually ignored and so are matters related to the role of the public versus the private sector interests. At the root of the problem lies the fundamental dichotomy between the legal system and the complex environmental and physical reality of the city.

Into the twenty-first century: recommendations and policy options

Few doubt that Rio faces substantial challenges to achieve a sustainable and equitable development. In many areas that will require decisive action the full range of available options has not been explored. What are the choices? Much rests on the performance of institutions, at the federal, state and municipal levels. Over the past two decades the world has learned that environmental protection is one area in which government must maintain a central role. The World Development Report of 1992 underlines this fact, and notes that, in spite of the lessons the world has learned,

and the generally positive experience it has had when it relies more on markets and less on governments to promote development, market mechanisms are poor protectors of the environment. This is not to say that traditional command and control instruments have had a good track record in protecting and restoring fragile ecosystems. Policy reforms are needed to improve environmental management. Technology choices, economic reforms, financial incentives, and environmental education are among the elements that will have to come together in a coherent manner if to reverse the accelerating degradation of the environment in Rio.

Rio's comparative advantage

Damage to the environment has costs that are reflected not only in fragile health conditions and diminished economic productivity but also in the reduced satisfaction that can be derived from a spoiled environment. Those issues have been discussed in this introduction and are explored at length in the contributions to this volume.

The costs of damaging Rio's amenities are not trivial. In Camargo's chapter, he argues for the consideration of Rio as a public good, and for the need to promote industrial and technological policies consistent with such an approach. His analysis calls for major conceptual shifts in urban and industrial policy-making as well as a new focus for urban public investment programs.

From the various papers in this volume we can conclude that, in the past, location decisions/land policies and public investments programs in Rio have failed to adequately compensate for the negative environmental impacts stemming from the utilization of certain types of infrastructure, transport, and industry. Access to less polluting technologies and the lessons learned from experience in other countries would be key in defining appropriate policy reforms now. The issue of a pluralistic choice of technologies is central. This is not to imply that Rio's environmental problems can be resolved through a quick "technological fix." Operating from a pluralistic perspective requires that the advantages and disadvantages of both cutting-edge and low-cost technologies be explored during the option identification process leading up to policies aimed at improved environmental sustainability. Additionally, it indicates that the range of policy options related to the adoption of specific advanced technologies is wide, and that exploring those options should be part of urban environmental decision-making. Many emerging technologies offer opportunities to implement new approaches to environmental protection, urban vulnerability reduction and risk management.

"Unanticipated" consequences in the use of technologies are no longer admissible. On this topic, it is argued that while it is often the case that "techniques or systems designed to fulfill one set of objectives, will, in the course of their development and use 'tip over' and cause 'unplanned' outcomes," only those outside the process can claim to be truly surprised. When the impact of certain technologies turns out to be detrimental or problematic, implementers usually argue that their consequences could not have been planned for, and label the results "unforeseen." In the authors' view, there is no such a thing as an unanticipated or unanticipatable consequence. The many decisions that for decades have affected the environmental development of Rio and the substantial degradation of its coastal environment provide a pragmatic illustration of how correct their argument is. The urban population of Rio is currently being threatened by the "unanticipated" consequences of a number of inappro-

priate and obsolete technologies in industry, transport, waste management and sanitation.

In Camargo's view, the abundant natural beauty in Rio provides the city with a special comparative advantage vis-a-vis other large cities in the world. Although tourism would seem to be a logical path to follow to development, it is neither the only nor the best alternative. The most logical use of Rio's comparative advantage would be to attract to the city high-paying, non-polluting, technology-intensive sectors that rely on highly-qualified employees and on high-quality productive structures. Camargo argues for policies targeted to attract the following industries: informatics, electronics, tele-communications, biotechnology, etc., in addition to specialized service sectors such as scientific and technological research, foreign trade support financial market firms, and (evidently) tourism. While in recent years, some countries, such as the newly industrialized countries (NICs), have shown a capacity to integrate new concepts in products and processes, absorb technological innovation, and utilize new communications systems; other countries have remained at the periphery of those developments (Kreimer, Munasinghe). The experience of the NICs seems to demonstrate that development is not a linear process, and there are opportunities to take shortcuts and make quantum leaps. In a similar manner, Camargo's argument leads to the conclusion that Rio's comparative advantage vis-a-vis other large cities requires that planners make the effort to "leapfrog" in the selection of new technologies. The journey will certainly be challenging, but the rewards outweigh the risks. The rest of this chapter describes some of the pieces of the road map put together by the contributors to this volume.

Using incentives to reduce negative externalities

An efficient way of reducing those externalities which are having a negative impact on Rio's environment would be to use taxes to pass the burden back to the agents creating the problem. Taxation could take various forms (e.g. high parking prices in congested destinations, tolls charged at certain strategic sites or even the closing of given areas to cars). Incentives for environmental preservation could be created by improving the quality of mass transportation (e.g. assign exclusive lanes to buses, improve the quality of mass transportation to reduce the use of individual cars). This strategy would require mass transportation to offer better quality and relatively lower prices. Investments on rail-based transportation (subway systems, modern streetcars, trains, etc.) are among the best ways of reaching this goal. Accordingly, the use of important public roads during rush hour for freight, hampering the flow of traffic, should be duly restricted through taxation or prohibitions.

Another strategy would be based on the reduction of externalities imposed on the dwellers of "corridor" neighborhoods. Individual cars coming from, for example, Barra da Tijuca would be charged a fee for using the areas that lie between it and the city center as a "corridor". Revenue collected from this fee would be applied towards the improvement of mass transportation.

Additionally, there is a need to introduce user's fees for the consumption of certain public goods, which can only be done through taxes and/or through the assignment of some form of property rights over these goods. Other urgently needed measures include: the introduction of charges for the generators of negative externalities; policies leading to the decentralization of economic as well as leisure activities in public sites (which could be done by increasing the supply of sites in under-utilized areas); and transportation improvements and fare rationalization (making mass transportation less expensive in under-utilized areas while raising charges in already over-utilized ones).

Environmentally-friendly investments

A pluralistic technological approach also requires the use of appropriate technologies. The Maimon and Rodrigues chapter provides numerous interesting examples of potential technologies that could be used, *inter alia* (a) rationalization programs in the industrial sector; (b) energy conservation and pollution reduction through energy substitution schemes; (c) lower end-product based energy consumption as a viable alternative; (d) in-house company assessment programs to help industries pinpoint, quantify and eliminate wasted energy; (e) modification of building standards to make better use of natural lighting and climatization factors, (f) energy savings in transportation; (g) low-cost decentralized sewage networks with sub-basin treatment to reduce water-body pollution; (h) potential water irradiation treatment as an alternative for industrial liquid wastes or pollutant sludge from chemical or physical treatment processes; (i) electrolytic treatment of hospital sewage; (j) innovative systems for garbage collection and disposal, making greater use of recycling, including also large-and small-scale selective garbage collection and recycling; (k) auctions of machinery and equipment, (l) plasma furnaces to dispose of industrial and medical wastes; and (m) re-use of water for industry and park lands.

Coastal zone management in Rio

Brazil's National Coastal Management Plan assigns responsibility for macro-zone implementation to State environmental agencies, with municipalities handling micro-zoning, working closely with Regional Administrations and local communities. Micro-zoning is still sporadic and haphazard. In order to set the Rio's Coastal Zone Management Program under way, computerized cartography equipment is required, together with satellite imagers and a geographical information system. A multi-disciplinary approach is needed, as well as training for environmental project managers in specialized environmental analysis courses. Detailed mapping and measuring in a variety of areas need to take place before a number of agencies will have the data that they require in order to contribute to the Program. Implementation of a coastal management program in the metropolitan region should respond to the following criteria: (a) specification of Project areas should be holistic; (b) coastal management project maps of metropolitan areas should be on a scale of no less than 1:25,000; (c) the taxonomic scale should follow the cartographic scale; (d) administrative regions and residents' associations should participate in micro-scale projects, coordinated by the municipality, which should also report back to the state (FEEMA) and federal (IBAMA) environmental agencies; (e) all involved parties should be integrated in the planning process; (f) universities, research centers and private specialized environmental-service companies should participate, to fine-tune the outputs of the Coastal Zone Management Program; and (g) air and water parameters should be coordinated by FEEMA and SERLA through monitoring key points.

Land management instruments to reduce environmental vulnerability

The main question with regard to efficient land management in the metropolitan region is how suitable land can be made realistically available to the majority of urban dwellers in the appropriate places. Urban planning authorities in Rio have long recognized the need to regulate the use of land to safeguard the basic interest of the community and to increase efficiency in the provision of services. Since the early 1950s, command and control mechanisms have been a central tool in government's attempts to manage urban expansion over unsuitable lands. However, in most cases, these regulations have not only failed to achieve their major objective, but have exacerbated some critical problems. For example, zoning and land-use controls have affected the price and quantity of land, generating strong economic interests and distortions which virtually exclude the poor from access to adequate land. Furthermore, as a result of limited financial and human resources, land-management agencies have been severely constrained in their ability to enforce existing regulations and policies.

One of the major difficulties lies in the inadequacy of the current laws to deal with the reality of the informal market that has resulted from the restricted access of low-income population to formal transactions. The rigidity and complexity of the present legal and regulatory system for land occupation has created high uncertainty for users and investors and acts as deterrent for private participation in infrastructure and housing development. A large part of land transactions occur underground. As a result, regulations are difficult to enforce, and the risk of arbitrariness and inconsistency is enhanced by the absence of institutional capacity and resources to monitor permits.

In any attempt to make the urban environment more sustainable, two important questions need to be answered: (a) To what extent should control and regulations mechanisms be the fundamental tool to achieve efficiency in managing urban growth in environmentally vulnerable areas? And (b) do the instruments envisaged reflect the particular circumstances of the city with regard to the co-existence of two separate land markets, and the reality of severe distortion in the operation of the legal market?

It is extremely important to decentralize urban infrastructure in order to reach a balance in the use of physical space in the City. Following the tradition of compensating the population for externalities created by overutilization, there is a trend to develop the infrastructure for water, sewage, waste collection, public schools, health centers, etc. in regions where overpopulation is already a problem and where the lack of such services is felt more acutely. The problem is that, to the extent that availability of urban infrastructure attracts more people, the expansion of such services in highly populated areas leads to an increase of the population, therefore, creating more demand for such services. On the other hand, less populated regions where these services are not available never become attractive.

An additional line of action that could bring about significant results is to share with the population the responsibility for costs and benefits resulting from the use and maintenance of public goods. This could be carried out through neighborhood and other grassroots associations and it could be particularly effective in poor communities and in slums where public authorities have a poor penetration. Thus, the role of the government would be to provide these associations with the support they need to meet the goals previously defined by both parties.

The main goal of such measures would be to rationalize the occupation of the soil, to prevent over-utilization of the city's physical space and, therefore, preserve its main asset—its natural beauty—while increasing the standard of living of the population.

Institutional and technical capacity building

There is no legal obligation for any government agency to consolidate its accounts and there are no uniform procedures, indeed 1985 was the last financial year whose accounts were fully investigated. Afonso reviewed Brazilian government financial statistics and found that most observers attack their range, consistency, and outdatedness. The author notes that definition of outlays on the environment is difficult and not standardized, and there are so many agencies and organizations handling the same programs and administrative changes are so frequent that accounts become extremely complex. Clearly, little can be done to improve the urban environment without the efficient management of the scarce resources available to the sector. Until more concern is shown over the quality and transparency of financial information by all levels of government, national accounts will continue to lag well behind, and rational management decisions will be difficult for implementing agencies.

Another key aspect to be taken into consideration and towards which public investments should be directed is the need to improve the level of education and skills of the work force. Two points must be stressed: (a) the need to develop a school curriculum addressing the physical conditions of the city; and (b) the need to provide the work force with training and other opportunities of acquiring and improving skills.

In order to promote the proper use of public goods, school curricula should address types of consumption that are not harmful to the ecosystem. On the other hand, in order to attract skilled labor-intensive sectors, an integrated program to upgrade the work force skill level should be implemented. Significant improvements in the quality of life require improvements in the quality of services, which can only be obtained with a more skilled work force. Considering the existence of a relatively large number of research institutions and professional courses in the City of Rio, public authorities, with the assistance of the private sector, could establish programs to provide consulting to companies and to train the work force.

With respect to companies, it is very important to improve the quality and reliability of products and services. For this purpose, consultant programs for companies should be implemented through agreements between the municipality and universities and research centers, paid by the companies. The universities and research centers would be responsible for making their staff available to companies during certain periods of the year, at the institutions where they work. The municipality would coordinate and disseminate the expertise available while consulting fees would be charged to companies. This system, in addition to improving the quality of products and services offered by companies of the City, could also promote the interaction between generators of knowledge - universities and research centers - and the private sector of the local economy. Moreover, this could be turned into an important source of financial support for Universities and research centers.

Future research

Participants at the World Bank-IBAM conference had the following suggestions to make regarding a future research agenda: (a) expand the outline of research institutions and their research presented to this Conference by Marcio Coriolano to include others such as collection, treatment and disposal of solid wastes, as well as geo-referenced data systems etc; (b) encourage appraisal of projects aimed at recuperation of the urban environment in the metropolitan region; (c) spur systematized, integrated discussion of academic contributions, public and private agencies, and NGOs, in order to resolve environmental degradation and urban vulnerability; (d) support implementation of a unified data base on technological research and development applied to Rio's urban environment; (e) open up a dialogue with research institutions regarding appropriate policies, programs and projects for intervening in the metropolitan urban environment. These institutions should be asked to rank priorities and alternatives for incorporating technical and scientific advances into ongoing work; (f) catalog sources of funding for research activities, assess their priorities for financing and investment and ascertain relevant conditions; and (g) encourage state and municipal governments to restore and foster expanded technical structures and staff training in applied environmental research and development.

Concluding remarks

Moving towards a sustainable urban environment in metropolitan Rio de Janeiro will require coordinated government action and the development of cross-sectoral approaches. Given the fact that the vulnerability of the Metropolitan Region of Rio de Janeiro to environmental degradation and natural and technological hazards is not only related to geophysical phenomena, but also to socioeconomic variables, the abatement of environmentally-related losses will also depend on establishing conditions to encourage efficiency in resource allocation and private sector participation.

Urban environmental planning in Rio should be based on a thorough assessment of the costs and effectiveness of policy options aimed at increasing market efficiency and private sector participation. An integrated strategy would enhance environmental safety through greater reliance on market forces, the elimination of overlapping responsibilities among different levels of governments, and the implementation of cost-effectiveness in the provision of basic services. The main task ahead lies in reconciling government's objectives at all levels, with the socioeconomic and the political reality of the region.

II. Conceptual Framework

Educational Framework

2. Rio de Janeiro:
Natural Beauty as a Public Good

José Marcio Camargo

1. Introduction

The City of Rio de Janeiro, as well as the state where it is located, has been suffering from prolonged social and economic deterioration. The economic performance of the metropolitan area has been relatively poor as compared to the Brazilian economy as a whole. There is a clear trend towards further degradation, standards of living began declining in the middle of this century and still continue deteriorating. In general, exogenous factors have been blamed for this phenomenon. Among these, the most frequently mentioned are the lack of federal support for solving the city's problems, the inability of local politicians to defend metropolitan interests, the transfer of the nation's capital to Brasília, and the compulsory merger into the State of Guanabara of the city and the former State of Rio de Janeiro.

When external factors are blamed for the economic decline there are two important aspects that stand out in the analysis. First, little emphasis is given to reasons directly associated with the actual structure and features of the city, such as its physical environment or the availability of exploitable resources, etc. Second, the assumption is implicit that the city should "naturally" have a performance equal to or better than the average for the country, and it could only be falling short of national figures due to the kind of outside circumstances mentioned above. It is precisely this notion—that the economic development of Rio is inevitable even given a context of prolonged economic deterioration—that causes analysts to be surprised. Once the initial assumption is accepted, however, the only possible explanation for the actual state of affairs is that there must be identifiable factors which are hindering development.

The widespread perception among the populace of Rio de Janeiro that the city's potential for development is being under-utilized can only be justified if it were possible to identify some unexploited natural resources that, if properly managed, could boost development. This chapter, without disregarding the factors identified by other analysts, explores the idea that the constraints on development in the City of Rio de Janeiro are directly linked to its physical features and the types of natural resources existing in the city. The most important point of the discussion that follows is that the main asset of Rio de Janeiro which, if utilized, could generate enormous potential for development, is its unique natural beauty and, as a consequence of its scenic attractiveness, Rio has the capacity to offer those who live there a quality of life which is potentially higher than that available in other cities.

A key aspect that has to be taken into account is the fact that natural beauty is a public good. As such, exploring its potential requires specific policies which are neither easily identifiable nor readily accepted by the general population for a variety of cultural and social reasons. Given the special nature of public goods, any development project for the City of

Rio de Janeiro which neglects these reasons will be a serious candidate for failure. In addition, the failure to treat natural beauty as a public good will hamper all possibilities of future development since such resources are easily destroyed as a result of the trend towards overutilization.

The following section of this chapter further develops the idea that the only asset in Rio de Janeiro that could constitute a possible "vocation" for development is its unique natural beauty. Consequently, the comparative advantage of the city would derive from its capacity to offer a certain quality of life, and this also represents a comparative advantage for the setting up in Rio of certain economic activities for which this factor is important. Based on this notion, section 3 of this chapter focuses on the analysis of this asset, its characteristics as a public good and the peculiarities and difficulties of using it as a lever for development. Two important aspects are highlighted: the incentive to exhibit a "free rider" type of behavior and the trend towards overutilization. These two factors have culminated in the impending physical destruction of the city, which can be seen as a consequence of current patterns of development. This suggests that the only possible type of development which can lead to the long-term betterment of Rio is sustainable development. In section 4 of this chapter, the concept of sustainable development as it should be applied to Rio is analyzed. Section 5 of this chapter introduces some economic policies that could help to reverse the current picture. Conclusions are presented in section 6 of this chapter.

2. The idea of "natural vocation"

The idea of a "natural vocation" is closely associated with the availability of relatively abundant resources (natural or man-made) either in the city or in its surrounding areas, which could generate significant economic growth. Such natural resources are not found in the city nor in the state. Land is relatively poor for agriculture and there are no mineral resources which could trigger economic development in the region.[1] The quality of the work force is above average and its consumer market ranks second in the country. However, the work force is a mobile factor, capable of moving to other cities and/or states offering better working and living conditions; moreover, the competitive edge provided by this skilled labor, when compared to the situation in other Southern cities, is not significant enough to be perceived as a relevant comparative advantage. Similarly, the relative size of the market, in spite of its importance for some industries, is not a strong enough reason to justify concentrating investments in Rio, especially when other industrial centers such as São Paulo and Belo Horizonte are not very distant.

The fact that, for over two centuries, Rio was the capital of the country imprinted on the city a certain vocation to function as an administrative center, both public and private. Nevertheless, development achieved during this period was not sufficient to keep up the growth rate after the capital was transferred to Brasília. In fact, when Brasília became the capital, the City of Rio de Janeiro was left in a situation similar to that of the state, which, since the decline of coffee plantations in the Vale da Paraíba at the end of last century, has not been able to maintain a growth pattern compatible with the national average, and which displays a performance similar to that of some Northeastern states.

It is true that the existence of abundant natural resources is not a necessary nor sufficient condition for the development of a given city or region. It is, nonetheless, a requirement for the idea of "natural vocation" to make sense. Without specific natural resources to be economically exploited, development in the region will have to rely on opportunities cropping up or policies being implemented rather than on a "natural vocation" to grow. Alternatively, if abundant natural resources are available, this could give the region a comparative advantage in the sectors which makes intensive use of this resource, thus creating a "vocation" relative to a certain development path, which could easily be explored.

But the unavailability, in the City of Rio de Janeiro, of abundant natural resources is merely apparent. Careful observation indicates the existence of an asset that, if properly explored from an economic viewpoint, could become an important source of development and lead to an improvement in the standard of living of the population: its unique natural beauty. Rio is, undoubtedly, one of the most beautiful cities in the world. There are large green areas dividing the city, long beaches that can be enjoyed throughout the year thanks to mild weather, forest-covered hills, not to mention an extremely valuable cultural and architectural heritage. Moreover, the physical layout favors mass rather than private transportation, there is a relatively large number of private and public universities and technological research centers, the quality of the labor force is good and the tradition of being the cultural center is deeply rooted.

The problem lies in the fact that the asset which is the only factor distinguishing Rio from other cities can, by its very nature, also be a liability. Inadequate use has generated, and may continue to produce, extremely perverse impacts on the development of the city and on the quality of life of its inhabitants. In this respect, some questions should be asked:

- What are the features of this asset which would hinder exploitation?

- What are the political, economic, and social conditioning factors that make its proper use on behalf of the population difficult or unfeasible?
- What social and economic policy tools can be used to maximize its potential?
- In what way can this asset function as an inhibiting factor for development instead of fostering it?

3. Beauty as a public good

When analyzing natural beauty as an asset to be exploited, the most important point for the purposes of this chapter is the fact that it is a public good. As such, the use one individual may make of it does not exclude that which others may as well make of it simultaneously. Therefore, it is difficult to assign property rights over it, just as it is equally difficult to set up a market where this good will be exchanged. Since consumption by one individual does not exclude consumption by others, a market does not emerge and the price of the public good is zero. However, the price of its production is not zero. Because its use is not exclusive, the market alone can not make users pay for its production, as occurs with private goods.[2]

For these reasons, consumers of public goods behave completely differently than consumers of private goods. Public goods provide an incentive for two types behavior that should be pointed out: 1) "free-rider" type actions; and 2) overuse of the public good.

In the case of private goods, their price represents the amount people are willing to pay in order to use them, which is another way of saying that the price represents their value for consumers. In a balanced competitive market, the price the last consumer will be willing to pay will be equal to the cost of the last unit produced.

In the case of public goods, this is not possible, as consumption by one individual does not exclude that by others. The only possible way of assigning a value to a public good would involve asking all consumers how much each of them would be willing to pay in order to use it. In other words, finding out the value from each individual and charging each one the amount indicated. This situation, however, offers an incentive for all of them to underestimate the value reported in their answers, minimizing the value of the public good in their particular situation and, consequently, reducing the cost involved in their use of it. In sum, the market cannot determine the value of a public good to each individual because its effective use does not depend on how much it will be paid for it.

Given these circumstances, everybody would like to use the public good but no one is willing to voluntarily pay for it. Everybody would like to have this good offered to them, however, for each one individually, the ideal would be that the others pay for its production. Since this is the type of behavior which gives the consumer the largest possibility of use, there is a major incentive for everybody to behave in this manner. This is the type of behavior called "free rider".

The second relevant point is that, for the same reasons mentioned above, there is an incentive to overuse a public good. Consumers tend to use it beyond the point where the cost of producing the last unit is equal to the value of the good to the last purchaser. This derives from the fact that the private cost of consuming a public good is zero, consequently it is consumed up to the point where it is no longer enjoyed by the consumer rather than up to a point at which has a relationship with the cost of producing the last unit. Because the social cost of producing a public good is positive, the question that naturally arises is who will pay for its production. In this context, the supply of a public good will almost invariably be less than that required to meet the demand from all consumers, thus generating overutilization. Overutilization, in turn, generates negative externalities which have an impact on the welfare of all users of public goods.

Public goods are found everywhere in the world. The most conspicuous case of a public good is the air in the atmosphere. Some of the main constraints to the development of the City of Rio de Janeiro are directly associated with problems deriving from the fact that the most striking feature of the city—natural beauty—is a public good.

The widespread "free rider" type of behavior is illustrated by the way Rio's inhabitants treat urban space and facilities: little respect is shown for traffic rules; cars are parked on sidewalks; public sites are subject to unplanned and unauthorized occupation by private interests (street vendors, restaurant tables, residences); construction occurs on mountain slopes in spite of the risks involved, etc. The trend towards overutilization can be observed in the demographic density of some of its most important neighborhoods (for example, Copacabana), as well as the excessive demographic density in the slums. Similarly, chaotic traffic conditions are due, on the one hand, to the poor quality of mass transportation and, on the other, to the excessive use of private transportation. While it is true that all these factors are found in other major Brazilian cities, they are found there to a lesser degree than in Rio.

One relevant aspect to be considered is that the very growth of the city tends to encourage "free rider" behavior, adding to the dimension of the problem.[3] This behavior only started being perceived as predatory in the 1980s, when accelerated growth was taking place. Up to now little or nothing has been done to prevent it.

It should be pointed out that all measures will have to be implemented by the government, since individual agents can do very little. Consequently, the development of institutions capable of creating the proper incentives for individuals is a prerequisite of preventive measures that can respond to overutilization and the "free rider" types of behavior. What seems to be a natural alternative in this context would be to adopt targeted rules and restrictions. However, although legal instruments are often the only available resource, in order to be effective, they require proper monitoring and enforcement, as well as a centralized decision-making process, all of which create opportunities for corruption and increase implementation costs. Therefore, it is often more effective to use the market itself in order to create the proper incentives.

This process results in extremely perverse outcomes for the city. On the one hand, it creates favorable conditions for ecological disasters to occur, such as landslides and floods during the rainy season, excessive air and sound pollution, etc. On the other hand, it significantly reduces the quality of life of the population, thereby diminishing the main comparative advantage of the city. Instead of functioning as a factor that promotes social well-being, natural beauty, because it is a public good, acts as a constraint to development.

Undoubtedly, the existence of a large supply of this public good in Rio has important positive aspects. It attracts tourists and visitors, indeed tourism is one of the major and most promising economic activities of the city. Furthermore, it is still capable of improving the quality of life for the population in general at a relatively low cost, if the proper measures are carried out correctly. On the other hand, some analysts might argue that one of the most interesting aspects of Rio is the irreverent nature of the people, their happy and laid-back attitude to towards life. This orientation is probably a

consequence of the large availability of public goods. If natural beauty is to be used as leverage for development, steps must be taken so that the benefits which result from such beauty, and which so positively distinguish this city from all others, are not destroyed.

The existence of abundant natural beauty in Rio has led some analysts to suggest that the city (and the state of Rio) should concentrate efforts on promoting tourism. Some have gone so far as to suggest it is the only path to growth. But industry based on tourism is only a small slice of the potential pie. The point is that the existence of this asset enables the city to offer a higher standard of living than other Brazilian cities, at a lower cost. In other words, while it can foster the growth of an important industry—tourism—it can also attract those sectors that pay attention to the quality of life of their employees. Considering that the higher the income level of employees, the stronger their demand for a better quality of life, the city could attract companies that require highly qualified and technologically sophisticated labor with relatively higher salaries.

The local comparative advantage should logically attract to the city non-polluting, technology-intensive sectors that rely on highly qualified employees and on high quality productive structures: sectors such as informatics, electronics, telecommunications, biotechnology, fashion, apparel, shoes, furniture, jewelry, etc., in addition to services such as scientific and technological research, cultural activities, foreign trade support, specialized insurance companies, financial market firms and, evidently, tourism.

It is worth noting that almost all these sectors were, or still are, the ones that prospered the most in the city. Nonetheless, the downward trend in the standard of living resulting from the inability to properly use the city's main source of wealth has reduced its attractiveness for these industries, and gradually they have moved to regions with more growth potential, less physical restrictions, and which offer better living standards to their employees. This, in turn, has accelerated economic deterioration in Rio.

Any strategy for the development of Rio, in order to be successful, has to respect its physical and natural features and focus on improving the quality of life. This implies that a key factor in this process is to stop the ongoing destruction of its natural resources. From this perspective, sustainable development is not just a goal to be pursued in order to avoid the destruction of an ecosystem, as in other regions, but rather the most effective way of adequately exploiting the growth potential of the City of Rio de Janeiro. Thus, the analysis of this concept is a step towards a feasible strategy for the development of the city.

4. Natural beauty and sustainable development

The idea that natural beauty is an asset to be exploited contains in itself the concept of sustainable development: beauty is both limited and renewable. Consequently, it is crucial that any possible degradation caused by its use as a resource be restricted in some way that is related to the capacity for renewal, either through natural or man-made mechanisms.

Issues associated with sustainable development contribute to a better understanding of the city's problem. One of the most relevant ones, as mentioned above, is the fact that the market alone cannot properly channel economic activity. The market can solve the problem of an optimal resource allocation (efficiency) but it cannot solve issues related to distribution (equity) and to optimal scale (sustainability). As the economy grows, the scale of the economy also grows, and the

optimal limit is provided by the capacity to regenerate or to absorb the ecosystem to which it belongs, whichever is less. The problem lies in the fact that maximum capacity does not necessarily correspond to optimal capacity. The focus of the discussion is, therefore, how to restrict the growth of scale in such a way that it remains within the limits of ecosystem sustainability. Four points should be taken into account in this respect (Daly 1990):

- Human scale should be limited to a point that, if not optimal, is nonetheless able of being sustained by the ecosystem.
- Technological progress aimed at sustainable development should lead to increased efficiency in the use of natural resources.
- Renewable resources should be exploited based on the principle of sustainable maximization of profits and, in general, should not be allowed to reach depletion, since they will grow in importance as non-renewable resources become unavailable.
- Nonrenewable resources should be exploited at a rate equal to the creation of renewable resources that replace them.

In a region where the main asset is a public good, the market alone will not provide adequate guidance for its use. Unplanned exploitation leads to the destruction of such assets, given that scale will be pushed beyond what the ecosystem is capable of absorbing. This has been one of the main problems of the City of Rio de Janeiro.

The way in which physical space has been used in Rio is a clear example of this phenomenon. Throughout the years, Rio has grown southward towards where the beaches and nicest areas are located. Governments, in order to make access to these parts of the city easier, have built tunnels, roads and urban infra-structure. As a result, the price of land in these new developments went up, housing structures grew more and more vertical while population density increased. At the same time, workers brought for the construction work occupied the neighboring mountain slopes where land was either vacant or belonged to the government. Occupation took place *de facto*, not by right. The fact that these unplanned neighborhoods are inhabited by low income unskilled workers, living in precarious conditions, with no infrastructure available, accounts for the accelerated expansion of slums ("favelização") in some of the most expensive areas of the city.

This process continues until profits obtained from the construction cycle in a given neighborhood come to an end, due to increasing demographic density, soaring costs of land and declining standards of living. At this point, activity is shifted to another area. However, the mountain slopes remain occupied by a poor and unskilled segment of the population, who depend on the demand for services in the area for their living, and earn low salaries and live under poor conditions. Wealth and poverty are found side by side, which exacerbates conflicts resulting from social and economic inequities, lack of urban infrastructure, risks of ecological disasters, and ultimately results in the destruction of the ecosystem.

Finally, the physical layout of city being such that one neighborhood follows the other almost in a straight line, as the city grows, the most recently developed area becomes a "corridor" leading to new developments. Consequently, almost all neighborhoods in the South zone function as "corridors"—areas through which those living further south have to go through on their way to work—contributing, thus, to greater deterioration of the quality of life.

The outcome of this process is the following: overpopulated neighborhoods, inadequate infrastructure and problems that seriously impact the living standards of

the population. Each new neighborhood is presented as a new paradise to be discovered. As the physical space is occupied, overpopulation changes the paradise into something far from it. Thus, the evolution of territorial occupation in the City of Rio de Janeiro is one leading to permanent destruction.

Moreover, poverty and inequality are fruitful media for the proliferation of anti-social behaviors, such as criminality and drug trafficking. The growing lack of safety impacts adversely on the quality of life of the population as a whole, including that of slum dwellers, creating a vicious cycle unlikely to be broken.

It should be stressed that providing the slums with urban infrastructure is not enough to solve the problem. In fact, from the perspective of the use of physical space, it may yield the opposite result, as it attracts more people, shoots demographic density levels even higher and increments the potential for the destruction of the ecosystem.

The fact that the City of Rio de Janeiro attracts people from other regions of the state and the country is particularly important in this respect. As more job opportunities are created, Rio will attract more immigrants, at a rate higher than the one justified by the real salary differential among regions, given that public goods in Rio have zero cost. As a consequence, pressure on the city's ecosystem grows stronger and the vicious cycle of poverty and ecological destruction, described above, is reinforced. An illustration of the magnet force of the city is the excessively high levels of concentration of the state population: 80 percent of the people live in the metropolitan area, 42 percent of which concentrated in the City of Rio de Janeiro.

Consequently, in order to benefit from the assets of the city, it is fundamental that tools to generate sustainable development (from an ecological perspective) be created in such a way that the scale of use of physical space can be kept at levels compatible with the city's ecosystem. This is the challenge that will allow the present trend towards degradation in the City of Rio de Janeiro to be reversed.

5. Rio as a public good

To adopt the view of Rio de Janeiro as a public good requires changing dramatically the way its development has been approached. It means creating conditions so that public goods available in large quantities in the city can be properly exploited by the population instead of being destroyed throughout the development process. This section of the chapter presents some policies that could contribute to reaching this goal. Many of them are difficult to implemented due to cultural, social and economic resistance. Nevertheless, the aim is to point out the direction in which the author believes the City should be heading in order to use its natural beauty as an efficient tool of sustainable development.

The first and probably the most serious problem to be solved is the trend towards overutilization of the existing physical space, which accounts for negative externalities and for the decline in the living standards of the population. This problem is particularly serious given the way externalities tend to be treated in Brazil, and especially in Rio de Janeiro.

The theory of externalities shows that, whenever an agent or a set of agents generate, through their actions, some type of negative (or positive) externality, the proper way of mitigating the problem is to tax (or to subsidize) the agent responsible for generating such an externality. The result is that this agent will have an economic incentive to find alternative ways of behaving (or of intensifying this behavior, thus increasing the positive externalities generated), which will reduce

its impact. A clear illustration is the use of private transportation, which increases CO_2 emissions in the atmosphere, hinders traffic flows, causes major traffic jams, while deteriorating the quality of life of the population.

An efficient and proper way of reducing this externality would be to tax the agents that make an intensive use of it. This taxation could take the form of high parking prices in main areas of destination, tolls charged at certain strategic sites or even the closing of given areas to cars. Another possibility would be to assign exclusive lanes and improve the quality of mass transportation so that the use of individual cars, given the limited space and high costs, would become less attractive to agents.

This strategy would require mass transportation to offer better quality and relatively lower prices. Investments on rail-based transportation (subway systems, modern streetcars, trains, etc.) are the best way of reaching this goal. Accordingly, the use of important public roads during rush hour for freight, hampering the flow of traffic, should be duly restricted through taxation or prohibitions.

However, instead of following this path, government has adopted the strategy of rewarding those responsible for negative impacts. Instead of imposing taxes on private transportation and improving the quality of mass transportation, new wide avenues are built to accommodate more individual cars, more parking places are made available in downtown areas, exclusive lanes for cars during rush hour are created, etc. The outcome is that the generator of the externality has no incentives to minimize it while there is an incentive for new agents to generate externalities and, consequently, benefit from the rewards given by the government.

The following example illustrates well this issue. During the 1970s, the government of the State of Guanabara decided to connect Barra da Tijuca to the center of the city through the South Zone.[4] For this purpose, tunnels had to be built through the mountains that separate these two regions and a long overpass was built along the coast. But, to reach downtown, those living in Barra da Tijuca have to go through all the neighborhoods of the south zone: Leblon, Ipanema, Jardim Botânico, Botafogo, Copacabana, etc. Thus, these areas were turned into "corridors" for the dwellers of Barra da Tijuca, bringing about a significant decline in the quality of life in such areas.

Considering the externalities imposed on the dwellers of such neighborhoods, the correct measure from an economic perspective, in order to reduce the generation of externalities, would be to charge individual cars coming from Barra da Tijuca a fee for using these areas as a "corridor". Revenue collected from this fee would be applied towards the improvement of mass transportation. However, instead of heading in this direction, municipal and state governments have been rewarding the generation of externalities with more express lanes, overpasses, etc. Each new express lane solves, for some time, a given type of problem. But the incentive to resort to private transportation, as a result of such policies, accounts for a relapse of the problem, each time compromising the future to a greater extent while generating more negative externalities. In spite of the operational and cultural difficulties involved in implementing a policy that would tax generators of externalities, this may be the only way of allowing the city to grow without destroying neighborhoods located in this "corridor".

The issue of the scale in which the ecosystem is used is particularly dramatic in Rio de Janeiro. This explains why it is of utmost importance to adopt policies disciplining the use of land, instead of allowing the market to do so. The classical tools to reach this goal are:

- Policies aimed at regulating the orderly use of the land.
- Fiscal policies, based on progressive taxes on real estate, taking into account the relative supply of public goods in different regions, with higher tax rates applying to regions where the supply of public goods is larger.
- A tariff structure for mass transportation that subsidizes transportation in regions where population growth is desired, penalizing the overpopulated areas.
- Investments in mass transportation and incentives given to projects aiming at replacing private by mass transportation.
- Policies aimed at providing land tenure to slum dwellers, coupled with investments for infrastructure in the slums. Costs of these investments should be duly allocated among the beneficiaries.
- Measures in order to discipline and restrict, when necessary, the use of public sites of the city—sidewalks, parks, beaches, etc.—by private agents (street vendors, cafes, etc.). Proper areas should be made available for such activities and better job opportunities offered to the agents involved, through programs to develop skills.
- Priority-based projects for urban infrastructure, contemplating areas where the inflow of people is desired at the expense of over populated regions.
- Policies aiming at decentralizing economic activities and restructuring access to regions where economic activities are concentrated. The creation of a flat rate for mass transportation can be a powerful tool to decentralize economic activities and housing distribution.
- Incentives to adopt technological innovations preventing the deterioration of public goods, such as the use of natural gas in mass transportation, the development of urban

L. I. H. E.
THE BECK LIBRARY
WOOLTON RD., LIVERPOOL, L16 8ND

infrastructure (water, sewage and waste collection, etc.) in the Baixada Fluminense and in areas where pollution reaches the beaches, the practice of companies providing transportation for their employees instead of offering private parking places, etc.

- Finally, investments in leisure infrastructure in polluted regions, such as the cleaning of the Guanabara Bay, which will contribute to decentralize leisure activities and avoid over consumption of those public goods that have not been over utilized yet.

It is not within the scope of this chapter to discuss in detail each one of these policies, nor is the author qualified to do so. However, there are some relevant initiatives, presently being implemented, that should be mentioned. The introduction of the concept of "created land" [taxing buildings for each story over an established maximum] is an important step towards the orderly occupation of the soil, as it turns construction work in densely populated and highly valued areas more expensive. Similarly, it is politically feasible to establish a flat rate for mass transportation and to improve the quality of this service. In this respect, international lending institutions have an important role to play in providing financing for the development of rail-based transportation to replace buses in mass transportation. In the long run, a legal settlement for the issue of land tenure in the slums, followed by investments in infrastructure, is rather costly but perfectly feasible.

One of the instruments to which the population would object the most would probably be the increase in the costs of private transportation as well as the possibility of replacing the awards given to the generators of externalities, such as new overpasses, express lanes for cars, etc. by financial penalties such as tolls paid in strategic sites or physical penalties that

could include assigning to mass transportation the express lanes presently used by private cars.

Similarly, the concentration of infrastructure and transportation investments in less populated regions would certainly be objected to by those presently living in areas with inadequate infrastructure.

However, the major points to be stressed are: the need to introduce user's fees for the consumption of public goods, which can only be done through taxes and/or through the assignment of property rights over these goods; the introduction of charges for the generators of negative externalities; and the importance of policies leading to the decentralization of economic activities as well as leisure activities in public sites, which could be done by increasing the supply of sites in under-utilized areas, improving and turning less expensive mass transportation in such areas while raising charges in already overutilized ones.

It is extremely important to decentralize urban infrastructure in order to reach a balance in the use of physical space in the city. Following the tradition of compensating the population for externalities created by overutilization, there is a trend to develop the infrastructure for water, sewage, waste collection, public schools, health centers, etc. in regions where overpopulation is already a problem and where the lack of such services is felt more acutely. The problem is that, to the extent that availability of urban infrastructure attracts more people, the expansion of such services in highly populated areas leads to an increase of the population, therefore, creating more demand for such services. On the other hand, less populated regions where these services are not available never become attractive.

In other words, the larger the population, the more inadequate the services provided, the larger the demand for jobs, the larger the volume of investments required from the state and the larger the migration to the region, thus creating a self-feeding process.

In fact, one of the main reason why the population of the State of Rio de Janeiro is concentrated in the City of Rio de Janeiro is the fact that infrastructure is also concentrated there. The percentages below are just a few examples of this situation: 50.3 percent of primary schools and 71.9 percent of secondary school are located in the metropolitan area; 80 percent of all hospital beds available in the public health system are located in the metropolitan area.

Apparently, at the root of this phenomenon is the fact that the city was the nation's capital for two centuries. Major investments from the federal public sector were channeled to the city while the State of Rio de Janeiro, since the decline of coffee plantations at the end of the century, was going through a process of economic deterioration and was unable to finance its own infrastructure.[5] In order limit the concentration in the city, which causes a saturation in its scale, it is necessary to steer infrastructure investments away from the city, to the interior of the state. From this perspective, efforts to improve the quality of life in the City of Rio de Janeiro have to include efforts to do the same in the interior of the state.

A second line of action that could bring about significant results is to share with the population the responsibility for costs and benefits resulting from the use and maintenance of public goods. This could be carried out through neighborhood and other grassroots associations and it could be particularly effective in poor communities and in slums where public authorities have a poor penetration. Thus, the role of the government would be to provide these associations with the support

they need to meet the goals previously defined by both parties.

The main goal of such measures would be to rationalize the occupation of the soil, to prevent overutilization of the city's physical space and, therefore, preserve its main asset—its natural beauty—while increasing the standard of living of the population.

6. Sustainable development and the quality of the work force

A key aspect to be taken into consideration and towards which public investments should be directed is the need to improve the level of education and skills of the work force. Two points must be stressed:

- First, the need to develop a school curriculum addressing the physical conditions of the city.
- Second, the need to provide the work force with training and other opportunities of acquiring and improving skills.

In order to promote the proper use of public goods, school curricula should address types of consumption that are not harmful to the ecosystem. Courses on environmental education, in public and private schools, can play a relevant role and should be implemented. Such courses could be very effective in inducing non-predatory types of behavior vis-a-vis public goods.

On the other hand, in order to attract skilled labor-intensive sectors, an integrated program to upgrade the work force skill level should be implemented. Significant improvements in the quality of life require improvements in the quality of services, which can only be obtained with a more skilled work force. Considering the existence of a relatively large number of research institutions and professional courses in the city of Rio, public authorities, with the assistance of the private sector, could establish programs to provide consulting to companies and to train the work force.

A first step towards this goal could be to require companies to offer professional training on a permanent basis in order to qualify to participate in bids for public constructions. These programs could be jointly carried out by companies and agencies such as SENAI and SENAC, for example. Similarly, the granting of municipal licenses to street vendors or any other activity should require the worker to devote part of his/her time to professional training. The aim of such policies is to differentiate the work force available in the city, thus creating a comparative advantage that will attract some industries to the city. Government should also devote a significant part of the annual budget to train and/or retrain the unemployed.

With respect to companies, it is very important to improve the quality and reliability of products and services. For this purpose, consultant programs for companies should be implemented through agreements between the municipality and universities and research centers, paid by the companies. The universities and research centers would be responsible for making their staff available to companies during certain periods of the year, at the institutions where they work. The municipality would coordinate and disseminate the expertise available while consulting fees would be charged to companies. This system, in addition to improving the quality of products and services offered by companies of the city, could also promote the interaction between generators of knowledge—universities and research centers—and the private sector of the local economy. Moreover, this could be turned into an important source of financial support for Universities and research centers.

7. Conclusions

This chapter is based on the assumption that the main asset of the City of Rio de Janeiro, one that accounts for its uniqueness in the country, is its natural beauty. Therefore, it is only logical to use this resource in order to foster development in the city. However, given its special characteristics, and in particular the fact of its being a public good; and the cultural, political and institutional limitations of the city and the country, this asset is difficult to exploit. Incentives for "free riders" and overutilization, coupled with the lack of proper policies to guarantee an orderly occupation of the land have created a permanent trend towards degradation and destruction. For this reason, in order to properly exploit this asset, the municipal governments and the general population must develop a permanent concern with the idea of sustainable development. In other words, any strategy to develop the city will have to be a sustainable one, particularly from an environmental perspective.

This chapter suggests some economic policies that could establish the criteria on which the city could use its main asset to leverage development, thus avoiding the vicious cycle of overutilization, ecological degradation and poverty that has characterized the recent past.

In addition to fiscal policies, the main thrust of this proposal is to encourage the upgrading of the work force and the permanent improvement of the quality of services and products. Such policies could reduce the scale in which ecosystems are being used, prevent their destruction, and allow the proper use of the city's main comparative advantage, which is ultimately the possibility of offering a higher quality of life. This would attract to the city those sectors that pay relatively higher salaries to their employees with higher level of skills; for these sectors the standard of living of their employees is an important factor that influences the decision of where to allocate investments. As a by-product, this strategy would promote productivity and income growth, consequently reducing the high levels of poverty among the population.

Notes

The author is a professor at the Catholic University of Rio de Janeiro in the Department of Economics. He thanks Pedro Otávio Prado for comments on a first version of this chapter.

1. Oil, recently found in Bacia de Campos, could be an excellent driving force for the future development of the State of Rio de Janeiro.

2. The expression "public good" is used here in the sense that economists usually attribute to it and not as it is popularly known, i.e., government produced goods. These two concepts are not interchangeable, in spite of the fact that many public goods are produced by the government and in spite of the difficulties implied in its production through the market.

3. About the proportion between the trend and the magnitude of the "free rider" behavior, see M. Olson (1982).

4. At the time, many specialists indicated that the most efficient way, from the perspective of urban planning and economics, would be to use the North Zone. However, real estate interests were able to induce the government to build the "Viaduto do Joá", an extremely expensive overpass connecting Barra da Tijuca to the South Zone. The value of land in Barra da Tijuca increased significantly and the externalities pointed out in this chapter were created.

5. See J. P. Almeida Magalhães and J. M. Camargo (1992) for an analysis of this phenomenon.

3. Coastal Zone Management in the Metropolitan Area of Rio de Janeiro

Mauro Sergio F. Argento

1. Introduction

As a result of the multiple uses which coastlines offer to the surrounding society, coastlines suffer great anthropic pressure, and the pressures placed upon the coastline by a metropolitan area create a dynamic due largely to the junction of air, landmass, and sea. Historically important for both conquest and trade, Brazilian ports grew into the major cities that today attract rural migrants who settle on lower-value coastal hillsides and lowlands, thus turning the shoreline into a giant garbage dump that needs systematic monitoring. Managing coastlines to take into account the needs of the cities and requirements of the environment demands a holistic overview of a wide geographic area and an understanding of the interaction between physical, human and biological agents in land, sea and air systems.

Brazil's Coastal Management Law 7,661, dated May 16, 1988, reflects this type of overview, especially in the delineation of the boundaries of the coastal zone which have been defined as including geo-morphological aspects both on and off-shore. This paper summarizes the main features in Brazil's National Coastal Management Plan, and suggests pragmatic actions to implement it in metropolitan areas such as Rio de Janeiro. The text is structured in the following manner: Section 2 of this chapter summarizes Brazil's National Coastal Management Plan, basic concepts and implementation methodology. Section 3 of this chapter presents suggestions for implementing coastal management plans in metropolitan areas on a micro-detail scale, particularly for Rio de Janeiro: treatment and infrastructure. Section 4 of this chapter analyzes current coastal management practices in Brazil and outlines projects for metropolitan areas such as that of Rio de Janeiro.

2. National Coastal Management Plan

Main aspects

Coastlines have always been the nation's most highly valued land. Brazil started to implement a National Coastal Management Plan in 1984, seeking integrated information on coastal systems through systematic data collection. The methodology was developed by the Interministerial Marine Resources Commission (CIRM) through the Coastal Management Project, covering 17 coastal States and some 7,408 kilometers of shoreline.

This modular program includes macro-zoning and monitoring, a Geographic Information System and State Boards. Macro-zoning has produced eleven 1:100,000 scale maps detailing the internal structures of coastal systems covering 30' latitude by 30' longitude. After geo-coding they enter the Geographical Information Data Bank to provide input for information plans that generate environmental scenarios to guide State Board decisions. Board members—representing the legislative and executive branches of government, as well as technical, scientific and civil communities—define properly-organized use of coastal areas in a Projected Use document. This program checks the dynamics of Coastal System functionality and notes inconsistencies between Projected Use and Actual Use, through Coastal Monitoring and data collected both in the field and from LANDSAT and SPOT satellites. Brazil's National Coastal Management Plan encourages decentralization, spurring each State to develop its own efforts in accordance with the methodology and objectives laid down nationwide by the General Coordination Dept.

State environmental agencies are responsible for implementation, and the environmentalist view colors all mechanisms in the National Coastal Management Plan. Aiming at environmental preservation, macro-zoning is carried out at State level, meso-zoning by municipalities, and micro-zoning by regional administrations. Provision is also made for training human resources at the research institutes that create methodologies, using state-of-the-art technologies.

Brazil's Coastal Management Project follows two basic principles:
- Decentralized coordination.
- Prior consultation with communities and other interested parties.

Operational limits of the Coastal Management Project have been set at the 20-meter bathymetric curve. Studies have indicated that surface distances vary from 6 to 100 nautical miles, depending on nearshore topography, particularly where major river mouths form underwater deltas. Mainland limits follow river basin watersheds that directly affect coastlines—criteria suggested by Argento and Azevedo—thus highlighting interactions between CAUSE and EFFECT of phenomena and facilitating coastal zone monitoring. In Rio de Janeiro State this onshore delimitation is simplified by the Serra do Mar range watershed.

Basic operational concepts

Successful implementation of Brazil's National Coastal Management Plan demands a conceptual basis for technical actions. Basic concepts include the following:
- *Theoretical basis for the coastal management process.* Multidisciplinary environmental actions based on structured. area data shown on single-topic maps. Coastal management decisions also rely on zoning and monitoring. Proper map scaling (macro/meso/micro) is crucial, within a holistic overview that defines environmental systems, pinpointing problems and offering solutions.
- *Practical content for development of the coastal management process.* As coastal management involves a specific geographical area, satellite-based remote sensing and radar provide vital input for computerized map-making using a Geo-environmental Data Bank, backed by field studies.

Coastal management methodology first defines a geo-systemic overview giving the operational limits of the coastline to be managed, presented in a single-topic map as specified previously. Shoreline areas are then macro-zoned as follows:
- Ecological conservation areas.
- Areas for use of profitable biological natural resources.
- Sites for ports and terminals.
- Areas for urban expansion.
- Sources of pollution.
- Tourism and leisure areas.
- National security areas.
- Areas for working energy-source natural resources.
- Historical sites and landscapes.
- Areas for scientific and technological development.
- Fish-farming areas.

- Farming and grazing areas.
- Forest activities areas.

Single-topic maps used in this macro-zoning process include the following:

- Topography, bathymetry, steepness, river and road networks, physical limits and urbanized areas.
- Geo-morphology.
- Geology and fasciology.
- Land use and ground cover.
- Agrarian suitability.
- Water quality.
- Plant and animal life.
- Oceanographic parameters.
- Climatological parameters.
- Existing plans and projects.
- Socioeconomic information.

Normally, more than one projected use scenario is defined for any given area. Coastal management methodology resolves conflicts through its multiple-representation Boards.

Next, a Geo-environmental Data Base supplies computerized topographical output for these scenarios. A Pilot Coastal Management Information System (SIGERCO) has been developed by the Rio de Janeiro Federal University and Brazil's Space Research Institute. Monitoring and data collection routines are then implemented to check changes in the area under study, using LANDSAT and SPOT satellites as well as socioeconomic population census data from the Brazilian Geography and Statistics Institute (IBGE). The projected use map (zoning) is then compared to the current use charts (monitoring) through the Geographical Information System, highlighting inconsistencies.

Coastal management is not responsible for correcting distortions; it rather advises the competent agencies so that suitable action may be taken. Coastal management defines environmental functions through single-topic maps in order to achieve specific objectives at each scale.

Macro-zoned pilot areas are already established in some Brazilian States (Rio Grande do Norte, Bahia, Espirito Santo, Rio de Janeiro, São Paulo, Parana); others are still preparing maps. Only the State of São Paulo has developed a coastal management monitoring project; the coastal management board structure has been tested in some States (Rio Grande do Sul, Paraná, São Paulo). More detailed scaling at the metropolitan level still needs definition, working along the same lines as regional macro-zoning.

Tools available at FEEMA for coastal management

Brazil's State Environmental Engineering Foundation (FEEMA) is responsible for implementation of Coastal Monitoring and Macro-zoning Projects in the State of Rio de Janeiro. Some technical staff is already available for coastal management, lacking only the necessary tools. FEEMA already has the infrastructure for collecting and processing data on air and water quality.

A map of the Lakes Region (Araruama) has been prepared, and macro-zoning of the Sepetiba Bay is currently under study. A coastal management plan for the Araruama Municipality has been drawn up, suggesting corrective environmental measures for implementation by the Town Council.

Progress is hampered by lack of autonomy in decision-taking, slow channeling of funds, lack of permanent technical staff, and limited political clout favoring specific-interest alterations pushed through by each new administration. Although halted since 1991 awaiting renewal of the implementing agreement, the Project is being restructured by temporary staff; activities should start up again soon.

3. Suggestions for implementation of coastal management plans in metropolitan regions

Coastal land use studies should consider scales of treatment that are vital to achieving objectives. Brazil's Coastal Management Project is currently detailing on a regional scale the principal products prepared by the various State Environmental Agencies, using Coastal Macro-zoning. More detailed municipal studies demand both conceptual and operational definition to become feasible. Mechanisms incorporating different methods and concepts are needed to minimize distortions due to varying viewpoints.

Management decisions for a metropolitan area should not concentrate on political, social, technical, economic or ecological factors. They should rather integrate all these characteristics, using social orientation, environmental education and executive action, each requiring different scales of detailing. Social orientation dovetails land use and the resulting impacts thereof. Environmental education should be included in normal schooling up to university level. Executive action should integrate the State, Business and the Community in decisions that weigh costs against social, economic and environmental benefits.

Geo-environmental data bases should be set up for each detail scale. In Brazil, regional macro-zoning is carried out on a scale of 1:1,000,000 (nationwide data base already in existence); municipal meso-zoning should be scaled at 1:50,000, and micro-scaling between 1:50,000 and 1:25,000.

The Rio de Janeiro Planning Institute - IPLAN-RIO already has a socioeconomic data base, although not arranged on the cartographic bases needed for preparation of environmental scenarios. We suggest an inter-relationship between IBGE and IPLAN-RIO to facilitate coastal management projects. Metropolitan areas obviously demand greater detailing, based on an environmental data base that should be set up.

Objectives of coastal management in the Metropolitan Region of Rio de Janeiro

Following the guidelines laid down by Brazil's National Coastal Management Plan, operational limits for the Rio de Janeiro metropolitan area should not be tied to densely-occupied areas. Adequate management of the city's urban and industrial areas should stretch as far as the Serra do Mar coastal range watershed and catchment basins for the area in question. Offshore limits can follow the 20-meter bathymetric curve.

Micro-zoning of Rio de Janeiro should be mapped on a scale of at least 1:25,000, with socioeconomic census data for the various Administrative Regions. This will streamline solutions for problem communities.

Important data base variables for mapping and consideration in coastal zoning decisions should include the following:
- Environmental protection areas—not for use: mangrove swamps, dunes, beaches, etc.
- Environmental conservation areas—controlled use: forests, bays, lakes, lagoons, rivers, bluffs.
- Port and terminal and tourism areas.
- Urban expansion areas.
- Tourism and recreation areas.
- National security areas.
- Historical sites and landscapes.
- Areas for working natural resources.
- Areas with renewable, profit-producing biological resources.
- Farming areas.
- Grazing areas.

- Urban areas: residential, commercial, industrial, airports, institutions.
- Areas at high environmental risk:
  - Air: acid rain, aerosols, radioactivity.
  - Water: sedimentation, pollution.
  - Land: forest clearing, silting, erosion, landslides flooding, social tensions, traffic jams, railroad junctions.

These 13 basic factors demand suitably-scaled single-topic maps:
- Plani-altimetric and bathymetric map.
- Geological map.
- Geo-morphological map.
- Soil map.
- Climatological map.
- Ground cover map.
- On/offshore water quality map.
- Plant/animal life map.
- Beach parameter map.
- Existing plans and projects map.
- Socioeconomic map.

These 11 maps would form the basis for the micro-zoning of the Projected Use Map, and should thus be highly objective. Data would be collected by duly-registered university-level Environmental Research and Study Centers. A geo-environmental data base, linked to a Geographic Information System for the Rio de Janeiro metropolitan area and backed by satellite monitoring, would ensure full compliance with coastal management objectives.

Demand and infrastructure for coastal management

Brazil's National Coastal Management Plan assigns responsibility for macro-zone implementation to State environmental agencies, with municipalities handling micro-zoning, working closely with Regional Administrations and local communities. Only macro-zoning is currently under way; micro-zoning is still sporadic and haphazard.

In order to set this Project under way, computerized cartography equipment is required, together with satellite imagers and a geographical information system. Human resources are another problem, as staff tends to be specialized, while a multidisciplinary approach is needed. Environmental Project Managers should be trained through specialized Environmental Analysis courses.

Efforts at both State and Municipal level are already seeking to firm up these interfaces, streamlining environmental project management. Plans also cover the participation of educational institutions, research centers and private companies, fostering the decentralized nature of this project and providing feedback.

4. Prospects for coastal management

Rising shoreline land values and ballooning populations pinpoint coastal management as the trend of the future, particularly along Brazil's extensive coastline. With a National Coastal Management Plan already established by federal law, and the methodology already in place, the future for coastal management in Brazil looks promising.

In terms of the current state-of-the-art, macro-zoning is under way in 14 coastal States The Brazilian Environment Institute - IBAMA is responsible for general coordination, and is currently reviewing coastal management methodological criteria.

Maps on a scale of 1:1,000,000 are at various stages of preparation in the States of Amapá, Pará, Maranhão, Piauí, Ceara, Rio Grande do Norte, Paraíba, Pernambuco, Alagoas, Sergipe, Bahia, Espírito Santo, Rio de Janeiro, São Paulo, Paraná, Santa Catarina, and Rio Grande do Sul.

In order to improve the implementation of coastal management plans in metropolitan regions, specifically Rio de Janeiro, the following measures are suggested:

- Specification of Project areas should be holistic.
- Coastal Management Project maps of metropolitan areas should be on a scale of no less than 1:25,000.
- The taxonomic scale should follow the cartographic scale, with basic headings suggested.
- Administrative Regions and Residents' Associations should participate in micro-scale projects, coordinated by the municipality, which should also report back to the state (FEEMA) and federal (IBAMA) environmental agencies.
- Integration is vital for the Regional Boards, responsible for ratifying the environmental plans laid out in the Projected Use map.
- Universities, research centers and private specialized environmental-service companies should participate, to fine-tune the Project.
- IBGE and IPLAN-RIO should be responsible for supplying socioeconomic census data.

This information should be presented in the following forms:

- Single-topic maps using parameters that include the labor force, equipment available and highway networks.
- Statistical tables that provide input for the Rio de Janeiro Coastal Management data base.
  - Air and water parameters should be coordinated by FEEMA and SERLA through monitoring key points.
  - Agencies involved should be supplied with the necessary equipment: Geographic Information System, Keying-in Center, Plotter, Digital Satellite Imaging Systems, etc.
  - Multidisciplinary Environmental Analysis courses should be set up to train Environmental Project Managers.

Coastal management is not a closed operation, but one that fosters adaptation to regional characteristics within master guidelines laid down by the basic methodology. Cost-benefit analyses of environmental impacts and preventive actions, favoring the environment and introducing social and economic improvements through sustainable development, need an operational base as outlined above in order to implement effective coastal management projects in metropolitan areas.

III. Institutional and Financial Framework

4. Institutional Framework of Environmental Policy in Brazil

Paulo de Góes Filho

Use of renewable natural resources is affected by political and institutional factors, with power relationships determining the ownership, distribution and use thereof. Too often this process results in *absolute* or *relative* scarcities and even shortages. Over the past two decades, increasing pressures from certain sectors of Brazilian society on agents of degradation and/or the government itself have produced some regulation of economic activities. Spurred by the 1972 U.N. Stockholm Conference, the Brazilian government established the following main objectives for the Special Environment Bureau—SEMA: analysis of national development and technological progress; assist environmental protection agencies; prepare environmental protection norms and standards; and strive for their enforcement. Environmental legislation was only consolidated in 1981, although water, forest and fisheries codes were already in effect at that time. However, they were not enforced very effectively, as was the Wildlife Protection Law.

The Water Code (1934, revised 1938) was effective only on paper. In 1984 the National Water Resources Plan was commissioned by the Ministry of Mines and Energy. Conflicts soon arose with SEMA and IBAMA over spheres of competence. Although Brazil's 1988 Constitution contains provisions for setting up a National Water Resources Management System, its makes no mention of how this should be done.

The Forest Code (1934, replaced in 1965) is vital to environmental protection,

setting standards for resource use and stipulating preservation areas for which the Brazilian Forest Development Institute—IBDF—was responsible until 1988. This law also created conflicts with other agencies.

The Fisheries Code and Wildlife Laws (1934/1967) split these living resources into two categories: forest wildlife is treated as a national asset. Fish are handled as economic assets, with the code placing greater emphasis on production rather than preservation of species. The Fisheries Development Superintendency (SUDEPE) has shown little concern with environmental protection.

Brazil's Environmental Law was only ratified in 1981. It stipulated the formation of a National System responsible for environmental issues nationwide. Today fully institutionalized, the National System forms the federal government's main tool for upgrading the environment and helping it to recuperate. The System has some serious drawbacks and weaknesses, however. Some are institutional, others are due to lack of funding. Its basic principle is that the environment is a public asset that must be protected.

The 1981 establishment of the National Environment System—SISNAMA was a benchmark in the institutionalization of Brazil's national environmental policy, allocating responsibilities and duties for environmental protection among the three spheres of government as well as integrating their efforts with civil society through the National Environment Council—CONAMA, set up by the same law to handle major environment problems. The main lines of SISNAMA's action are:

- Rationalization of land, water, and air use.
- Planning and supervision of natural resource use.
- Protection of economic systems and preservation of ecologically important areas.
- Control of potentially or effectively polluting activities.
- Recuperation of degraded areas and protection of areas threatened with degradation.
- Environmental education at all levels of schooling (see Box 4.1).

Various instruments were defined to implement these activities:

- Establishment of environmental quality standards.
- Environmental zoning.
- Licensing and supervision of potentially or effectively polluting activities, with appraisal of environmental impacts.
- Incentives for production and application of environmentally-friendly technologies, processes, and equipment.
- Federal, state, and municipal environmental protection areas, ecological reserves, extractivist reserves, etc.
- Development of a national environmental data system, with a technical listing of environmental protection tools and activities.
- Enforcement of penalties for noncompliance with environmental protection measures.

Acknowledged as among the most advanced in the world, Brazil's environmental protection legislation lacks the institutional framework needed for implementation and enforcement. This is largely due to unstable official spheres of competence, excessive state intervention, and a chronic shortage of funding.

The 1989 establishment of the Brazilian Institute of the Environment and Natural Renewable Resources (IBAMA) brought together the Rubber Superintendency (SUDHEVEA), the Fisheries Development Superintendency (SUDEPE), the Brazilian Forest Development Institute (IBDF), and the Special Environment Bureau (SEMA). A 1991 Decree defined four IBAMA Divisions: Control and Supervision; Natural Renewable Resources; Eco-Systems; and Fisheries Incentives, as well as an Administration and Finance Department. It maintains a Superintendency in each State, which is of strategic importance in implementing the SISNAMA Plan at state level. It also includes three Boards: The National Wildlife Protection Council; the National Conservation Units Council; and a Technical and Scientific Committee. In 1990 IBAMA was made subordinate to the Presidential Environment Bureau.

Earlier outstanding events were the second National Development Plan and implementation of direct state government elections in 1982. Another major institutional benchmark was the 1975 Industrial Pollution Control and Prevention law, which pinpointed seven of Brazil's nine metropolitan regions as critical areas, and made SEMA responsible for basic environmental zoning guidelines.

The 1980s brought significant advances in this institutional framework. Supplementary Law No. 40 (1981) made the Ministry of Justice responsible for criminal and civil lawsuits involving environmental protection. Law 7,385 (1985) covered damage to the environment and historic/artistic/landscape assets. The Ministry of Justice set up Environmental Boards of Curators in major cities, and environmental protection associations won the right to bring suit. Decree 91,195 (1985) set up the Ministry of Urban Develop and the Environment, which also took over SEMA. The 1988 Constitution featured an entire chapter devoted to environmental issues and established the right of all Brazilians to a healthy, ecologically-balanced environment, giving states and municipalities unprecedented autonomy in legislative competence. Congress was assigned responsibility for nuclear matters.

The federal government's *Nossa Natureza* environmental protection program prompted the establishment of IBAMA, the National Environment Fund (FNMA) and Law No. 77,802 (1989) controlling pesticides; ecological zoning, particularly for the Amazon, Pantanal, and Atlantic Forest; an Interministerial Work Group (Decree 96,994/1988); tighter Forest Code restrictions on clearing and logging, with suspension of tax incentives and government loans for such projects; and a World Bank loan to cover investments of some US$166 million in National Environment Plan programs.

Law 8,028 (1990) made deep-rooted alterations in Brazil's federal administrative structure, setting up the Presidential Environmental Bureau to plan, coordinate, supervise and control National Environment Policy activities. The Bureau is intended to place a clear-cut emphasis on environmental protection, recuperation of degraded areas and sustainable development. However, disputes and conflicts arose between the three levels of government due to blurred definitions of their spheres of competence in environmental matters, often leading to environmental degradation as a result of favoring private interests.

State environmental structure

Prior to 1981, state involvement in environmental protection was largely restricted to attempts to control industrial pollution in São Paulo and implementation of basic Sanitation schemes elsewhere. After the 1982 election, state environmental agencies came under double pressure, as social demands bore down heavily on their already-fragile institutional frameworks. A 1987 survey by the Brazilian Association of Environmental Agencies (ABEMA) showed that only three states lacked environmental agencies, although the work force was concentrated in Rio de Janeiro and São Paulo. The latter had 52.3 percent of the work force, with 19 percent located in Rio de Janeiro. Of a total budget of some US$61 million, São Paulo absorbed around 75 percent and Rio de Janeiro took 6 percent of public expenditures in this area, some US$4 million.

Various states currently have Environmental Councils, whose members come from various social strata reflecting local idiosyncracies. They seem to become more effective as their power of decision increases and their members find new ways to participate.

The State Environmental Engineering Foundation (FEEMA) was set up in 1975 when the States of Guanabara and Rio de Janeiro merged. By 1984 the federal government still maintained authoritarian control over state affairs. The first Rio de Janeiro State Economic and Social Development Plan devoted a chapter to environmental protection and the use of natural resources, setting up FEEMA and the CECA Environmental Control State Board, widening the scope of environmental policy beyond just the control of industrial pollution.

In 1977, after heavy opposition, Decree 1,633 set up the Rio de Janeiro State Polluting Activities Licensing System (SLAP), later adopted nationwide. It fell into virtual disuse during subsequent administrations, although in 1989 the State Constitution devoted a long chapter to environmental issues and a project was undertaken to clean up the Guanabara Bay. Once the selection of Rio was confirmed in 1990 as host to UNCED/Rio-92, both the municipality and the state began to concentrate on environmental matters. Federal, State and foreign funding

Box 4.1: Environmental Management Training Programs Developed by the Brazilian Municipal Administration Institute

Mara D. Biasi Ferrari Pinto

Municipal administrations need strengthening and streamlining in order to serve their communities more effectively, through intermunicipal associations that share costs, staff and materials needed to study, analyze and implement solutions, highlighting the importance of smooth-running interplay and coordinated efforts. Well-structured municipal human resources policies are vital, particularly as public competitive entrance examinations for the civil service are required by the 1988 Constitution, thus imposing increased professionalism.

The major sponsor of municipal administration training programs held between 1977 and 1991 was the federal government. Limited information and the dispersion of FUNDREM functions make it difficult to portray the current situation. However, as development policies make no provision for integrated training, isolated actions cannot be sized to handle collective municipal staff training requirements.

In 1990 ENSUR held its first graduate course (360 hours) in Formulation of Municipal Urban and Environmental Development Policies. Backed by the federal and state governments, it covered urbanization and environmental issues and controls, master plans and urban management, municipal housing and urban services, social welfare and environmental policies.

Shorter courses (120-480 hours) covered Project Management and Municipal/Urban Development, with fresh emphasis on Environmental Management, Health and Sanitation, and Community Participation. IBAM also provided technical assistance to local municipal administrations, particularly for finance, budget and human resources administration; no demand was noted for help with environmental management.

From 1977 to 1987, programs developed by FUNDREM for town councils focussed on modernization, master plans and finances. In 1981-82, Technical Assistance Programs planned and restructured municipal garbage collection services, and upgraded technical records and information systems. Priorities continued unchanged from 1983 to 1987, with the addition of zoning and land subdivision law review, community participation in planning, public transportation, low-cost housing development, infrastructure mapping, urban services, the Guanabara Bay, rivers, coastal lagoons and the road system. Courses also covered Social Welfare and Economic Planning and Policies, Democratization, Urban Law, Alternative Garbage Removal/Treatment Systems, and Simplified Basic Sanitation. IBAM training activities in 1988-91 highlighted Trends and Outlooks for Master Plans, Social Welfare Policies, Environmental Sanitation; Urban Cleaning and Project Management.

Some municipalities are already preparing career plans and training programs. In 1992, the Rio de Janeiro City Council set up the João Goulart Foundation Public Administration Institute to handle the planning, organization, implementation and coordination of integrated actions designed to upgrade its professional and technical staff. Its activities include organizing public competitive civil service examinations, planning, implementation and coordination of training programs, and encouragement of scientific output through public administration research projects. It also holds specialized courses in administration, such as the Municipal Government and Administration Course organized jointly with IBAM. Transdisciplinary, it highlights decision processes, analysis of sectorial policies and study of the government's managerial abilities, with particular reference to Rio de Janeiro.

Box 4.1 (continued)

Human resources policies should be compatible with local requirements; a collective approach to regional development should—over the medium term—boost town councils' capacity for effective actions, resolving typical community problems, with added emphasis on environmental issues at all levels. The following list specifies the environmentally related training which IBAM has offered:

- Once-off courses, seminars, and on-the-job training in municipal administration in response to specific needs and requests from Metropolitan Region of Rio de Janeiro municipal administrations, largely indicated by FUNDREM—Brazil Metropolitan Region Development Foundation (established in 1977, closed down in 1989) and then by various state works and services boards.
- Ongoing courses for municipal employees held by ENSUR—National Urban Services School, providing staff for municipal administrations trained in urban systems engineering, organizational and institutional development and administration, and urban development. Recognized internationally, these full-time advanced training courses lasted one to two weeks; full graduate courses took eight months, while shorter versions varied from one to eight months. Topics included municipal modernization and planning, budgets, taxes, law, records, supervision and management, as well as housing and recreation, lighting, roads and transportation, food supplies, cemeteries, drainage, sanitation and garbage removal. Courses also included practical field studies.

backed major projects designed to solve environmental problems. These became the responsibility of the State Environment and Special Projects Bureau (SEMAM), set up by Decree 16,520 in March 1991, and coordinating the State Environment Council (CONEMA), the State Environmental Control Commission (CECA), the Special environmental Control Fund (FECAM), and the Shoreline Protection Committee (CODEL/RJ), supplemented by FEEMA, SERLA and the IEF. Throughout this period, the Vice-Mayor also acted as State Environment Secretary.

Municipal environmental structure

Although community pressures demanding solutions to environmental problems are first felt at the municipal level, Brazil's four thousand municipalities have very few agencies specifically assigned to environmental issues, despite the 1988 Constitutional requirement of master plans for all municipalities of over 20,000 people. Some plans result from local efforts and Town

Council discussions, but many have been prepared by outside consultants and feature the same shortcomings, based on underpowered municipal legislation, as the Integrated Local Development Plans (PGLIs) of the 1960s and 1970s.

Urban legislation in Brazil is municipal, based on Law 6,766 (1979), covering land use, with states responsible for defining special protection areas; Law 6,803 lays down basic guidelines for industrial zoning in critical high-pollution areas. Both assume the existence of metropolitan agencies that were abolished by Brazil's 1988 Constitution. This reemphasized the importance of local government through master plans that set basic standards such as: population densities; infrastructure networks; and road widths; as well as the consumption of building materials that could put pressure on natural resources, which are in step with technological development trends for urban-industrial societies. Compliance with these standards in fulfilling the pent-up demand for housing, infrastructure and urban services would need an enormous stock of natural resources.

Energy use to satisfy basic needs is a criterion of consumption and consequent environmental damage in any given society. A US citizen uses twice as many resources as a Swedish or USSR citizen, 13 times more than a Brazilian, 35 times more than an Indian, 140 times more than a Bangladeshi or Kenyan, and 280 times more than a person living in Chad, Rwanda, Haiti or Nepal. By the same token, an urbanized, high-density *favela* slum uses far fewer resources than a luxury condominium. The infrastructure for a density of 15 families per hectare (the average in medium-size towns) costs around US$3,529; at 60 families per hectare (a comfortable ratio in cities) this infrastructure cost drops to US$2,227.

Urban planning decisions should determine the costs of service. Paving and drainage account for some 60 percent of these total costs; water, sewage and electric power systems take up another 20 percent. Skillfully reworked settlement plans can slash urban costs and the demand for nonrenewable natural resources. At an average urban settlement cost per head of US$1,000 for infrastructure and basic services, US$2 billion would be needed annually just to keep up with the demands imposed by an urban population rising by two million people every year.

The relationship between urban development and environmental policies is largely shaped by legislation that fosters sustainable development and sets clear-cut standards for land subdivision, occupation and use, (e.g., urban works and sanitary codes, garbage removal, etc.), although it fails to reflect advances at other levels. Unification of these laws and their harmonization with those of other spheres of government has been given much importance. In some cases, in water source

protection, for example, it has proved quite possible to codify and consolidate applied norms. However, for pollution control, environmental licensing, recovery of degraded areas, risk analysis and integrated supervision, joint actions are still fairly unlikely in most Brazilian municipalities.

In the City of Rio de Janeiro, environmental issues fall under the Municipal Urban Improvement and Environment Bureau, set up by Decree 8,858 in October 1989. The Municipal Environmental Protection Council (CONDEMAM) is also part of this structure.

The Rio de Janeiro Municipal Charter details responsibilities for environmental issues in Chapters V (Urban Policy), VI (Environment), and VII (Basic Sanitation), with appraisal of both urban and environmental impacts required. This introduces the need for Environmental Impact Studies (EIAs) and Environmental Impact Reports (RIMAs), with active public participation being a sensitive issue.

Many environmental control activities have recently been transferred to the municipality by the state, unfortunately not accompanied by the necessary funding. This is particularly serious in metropolitan areas, where environmental control becomes extremely complex due to licensing and supervision activities.

Laws passed in the early 1970s define metropolitan services as planning for inte-grated economic and social development. Basic sanitation—particularly water, sewage and garbage collection, land use, public transportation and the road system, production and distribution of gas mains, use of water resources and control of environmental protection—are all compat-ible with sustained development. However, outdated metropolitan laws generally produce a serious institutional vacuum. New alternatives should be sought for participatory management models that involve various sectors of society.

Economic aspects

Environmental control sets minimum standards and supervises the quality of water and air. Since 1973 Brazilian water has been graded to facilitate pollution control, with four classes of use. Licensing of polluting activities, mainly industry and pesticides, helps spur corrective actions.

A 1986 CONAMA Resolution beefed up environmental controls, banned certain water-polluting activities and strengthened catchment area management. Currently, the PROAGUA National Water Quality Program and the Marine Environment Quality Management Program are being developed to boost the effectiveness of environmental protection.

In 1989 CONAMA instituted the National Air Quality Control Program (PRONA), which monitors air quality, administers pollution source licenses, and maintains a nationwide inventory of sources of pollution. The National Vehicle Pollution Control Plan (PROCONVE) is more restrictive, setting limits on auto emissions deadlined for 1997 and interfacing between municipal and state governments on streamlining traffic flows and implementing innovative mass transportation projects, preferably electric-powered.

The National Environment Fund could constitute an excellent source of financing, but funds channeled to IBAMA frequently get backed up in the bureaucratic pipeline, perhaps due to institutional rivalries.

Although environmental licensing of polluting activities has been in force in some states since the 1970s, it was only implemented nationwide in 1989; the legislation was modified in 1989 to include IBAMA as the agency responsible for licensing polluting activities. Licensing takes place in three stages: prelicense,

installation license and operational license. Petrochemical and Chlorochemical complexes may be licensed only by the federal government, after hearings with the states and municipalities involved. Nuclear installations fall under the National Nuclear Power Commission (CNEN). More recently, some states, including Rio de Janeiro, have successfully transferred to municipalities the responsibility for exercising environmental control over activities with a localized impact, including the requirements for EIAs and RIMAs.

Health care

Although vaccination campaigns and improved sanitation have reduced infant mortality due to infectious diseases over the past few years, diarrheas are still a major public health problem, especially in the Northeast. Some diseases once considered extinct—dengue, yellow fever, and cholera—are reappearing, parasite-borne illnesses are on the rise, and rates are rising for hanseniasis, tuberculosis, hepatitis and some sexually-transmittable diseases. Neither endemic nor epidemic processes can be explained solely by hard-to-eradicate pockets of poverty, but they do seem to relate to certain environmental problems such as pollution, due either to a lack of preventive measures or to disasters and accidents.

In ten years, over 10.5 million insured workers were involved in accidents, of whom 41,000 died and some 250,000 were permanently incapacitated. The most frequent injuries include: noise-induced deafness, occupational dermatoses, metal (particularly lead) poisoning, exposure to solvents and other poisons, particularly pesticides, and the wildcat gold miners in the Amazon suffering from mercury poisoning.

The Single Health Care System (SUS Law 8,808/1990) municipalizes health care, aiming at the decentralization of services and executive-level integration of health care, environmental and sanitation activities. The SUS program ran into opposition from private medicine and medical groups at the federal and state government levels, and is further hobbled by some governors refusing to pass funds on to political adversaries. It has also run up against the resistance of certain municipal leaders.

Basic sanitation

Bodies of water in urban areas are often polluted by sewage and drainage systems. In 1970 some 55 percent of urban households had water connections and 22 percent had sewage connections. Eighteen years later, estimates are that some 81 percent of Brazil's population is supplied with water, and 95 percent of urban centers have water. Figures for sewage networks are far more modest, rising from 22 percent to 35 percent over the same period, with only 10 percent of total sewage collected receiving proper treatment. This means that some 10 billion liters of raw sewage are discharged every day into the ground or water-courses. This mainly affects low-income homes, where 72 percent of 5.9 million urban households without water or sewage connections sheltered families earning under three minimum wages, causing disease and death.

The 1971 National Sanitation Program (PLANASA) aimed to supply water and sewage services to much of Brazil's population through subsidized loans. However, financing was to come from higher rates penalizing domestic rather than industrial consumption, and anti-inflationary policies nibbled away the real value of these overcharges. Restrictions on government spending, plummeting income levels and the concentration of services in state companies all reduced this financing capacity to virtual stagnation. In any event, most pollution came from industry, and while rates and fines were negligible, pollution control measures were of little interest to industrialists.

Garbage collection

The average Brazilian produces 600 grams of garbage daily, a figure that rises with income and in large towns. Garbage collection services are provided to less than 50 percent of the population. While only 3 percent of urban rubbish receives adequate disposal, 63 percent goes into water-courses, and 34 percent is dumped, causing environmental degradation and proliferation of disease vectors. CONAMA recently established special norms for hospital refuse.

Drainage

Urban construction demands earth-moving that frequently silts up riverbeds and causes flooding. Flooding problems grow worse during the rainy season, due to pavement runoff. Poor urban settlement patterns cause environmental degradation that increases the risk of floods and landslides: Brazil's South Region in 1983 had losses of US$1.3 billion; the Northeast Region suffered a series of floods in 1984-85; and a series of flash floods and landslides in Rio de Janeiro caused much loss of life and financial damage that reached US$1 billion in 1988. Between 1979 and 1989, cloudbursts followed by flash floods and landslides took over 5,000 lives in Brazil and left 3.6 million homeless, damaging 111,770 homes and destroying 101,000 houses completely.

Basic sanitation and Guanabara Bay

The Guanabara Bay covers an area of some 4,000 square kilometers, with some 35 important rivers, 44 square kilometers of islands and islets, a perimeter of 131 kilometers and a volume of 2 billion cubic meters of water. Only a narrow strip some 40 kilometers long remains of its original mangrove swamps and sand-spit vegetation, they have melted away in the face of disorganized urban growth and industrial complexes. There is a lack of infrastructure to prevent degradation: some 6,000 industries cause around 25 percent of the pollution of the bay and almost all effluent is contaminated by heavy metals, particularly pollution coming from the Duque de Caxias and Manguinhos Oil Refineries and the two ports.

In 1987 the state tovernment set up the Guanabara Bay Gradual Eco-System Recuperation Project, financed by the Japan International Cooperation Agency (JICA) with US$5 million, and US$450 million from the IDB.

Conclusions

From both the institutional and legal viewpoints, Brazil is well prepared to implement an environmental policy that dovetails with the demands of urban development. However, the current economic crisis inhibits growth and hampers structural reforms that are needed to reformulate economic and social policies in order to foster environmental protection and spur growth in compliance with Agenda 21. Implementation of Brazil's National Environment Policy also demands clearer definition of the roles of state and federal government, as well as increased participation from various sectors of society as a whole.

5. Historical Perspective on the Institutional Framework for Urban Policy

Braz Menezes

The recurrent theme throughout the conference was the institutional confusion resulting from the proliferation and overlapping roles and responsibilities of institutions responsible for urban and environmental management. This did not happen overnight, but evolved as a natural consequence of Brazil's attempts to cope with urbanization, and more recently with the provisions under the 1988 Constitution.

After a period of steady growth between the 1930s and mid-1960s, Brazil became acutely aware of urban problems. The rapid urbanization of Brazil created heavy demands for housing, social services, and infrastructure. State and local authorities, traditionally responsible for meeting these needs, became increasingly unable to meet their growing financial obligations. An attempt was made to develop an urban planning policy and introduce coordinated regional and urban development. The Ministry of the Interior (MINTER) was given the mandate to coordinate sectoral and subsectoral services.

In 1964, the government took measures to centralize housing and infrastructure development by creating the National Housing Bank (*Banco Nacional da Habitação*, BNH) to provide financing for a broad range of shelter-related urban services. In 1976 the Brazilian Urban Transport Company (*Empresa Brasileira de Trens Urbanos*, EBTU) was established to implement urban transport policy and to finance urban transport investments. At the same time, the Brazilian Transport Planning Agency (GEIPOT) was created to assist in the preparation of both urban and interurban transport policies and investment plans. In 1984, the Brazilian Urban Rail Company (*Companhia Brasileira de Trens Urbanos*, CBTU) was formed to take over suburban rail functions from EBTU including planning, operation, and financing of the majority of suburban rail systems. From 1979 to 1985, the National Urban Development Council (CNDU) had the primary responsibility for urban development coordination within the federal government and with other levels of government.

In March 1985, the incoming Sarney administration replaced MINTER. The Ministry of Urban Development and the Environment (MDU) was established and took over a broad range of responsibilities, including the CNDU, BNH, and a few months later, the EBTU. The urban sections of GEIPOT were also merged with EBTU. Since MDU was also responsible for urban transport policy formulation, those institutional changes were intended to improve urban planning, coordination, and the formulation of environmental policy. CBTU remained within the Ministry of Transport (MT). Further changes were introduced by the Collor administration in 1990 with the extinction of MDU and the birth of the Ministry of Social Welfare (*Ministério da Ação Social*, MAS) primarily responsible for urban issues. Urban policy never really got a foothold. In late 1992 a new administration juggled the ministries around again. Some familiar-sounding ministries from days gone by reappeared.

In summary, the past five years have been chaotic with institutions transferred back and forth between ministries, yet with overlapping responsibilities never clarified. Two significant events, beyond those noted above, added complexity to the institutional framework, and hence further influenced the direction of recent urban policy: the 1988 Constitution and the extinction of BNH.

In 1988, Brazil enacted a new federal constitution. This constitution shifted the burden for urban development back to the municipalities, which had legally been responsible for planning and administering local services, but which had temporarily been deprived of effectively fulfilling their role during the military regime between 1964 and 1975. The result was the reemergence of dormant municipal agencies and some new ones to add spice to an already complex network of state and federal agencies.

The extinction of BNH and the transfer of its responsibilities to the *Caixa Econômica Federal* (CEF) in 1986 fundamentally changed the pace of implementation of projects and programs that were targeted towards ameliorating the urban environment. BNH administered funds from the *Fundo de Garantia do Tempo de Serviço* (FGTS). A substantial portion of these funds were earmarked for housing, water supply, sanitation, and drainage, and their distribution was mandated under policies determined by MDU and later the MAS. Various reasons have been put forward as justification for terminating BNH, which include among others, the pressures of the macro-financial situation facing the country, and for a reform of the public sector. Speculation continues on a host of possible reasons. CEF as a financial institution was governed by broader policies defined by

the Ministry of Economy and Planning, but urban (social) policies remained with the sectoral ministry. Almost overnight, it seems, further and accelerated institutional deterioration set in. As a result of the apparently ad hoc transfer of BNH to CEF, new problems, as described below, emerged to replace familiar ones, and urban policy did not take a step forward.

Costs May Often Outweigh Benefits

Sometimes the costs of unplanned or uncoordinated institutional change may outweigh the benefits. The merger of BNH into CEF provides a useful example. The problems of CEF are only a microcosm of global institutional confusion that has to be addressed. The costs to the national economy are incalculable. In the case of CEF, the administration that assumed responsibility in October 1992 is taking rapid corrective steps to address the many problems of a dysfunctional institution.

Much of what was achieved in the Rio flood project (see section IV of this volume) over the past five years has been due largely to the dedication and professionalism of a number of very committed and hard-working individuals—both ex-employees of BNH and employees from CEF that kept hope alive—in spite of frequently difficult conditions. The observations below are made in good faith as a tribute to those individuals. The problems, however, are generic to institutions in transition, and a careful evaluation is recommended when considering such institutional reorganization.

The problems of CEF seem to arise from a number of factors:

- **The institutional schizophrenia of CEF.** Following the extinction of BNH in November 1986, the role, functions, and staff of BNH were merged into CEF, which is 150 years old and well established as a separate first-line financial institution with a different role and functions from BNH. To our knowledge, no significant attempt has been made since the merger to rationalize the conflicting institutional cultures—first-line banking with development banking—of the combined staff of CEF. The management and *modus operandi* culture remained that of CEF—a savings bank. The development bank role and functions of BNH were given only cosmetic treatment.

- **Constant changes in CEF.**
  The abolition of BNH—without provision for a substitute apex sector institution—created a deterioration of the national system for institutional financing of social services, which took almost two decades to build up. Since 1988 each ministerial change has been accompanied by a new appointment to the presidency of CEF (four so far); this, in turn, has led to constant changes in the top echelons of CEF management, which has affected staff continuity. These changes have in most cases been accompanied by new "operating policies" or bureaucratic changes. The practice of patronage "clientelism" reached new levels.

- **The demoralization of experienced BNH staff.**
  As a consequence of this institutional schizophrenia and the politicization of loan approvals, it is alleged that better qualified and experienced staff of the erstwhile BNH became demoralized and have retired or resigned from active service. Others are naturally inclined to maintain a low profile. With a few exceptions, most avoid taking decisions or assuming responsibility because they are afraid of "political repercussions." This results in low efficiency, low productivity, and absolutely no accountability.

- **The unpredictable flow of counterpart funds.**
  The smooth flow of these funds has in the past been adversely affected by the receipts of the FGTS contributions during a prolonged recessionary period, and by the constant introduction of regulatory mechanisms governing the financial sector. Media reports in Brazil have highlighted the ad hoc redirection of funds by CEF management, often to a focus on clientelistic objectives. The flow of funds, when savings permit, are apparently often manipulated to bargain, reward, or punish state and municipal sub-borrowers in return for other (political) favors. The most recent example is the well-publicized pre-impeachment plunder of CEF resources that allegedly took place in mid-1992.

- **The absence of clear operating practices.**
  Excessive centralization has been a natural consequence of some of the above-mentioned policies. All final approvals for projects, subprojects, and even detailed technical minutiae, are referred to Brasilia where no adequate technical support exists. Regional offices and technical coordination teams appear helpless and remain in the dark.

- **Cumbersome bureaucratic practices.**
  Little attempt appears to have been made to reconcile the processing needs of a "development bank" (such as BNH) and the traditional practices of a savings institution. There appears to be a great deal of scope for reducing the paperwork for the internal processing of subprojects, and the administration of loan amendments, notices, approvals, and related activities.

- **Weak technical capacity to monitor and manage projects.**
A direct consequence of CEF institutional environment, as described above, has led to a deterioration of CEF investment in human resources and, hence, in its technical capacity to supervise project execution, verify costs, and identify irregularities when they occur. These conditions provide a fertile breeding ground for many cases of misprocurement, price collusion, and other practices.

In summary, institutional clarity for urban environmental policy is still a distant reality. There is a general consensus that change is necessary. The Rio Earth Summit (UNCED) brought the issue of coping with urbanization to the forefront. International finance institutions are also reorganizing to respond to and/or guide this effort. There is a continuing debate within Brazil of the issue. At least while the debate is being actively pursued, there is hope!

6. Government Expenditures and Financing on the Environment in Brazil and Rio de Janeiro

José Roberto Rodrigues Afonso

I. Introduction

This study analyzes government expenditures and financing of environment-related activities in urban areas of Brazil, particularly Rio de Janeiro, with emphasis on health care, sanitation, and environmental protection programs. The availability and quality of statistics on public expenditures in Brazil are limited, particularly when broken down into federal, state, or municipal categories in a specific region. Any short-term survey such as this is thus constrained by having to adopt a methodology that (a) surveys available statistics (section II of this chapter); (b) concentrates on expenditures by level of government (section III of this chapter); (c) surveys the development of federal outlays during the 1980s (section IV of this chapter); (d) examines the structure of outlays by functional classification and economic category (section V of this chapter); (e) surveys funding currently allocated by the National Treasury (section VI of this chapter); and (f) surveys recent outlays by the Rio de Janeiro state and municipal governments (section VII of this chapter).

This study covers the direct and decentralized civil service (independent agencies, foundations, and funds) where most health care and environmental protection activities are concentrated. It does not include state-owned companies, except where they are responsible for sanitation. Added to statistical and methodological difficulties is the political and financial independence and participation of state and municipal governments in generation and allocation of public funds. This decentralization grew more marked during the 1980s. Today local governments in Brazil are highly autonomous in tax legislation, collection, and application. Backed by the 1988 constitution, they regulate a wide range of action in basic health care and sanitation, in part because they are funded locally. A study of central government data alone would give only a partial view of its constantly-decreasing outlays.

II. Statistics: Constraints and Handling

Statistics on Brazilian government finances have limited range and consistency, and are outdated. The only surveys that include data from all levels of government are carried out by the Institute Brasileiro de Geografia e Estatistica [Brazilian Institute of Geography and Statistics] (IBGE) and Fundação Getulio Vargas [Getulio Vargas Foundation] (FGV) of national accounts and the *Government Finance Statistics Yearbook* published by the IMF. Little concern for the importance of collecting broad-based information is shown, even by the central government. Surveys of national accounts lag well behind; although the IBGE survey is annual, and the FGV survey is carried out every five years, 1985 was the last financial year whose accounts were fully investigated. Government agencies are not legally obligated to consolidate their accounts; hence, there are no uniform procedures, and soaring inflation hampers measurement of outlays. Cross-referencing of expenditures is more difficult still; only IBGE and FGV surveys detail and cross-reference book outlays against actual expenditures. Defining outlays on the environment is also difficult and not standardized. So many agencies and organizations handle the same programs, and administrative changes occur so frequently that accounts become extremely complex.

III. National Expenditures by Level of Government

A starting point for a study of public expenditures on the environment is the distribution of expenditures by sphere of government in the national accounts. The latest figures available date from 1985 and indicate that the central government spent some 2.65 percent of gross domestic product (GDP) on health care and sanitation, equivalent to some US$11.4 billion at 1991 average foreign exchange rates. Of this, 59 percent went to the central government, 27 percent went to states and municipalities, respectively, and the remainder went to national expenditures (see Figure 1). The Southeast absorbed around one half (see Figure 2).

During the second half of the 1980s, and particularly in 1990/91, there was an increase in the participation of subnational governments in tax collections and allocations. It is expected that this same process of participation of subnational governments in tax-related issues would have occurred in the 1990s with outlays on health care and sanitation, reducing the concentration registered in 1985 levels. This hypothesis is confirmed by the analysis of national, state, and municipal treasuries in Table 1, although central government outlays are underestimated. A

marked cyclic increase in outlays on health care and sanitation is also expected, although they dropped sharply in 1990 because of cuts in government expenditures. However, the second half of the decade was marked by outlays that expanded faster than the population and the economy. The latter was virtually stagnant.

IV. Real Growth of Federal Government Expenditures (1980/91)

Focusing on federal government outlays on health care, sanitation, and environmental protection, this section of the chapter uses as its basic source a survey carried out by Instituto de Pesquisa Economica Aplicada [Institute of Applied Economic Research] (IPEA)/Brasilia entitled "Social Outlays—Consolidated Accounts." The survey split social outlays into health care programs, and sanitation and environmental protection (Table 2), accounting for an average of 23 percent of federal government outlays on social welfare between 1980 and 1991. However, sanitation and environmental protection accounted for only 3.5 percent of consolidated expenditures.

In 1991, central government outlays on health care reached US$7.9 billion (higher than pre-1986 levels, lower than over the four previous years—US$11.5 billion in 1989); US$1.2 billion went toward sanitation and environmental protection, for a total of US$9.1 billion (higher than 1989/90, less than 1987/88). Total social welfare expenditures reached US$41.1 billion (Table 2). *Per capita* federal outlays on health care, sanitation, and environmental protection followed the downward trend (Table 3). Health care programs took US$53 per inhabitant, while sanitation and environmental protection reached a mere US$8—a total of US$61, or only 2 percent of Brazil's *per capita* income.

Tightened federal purse strings at the start of the Collor administration (1990/91) cut health care outlays in particular by one-third. Per capita sanitation and environmental protection outlays were 28 percent lower than in 1980, showing that the 1990s was a decade of dwindling federal outlays on social welfare in general (Table 4). The same trend is repeated when comparing central government social welfare expenditures against GNP (Table 5). Health care outlays for 1991 reached only 1.9 percent of GDP, and sanitation and environmental protection scraped by with 0.3 percent.

Table 6 gives the origin of funding, identified by expenditure center, between 1985 and 1991 (preliminary data). Federal health care programs were basically (80 percent) financed by the social security funds (FPAS) Social Welfare Fund income, paid by both employees and employers on income and payroll, from 1985 to 1990. In 1991 this seems to have been drastically modified, with National Treasury funding rising to almost half. Sanitation featured a nonbudget source—loans from the workers' patrimonial funds (FGTS) Length of Service Guarantee Fund. Between 1985 and 1989, this financed some 80 percent of federal outlays on these programs, but in 1990/91 the situation changed, and some 30 percent came directly from the National Treasury. This reflects the inclusion of sanitation programs in social welfare budgets, which allowed financing to come from social welfare levy revenues.

During the second half of the 1980s, funds came largely from the FPAS and FGTS, although they dropped sharply in 1990/91. These recent changes in federal funding for health care and sanitation may well drop still further, as they reflect increasing dependence on social welfare

levies and company profits (FINSOCIAL), whose validity is being widely challenged in court, along with tax evasion and reform.

V. Expenditures on Health Care and Sanitation

FGV and IBGE surveys discriminate between and compare classifications of government outlays by category up to 1985. Although not up-to-date, they reveal the structure by category, which should not in principle change greatly over the short or medium term. Table 7 presents FGV data aggregated to federal and state outlays in 1985. Health care and sanitation represent 98 percent of total expenditures. The remainder is split between preservation of natural resources and reforestation (agriculture) and historical assets (education).

Outlays on the environment totaled US$10.5 billion at 1991 prices, excluding FGTS loans—only 5 percent of consolidated government expenditures. Staff salaries accounted for over 30 percent of expenditures, with slightly less taken up by social welfare assistance and medical or hospital aid. Apart from health care and sanitation, the only sizable subprogram in 1985 was Preservation of Natural Resources (Agriculture), with US$122 million—just over half of what was spent on environmental protection.

Under health care and sanitation, federal and state outlays were strongly concentrated (over two-thirds) in medical and sanitary assistance. Sanitation (85 percent) and environmental protection accounted for only 14 percent of outlays, a negligible 1.3 percent of total consolidated nonfinancial outlays. Feeding and nutrition and administration also had a relative weight. Little attention is given by the Brazilian government to preventive health care, as is shown by proportionately low outlays on sanitation and disease control programs.

Leaving aside health care programs (where major institutional changes took place after 1985 with the introduction of the Single Health Care System), in an analysis of outlays at the two upper levels of government (Tables 8 and 9), direct action is concentrated markedly in sanitation at the state level, with outlays 10 times higher than federal expenditures, excluding FGTS investments. The opposite occurred with environmental protection, where the central government spent four times more than the state governments.

By category of expenditure, and in contrast to health care, capital outlays were high for sanitation and environmental protection. Central government investments in these two programs were higher than current outlays (Table 7); and in sanitation 8.5 percent of overhead was passed on to lower spheres of government. In their turn, the states' current expenditures grew (Table 9), with most funds going to subsidize state water and sanitation companies.

In municipal metropolitan region administrations (Table 10), outlays on health care and sanitation in 1985 reached some US$720 million. Although lower than in other spheres of government, this amount nevertheless accounted for some 10 percent of total expenditures, which was higher than for the state and federal governments. Similarly, 1985 municipal outlays on sanitation and environmental protection were greater than figures for the central government—with environmental protection alone accounting for 17 percent (Table 10).

The structure of local government outlays by economic category is similar to that of other spheres, with overhead taking up over 90 percent of health care programs (60 percent on staff), which emphasizes that municipal sanitary actions concentrate on services rather than on expanding the hospital network. Overhead also predominated in environmental

protection managed by decentralized civil service agencies. Fixed investments accounted for most sanitation costs. IBGE statistics (Table 11) for the Rio de Janeiro metropolitan region reveal no surprises. Health care and sanitation absorb the same proportion (10 percent) of the consolidated municipal budgets, and overhead accounts for much health care funding, while capital outlays are high in sanitation. Medical and sanitary assistance are more costly than environmental protection, which is proportionate to other Brazilian state capitals and metropolitan regions.

VI. National Treasury Funds for the Environment: Diagnosis 1991

An analysis of the 1991 Central Government General Balance Sheets mirrors the attitude of the National Treasury toward the environment. Amounts differ from those under the social outlays account (Tables 2-6) because of FGTS funding and income going directly to these agencies. However, both sources include FPAS funding passed to Instituto Nacional de Previdencia Social [National Institute for Medical Assistance and Social Security] (INAMPS).

In 1991 the National Treasury contracted health care (93 percent) and sanitation outlays of US$6.5 billion (Table 7). However, revenues were considerably lower (60 percent) than expected for health care and sanitation, due largely to inflation, despite being authorized by law to contract 1.6 more outlays than in 1991. Additionally, 18 percent were booked as still to be paid. Sanitation and environmental protection programs were relatively more affected than health care schemes, particularly with regard to delays in release of funding.

For sanitation, 57 percent of federal budget funds were not used in 1991, with 83 percent booked as still payable, meaning that the National Treasury postponed to 1992 the payment of US$366 million contracted for sanitation in 1991, against US$75 million contracted and paid nationwide. This was less than São Paulo, with US$85 million (Table 17).

With regard to the Environmental Protection Program, federal balance sheets show that in 1991 only 44 percent of allocations were used, while exactly 50 percent of outlays were held over for settlement in 1992. The National Treasury thus contracted and effectively paid only US$20 million on environmental protection, almost the same amount as the Rio de Janeiro state budget on these programs.

Table 12 details the main characteristics of outlays contracted:

- Apart from health care and sanitation, few environmental protection programs were financially important, apart from an urban sanitation project that cost US$87 million, of which 28 percent came from FINSOCIAL contributions—100 percent were intergovernmental transfers with 85 percent from municipalities and 15 percent from states—and 82 percent were held over for payment in 1992.
- Health care funding represented 93 percent of those classified as environmental funds, or 1.5 percent of GDP. About 75 percent went to medical and sanitation subprograms; feeding and nutrition topped US$500 million, largely on school lunches, free milk, and control of vector-transmitted diseases.
- National Treasury allocations for sanitation were negligible at under 0.1 percent of GDP, concentrated (68 percent) in the general sanitation subprogram, with US$117 million from foreign loans going to emergency social welfare programs, 75 percent being assigned to states, and 25 percent to municipalities, although in fact no

measures were carried out, and no money was actually released.
- In 1991 the Treasury contracted only US$40 million, less than half the amount earmarked for Instituto Brasileiro do Meio Ambiente e Recursos Naturais Renovaveis [Brazilian Institute of the Environment and Renewable Natural Resources] (IBAMA).

Table 13 shows total National Treasury funding: 50 percent from ordinary funds, 25 percent from FINSOCIAL, earmarked largely for water supplies and sewage, and the remaining 25 percent from foreign credit operations.

VII. Government Expenditures on the Environment in the State and Municipality of Rio de Janeiro

The latest data available date back to the mid-1980s and are not very informative, since changes have probably occurred since then because of the clampdown on federal outlays and shifts in priorities, particularly for capital expenditures—vital in sanitation programs.

Attempting to reduce red tape, federal law relieved small municipalities of the obligation to account for expenditures under a function-program system. Few other statistics are available, except for state capitals. For the vital post-1988 Constitution period, with reinforced state and municipal outlays, the sole sources of information are the annual surveys carried out by the National Treasury of major balance sheet data and direct consultations with the government.

1. Main Federal Outlays in the State

Federal government actions in environmental protection feature the following: FGTS-funded Caixa Economica Federal (CEF) loans for urban infrastructure and sanitation, and health system transfers to the INAMPS. FGTS-funded CEF loans allocated to the State of Rio de Janeiro in 1991 (Figure 3) reached US$150 million, with state participation reaching 12.9 percent of national expenditures, relatively high compared with the national average of 8.6 percent. Only 63 percent, or nearly US$95 million, was actually released, equivalent to 70 percent of 1991 state and municipal government outlays on sanitation.

The FGTS loaned some US$50 million for state urban infrastructure projects, but actual cash released was less than US$13 million, equivalent to only 1.3 percent of state and municipal outlays on Housing and Urban Improvements. The year-end 1991 debit balance with the FGTS for sanitation and urban development contracts in the State of Rio de Janeiro reached US$398 million, less than that of smaller states, such as Bahia and Goias. Only 1.5 percent of the total debt was in breach of payment, 80 percent being owed by the National Sanitation Works Department, and the remainder by the Niteroi Town Council. Nationwide, overdue debt accounted for 9 percent of total sanitation indebtedness, although the debt accounted for 21 percent in São Paulo.

Figure 4 shows the distribution of FGTS debt for urban development and sanitation in Rio de Janeiro, concentrated (89 percent or US$398 million) in the state sector. Municipal debt on sanitation was negligible—US$30 million for Rio itself, less than 1991 investments, and only 1.4 percent of net annual revenues. The 1992 FGTS budget indicates state outlays on sanitation of US$98.5 million, although only US$17 million had been released by July. Rio is penalized more than other states. Urban infrastructure budget allocations reached some US$14 million, with only US$5.7 million effectively released for Rio by mid-year, and 4.5 percent of funds passed on nationwide.

This is yet another example of the exhaustion of federal government funds. From January through June 1992, FGTS funds released for sanitation and infrastructure reached US$22.8 million, a mere 3 percent of city council outlays on health care, sanitation, housing, and urban improvement over the same period.

The Sistema Unificado e Decentral-izado de Saude [United and Decentralized Health System] (SUDS) health care system transferred funds to the INAMPS to cover hospital network maintenance, treatment agreements, and hospitalization in state, municipal, philanthropic, and private hospitals, with the effective release to the State of Rio de Janeiro of some US$1.311 million in 1990 and US$792 in 1991; the amount was slashed by 42 percent in a single year (Figure 5). State participation in the national SUS funding dropped from 22 percent to 17 percent, although it was still high compared with national averages. In 1991, per capita outlays in Rio were US$58 per inhabitant against US$29 nationwide, reflecting the advanced extension of the federal health care network, due to Rio de Janeiro having been the nation's capital for over 100 years.

2. Developments over the Decade and the Current Structure of State and Municipal Expenditures

Table 14 shows the development of real outlays (state and municipal civil service) on health care and sanitation between 1980 and 1991, with two distinct stages. Up to 1984 outlays sagged, particularly in the state. From 1985 to 1989 there was a sizable ongoing expansion, with state outlays on this function reaching US$615 million by the end of the decade, 4.2 times more than five years previously. Rio de Janeiro outlays reached US$179 million, almost doubling. The gap between state and municipal outlays widened, and health care and sanitation allocations reached 15 percent in the 1989 state budget, three times higher than figures at the start of the decade. Its 11 percent slice of the 1980 municipal budget was already reasonable, and remained stable, except for a sharp hike in 1987. However, local outlays on health care and sanitation ballooned in general, along with the entire municipal budget. This was partly due to changes in budget procedures and the handling of cash transfers—particularly SUS funding—from higher levels of government. This changed in 1991 with the implementation of a special fund to handle state SUS funding, holding down expenses by 56 percent in this function (Table 14).

Table 15 shows Rio de Janeiro state direct civil service outlays on the environment. Health care accounts for almost half, and general sanitation items were concentrated on projects—almost US$100 million, but only 2 percent of the state budget. Some US$20 million went to pollution control—less than 0.5 percent of the state budget. Table 16 gives the same structure for 1991 outlays by the Rio de Janeiro City Council: environmental actions took up over US$200 million, 90 percent financed by ordinary funding, with this sector allocated higher priority than in other spheres of government. Three quarters went to health care programs, and general sanitation accounted for one fifth. Table 17 shows 1991 environmental expenses for the São Paulo City Council. Health care and sanitation are given high priority with 17 percent of the local budget, reaching almost half a billion dollars. General sanitation took 3 percent, or US$85 million, with two-thirds applied to expansion projects. The responsibility for environmental protection doesn't seem to belong typically to this sphere of government.

3. Development of Outlays on Health Care and Sanitation in the Region's Largest Municipalities after the 1988 Constitution

National Treasury Department data show that after the 1988 Constitution, there was a marked hike in Rio de Janeiro state municipality outlays, in both global terms and specifically on health care and sanitation, in step with trends in the national accounts. Figure 6 shows consolidated municipal outlays rising from US$191 million in 1988 to US$318 million in 1991, an unprecedented two-thirds' increase in only three years. Outlays in the Metropolitan Region of Rio de Janeiro were analyzed in the eight largest municipalities: Rio de Janeiro state capital, Nova Iguaçu, São Gonçalo, Duque de Caxias, São João de Meriti, Niteroi, Itaborai, and Nilopolis. In 1991 they held 96 percent of the metropolitan population, and 76 percent of the state population, and accounted for 84 percent (1988) and 81 percent (1989) of aggregate municipal outlays on health care and sanitation.

Table 18 gives the internal distribution by municipality, with the Rio de Janeiro municipality spending more per inhabitant (US$33) on health care and sanitation than other municipalities in the region (US$12), shown in Table 19, and totaling US$257 million, or US$23 per inhabitant on average. This is extremely low (less than half the National Treasury calculations given in Table 12), and well below São Paulo's US$56 per inhabitant, which totaled over 50 percent more than Rio de Janeiro. Long distances aggravate the problem, since in 1991 the capital itself spent US$38 per inhabitant on health care and sanitation, while outlying, poorly-developed São Gonçalo, Niteroi, and São João de Meriti reached only US$11, reducing the regional average to US$17.

However, recent real upgrading of municipal outlays on health care and sanitation are promising. They rose 16 percent (Table 19) between 1988 and 1991, with 1991 real outlays six to seven times greater than in 1988. Although the 1991 per capita outlay was not satisfactory, it had improved greatly and rapidly, boosted by a certain decentralization and despite cuts in federal aid to the State of Rio de Janeiro. The high priority given to health care and sanitation by municipal government can be seen in their respective budgets (Table 10), which remained around 12 percent of total outlays from 1988 to 1991. Local government budgets expanded rapidly, although the aggregate results are much influenced by the capital, where health care and sanitation dropped from 12 percent to 9 percent of total outlays between 1988 and 1991.

The highest local budget allocations were in the Baixada Fluminense lowlands municipalities, in 1991 accounting for 30 percent of total outlays in Nova Iguaçu, 25 percent in São João de Meriti, and close to 20 percent in the other municipalities. Lower rates were noted in the capital (9 percent) and Niteroi (7 percent). This is confirmed in Table 20 by the comparison of the variation in functional outlays with the variation in total outlays. Health care and sanitation accounted for a considerable slice of recent growth in outlays, with health care and sanitation taking only 10 percent of the total budgets of Rio de Janeiro and Niteroi, while reaching 29 percent in Nova Iguaçu and 24 percent in São João de Meriti. Cash-starved local governments in the underdeveloped Baixada Fluminense were forced to cut expenditures on health care and sanitation, to some extent because

administrative structures penalize low-income dormitory areas with little industry to generate tax revenues.

Table 21 compares the 1988-91 growth in municipal outlays on health care and sanitation with the rise in major expenditure and income aggregates in the Rio de Janeiro metropolitan region, with total outlays expanding an average of 26 percent annually, slanted more heavily toward capital investments (60 percent) than to overhead (20 percent). In six of the eight municipalities, revenues rose in parallel with or more than outlays. Rio itself chalked up revenues 40 percent higher—almost double the expansion rate of outlays. Transfers of state taxes on goods and services (ICMS) also rose by around one third during 1988/91, particularly in Duque de Caxias, due to its huge oil refinery.

VIII. Final Comments

Despite the haphazard nature of many statistics on public finances, data available on outlays for health care, sanitation, and environmental protection leave no doubt that deep-rooted—if somewhat unplanned—structural changes are under way in the financing and expenditure standards for these programs. There are striking discrepancies between the rapidly drying-up sources of federal public sector funding and those of state and municipal incomes, with unparalleled fiscal adjustments, particularly for the Rio de Janeiro metropolitan region. This across-the-board process at the national level may well help avert the near bankruptcy of the country's social welfare systems.

Annex of Figures and Tables

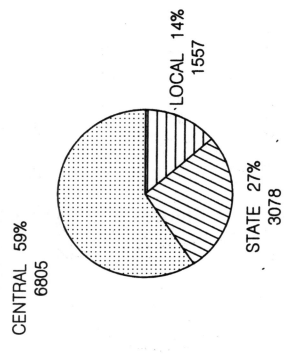

FIGURE 1

OUTLAYS ON HEALTH-CARE AND SANITATION IN 1985 DISTRIBUTION BY LEVEL OF GOVERNMENT

LOCAL 14%
1557

STATE 27%
3078

CENTRAL 59%
6805

TOTAL = US$ 11,440 MILLION
(AT 1991 FOREIGN EXCHANGE RATES)

TOTAL OUTLAYS BY FUNCTION, EXCLUDING
INTER AND INTRA GOVERNMENT TRANSFERS
SOURCE: FGV/CEF/REGIONALIZATION

FIGURE 2

OUTLAYS ON HEALTH-CARE AND SANITATION IN 1985
DISTRIBUTION BY REGIONS

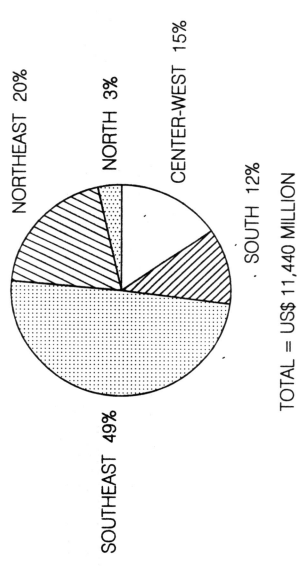

NORTHEAST 20%

NORTH 3%

CENTER-WEST 15%

SOUTH 12%

SOUTHEAST 49%

TOTAL = US$ 11,440 MILLION
(AT 1991 FOREIGN EXCHANGE RATES)

GOVERNMENT = THREE LEVELS
TOTAL OUTLAYS, EXCLUDING GOVERNMENT TRANSFERS
SOURCE: FGV/CEF/REGIONALIZATION 1985

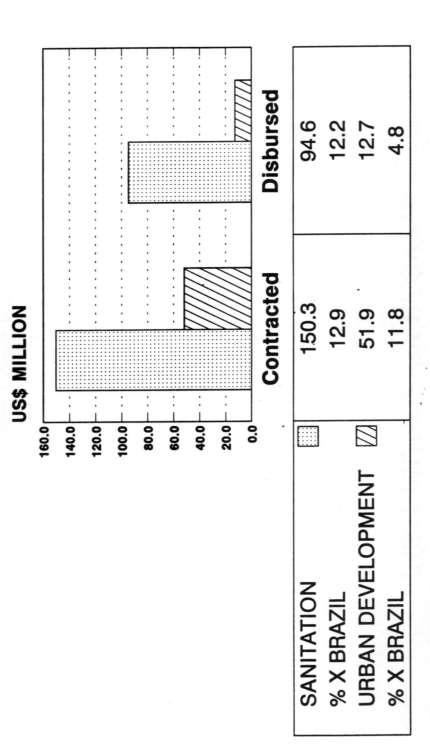

FIGURE 3

FGTS APPLICATIONS IN RIO DE JANEIRO
SANITATION AND URBAN DEVELOPMENT - 1991

US$ MILLION

	Contracted	Disbursed
SANITATION	150.3	94.6
% X BRAZIL	12.9	12.2
URBAN DEVELOPMENT	51.9	12.7
% X BRAZIL	11.8	4.8

CONTRACTING IN UPF FINANCIAL UNITS: SANITATION: 233,0122,000
URBAN DEVELOPMENT: 7,944,000
SOURCE: CEF (EXCLUDING HOUSING PROJECTS)

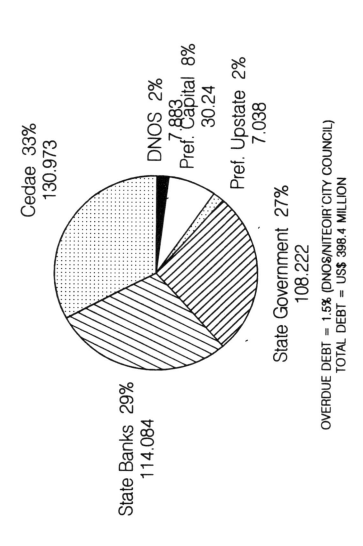

FIGURE 4
RIO DE JANEIRO/FGTS DEBIT BALANCE SANITATION - DECEMBER 1991

Cedae 33%
130.973

DNOS 2%
7.883
Pref. Capital 8%
30.24

Pref. Upstate 2%
7.038

State Government 27%
108.222

State Banks 29%
114.084

OVERDUE DEBT = 1.5% (DNOS/NITEOIR'CITY COUNCIL)
TOTAL DEBT = US$ 398.4 MILLION

INCLUDES URBAN DEVELOPMENT PROJECTS
OVERDUE DEBT = 1.5% (DNOS/Pr.Niterol)
SOURCE: CEF (EXCLUDES HOUSING)

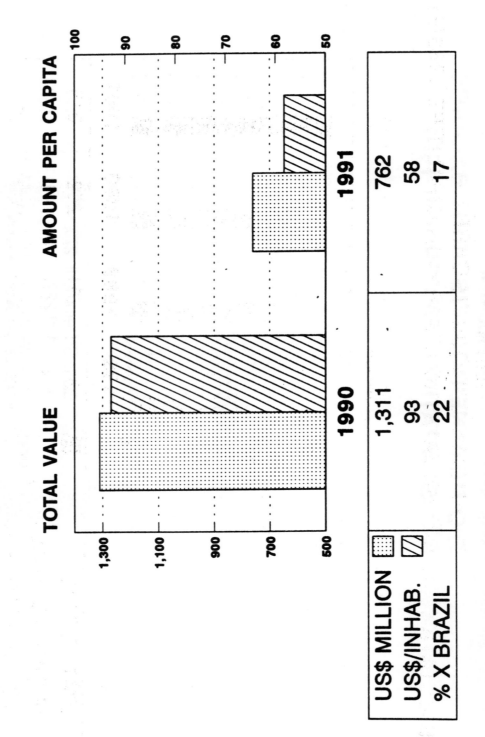

FIGURE 5
SINGLE HEALTH SYSTEM - SUS TRANSFERS
TO RIO DE JANEIRO IN 1990/91

AGREEMENTS, HOSPITALIZATION AND MAINTENANCE OF OWN NETWORK
SOURCE: HEALTH MINISTRY/INAMPS

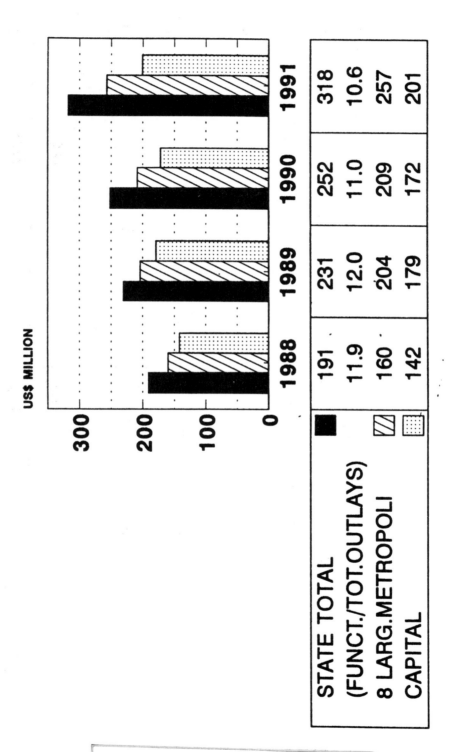

FIGURE 6
OUTLAYS ON HEALTH-CARE
SANITATION BY RIO DE JANEIRO STATE MUNICIPALITIES 1988/91

US$ MILLION

	1988	1989	1990	1991
STATE TOTAL	191	231	252	318
(FUNCT./TOT.OUTLAYS)	11.9	12.0	11.0	10.6
8 LARG.METROPOLI	160	204	209	257
CAPITAL	142	179	172	201

AT AVERAGE 1991 PRICES AND FOREIGN EXCHANGE
SOURCE: MINISTRY OF THE ECONOMY, FINANCES AND PLANNING/DTN
DEFLATOR: IGP

L. I. H. E.
THE BECK LIBRARY
WOOLTON RD., LIVERPOOL, L16 8ND

Table 1. Outlays on Health-care and Sanitation in Financial Balances
1985 - 1991

Item	1985	1986	1987	1988	1989	1990
% GDP	1.18	1.39	1.61	1.83	2.41	2.08
Real Development	100.00	129.00	145.00	157.00	214.00	166.00
% Total Outlays	5.25	4.83	5.32	5.01	5.88	5.69
Distribution by Gov't						
Central	28	32	37	23	36	24
State	61	58	53	66	57	65
Capitals	11	10	10	10	7	11

Source: Data taken from Guedes, Ohana and Mussi (1991), statistical annex. Based on the
Federal Government Balance Sheets (including supervised agencies) of States and
Capitals. Includes overhead plus capital, excluding amortizations and inter-governmental
transfers.

Table 2. Consolidated Central Government Outlays on Health-care
Programs, Sanitation and Social Welfare - 1988/91
(constant values/in average 1991 US$)

| Year | Health Care | Sanitation and Env. Protection | Sum | Total Outlays Soc. Welf. Areas | Relative Participation | | |
	A	B	C=A+B	D	E=B/C %	F=B/D %	G=C/D %
1980	7,431	1,375	8,805	39,025	15.6	3.5	22.6
1981	6,917	1,737	8,654	40,253	20.1	4.3	21.5
1982	7,222	1,615	8,837	42,375	18.3	3.8	20.9
1983	5,764	1,149	6,913	35,963	16.6	3.2	19.2
1984	6,018	709	6,727	31,207	10.5	2.3	21.6
1985	6,928	1,359	8,287	36,521	16.4	3.7	22.7
1986	7,416	1,205	8,621	41,266	14.0	2.9	20.9
1987	10,731	1,828	12,560	44,171	14.6	4.1	28.4
1988	10,129	1,645	11,775	45,801	14.0	3.6	25.7
1989	11,461	1,106	12,567	48,810	8.8	2.3	25.7
1990	9,532	1,016	10,548	46,936	9.6	2.2	22.5
1991	7,945	1,207	9,152	41,136	13.2	2.9	22.2

Sources: IPEA/CPS Consolidated Social Welfare accounts: primary data - balance sheets of the Central Government, INSS, CEF and others. Outlays: accrual accounting. Annual values updated to average 1991 prices (Deflator: IGP-DI) and converted into dollars at the average 1991 foreign exchange rate (Cr$/US$408.73). Consolidated Central Government figures include: National Treasury, Social Welfare Fund, FGTS, FINSOCIAL funding, FAS direct and decentralized civil service. Outlays in the Social Welfare area also include those under feeding and nutrition schemes, education and culture, housing and urban improvement, labor, assistance and social welfare, (including retired federal civil servants and INSS pensioners).

Table 3. Consolidated Central Government Per Capita Outlays
in Health-care, Sanitation and Social Welfare Programs - 1980/91
Constant Values (1991) in US$/Inhabitant

Year	Health Care A	Sanitation and Env. Protection B	Sum C=A+B	Total Outlays Soc. Welf. Areas D
1980	61.3	11.3	72.6	321.8
1981	56.0	14.1	70.0	325.7
1982	57.4	12.8	70.2	336.5
1983	44.9	9.0	53.9	280.3
1984	46.0	5.4	51.5	238.7
1985	52.0	10.2	62.2	274.2
1986	54.6	8.9	63.5	304.1
1987	77.7	13.2	90.9	319.7
1988	72.0	11.7	83.6	325.3
1989	79.9	7.7	87.6	340.3
1990	65.2	7.0	72.2	321.1
1991	53.4	8.1	61.5	276.2

Sources and notes: See Table. Population - IBGE, 1991 Census.

Table 4. Development of Central Government Per Capita Outlays in
Health-care, Sanitation and Social Welfare Programs - 1980/91
index figure: base 1980 = 100

Year	Health Care A	Sanitation and Env. Protection B	Sum C=A+B	Total Outlays Soc. Welf. Areas D
1980	100	100	100	100
1981	91	124	96	101
1982	94	113	97	105
1983	73	79	74	87
1984	75	48	71	74
1985	85	90	86	85
1986	89	78	88	95
1987	127	117	125	99
1988	117	103	115	101
1989	130	68	121	106
1990	106	61	99	100
1991	87	72	85	86

Sources and notes: See table (Deflator: (IGP-DI).

Table 5. Consolidated Central Government Outlays in Health-care
Sanitation and Social Welfare Programs, in Proportion the GDP
1980/91 (in percentage; in proportion the GDP)

Year	Health Care A	Sanitation and Env. Protection B	Sum C=A+B	Total Outlays Soc. Welf. Areas D
1980	1.76	0.33	2.09	9.25
1981	1.74	0.44	2.17	10.10
1982	1.72	0.38	2.10	10.09
1983	1.51	0.30	1.81	9.39
1984	1.53	0.18	1.71	7.94
1985	1.60	0.31	1.92	8.44
1986	1.57	0.25	1.82	8.73
1987	2.34	0.40	2.74	9.63
1988	2.32	0.38	2.70	10.49
1989	2.53	0.24	2.78	10.78
1990	2.34	0.25	2.59	11.52
1991	1.93	0.29	2.22	9.98

Sources and notes: See table. GDP-IBGE: National Accounts.

Table 6: Development of Origins of Financing for Consolidated Central Government Outlays in Health-Care, Sanitation and Environmental Protection Programs

Year	In average 1991 US$ million					Composition of Origins		
	National Treasury	Social Welfare Fund	FGTS	FAS	Sum	National Treasury	Social Welfare Fund	FGTS
Health-care								
1985	1,274	5,417	-	237	6,928	18	78	-
1986	1,660	5,700	-	56	7,416	22	77	-
1987	2,084	8,610	-	37	10,731	19	80	-
1988	2,014	8,049	-	66	10,129	20	79	-
1989	3,156	8,277	-	27	11,461	28	72	-
1990	2,024	7,546	-	0	9,570	21	79	-
1991*	3,769	4,177	-	0	7,945	47	53	-
Sanitation and Environmental Protection								
1985	128	-	1,231	-	1,359	9	-	91
1986	219	-	986	-	1,205	18	-	82
1987	397	-	1,431	-	1,828	22	-	78
1988	254	-	1,391	-	1,645	15	-	85
1989	209	-	897	-	1,106	19	-	81
1990	258	-	759	-	1,016	25	-	75
1991/e	403	-	804	-	1,207	33	-	67
Health-care, Sanitation and Environmental Protection								
1985	1,402	5,417	1,231	237	8,287	17	65	15
1986	1,879	5,700	986	56	8,621	22	66	11
1987	2,482	8,610	1,431	37	12,560	20	69	11
1988	2,268	8,049	1,391	66	11,775	19	68	12
1989	3,365	8,277	897	27	12,567	27	66	7
1990	2,281	7,546	759	0	10,586	22	71	7
1991/e	4,172	4,177	804	0	9,152	46	46	9

Sources and notes: See Table. National treasury: includes ordinary and linked funding (such as FINSOCIAL levies and Profits) allocated directly by area. Social Welfare Fund: Social Welfare levy funding (payroll) and others allocated to the fund, including from FINSOCIAL.
(*) own estimates, based on 1991 Central Government Balance Sheets

Table 7. Amount and Structure of Outlays on Environment Programs in 1985
Consolidated Central Government and States

Selected Programs	Outlays - 1985 US$ in mil 1991 A	In % x Outlays Total B	In % x Outlays Net C	In % x Outlays Function D	Distribution by Economic Category and Function Total E	Staff F	Other Purchases G	Social Welfare H	Overhead I	Fixed Investments J	Capital Expenses K	Own Expenses L	Inter-Governmental Transfers M
Pres. National Renewable Resource	122.3	0.1	0.1	2.1	100.0	51.3	26.0		81.9	9.5	16.9	98.8	1.2
Reforestation	25.9	0.0	0.0	0.5	100.0	2.4	13.4		15.7	3.1	84.3	100.0	
Meteorology & Climatology	4.8	0.0	0.0	0.1	100.0	64.0	32.4		96.5	3.4	3.5	100.0	
Agriculture	5,693.3	2.6	5.0	100.0	100.0	12.9	10.9		62.0	1.9	37.3	89.3	0.7
Art/Archeol. National Assets	24.2	0.0	0.0	0.2	100.0	74.7	15.9	0.4	91.0	7.3	9.0	100.0	
Education and Culture	10,981.0	5.1	9.6	100.0	100.0	70.5	10.3	2.8	83.7	7.4	7.7	91.4	8.6
Administration	414.9	0.2	0.4	4.0	100.0	68.1	26.1	0.1	94.3	3.8	3.8	98.1	1.9
Studies, Surveys, Research	36.3	0.0	0.0	0.4	100.0	60.0	17.5	6.2	83.6	16.2	16.2	99.9	0.1
Personnel Training	1.8	0.0	0.0	0.0	100.0	36.9	24.3		61.3	0.0	0.0	61.3	38.7
Sanitary Medical Aid	7,068.1	3.3	6.2	68.3	100.0	36.6	13.8	41.0	91.6	2.8	2.8	94.4	5.6
Control/Erad Transm. Diseases	257.3	0.1	0.2	2.5	100.0	59.9	31.5	0.0	91.4	6.9	6.0	97.4	2.6
Specialized Assistance	31.9	0.0	0.0	0.3	100.0	57.7	30.8		93.4	6.6	6.6	100.0	
Feeding and Nutrition	756.0	0.4	0.7	7.3	100.0	1.3	84.9		95.5	0.0	0.2	95.7	4.0
Sanitary Supervision and Inspection	8.9	0.0	0.0	0.1	100.0	84.4	14.3	0.0	98.7	0.0	1.2	99.9	0.1
Therapeutic/Prophyl. Products	233.2	0.1	0.2	2.3	100.0	2.5	94.5	0.0	97.9	1.2	2.1	100.0	
Mother/Child Care	97.6	0.0	0.1	0.9	100.0	63.0	28.4	0.2	91.6	0.6	0.1	91.7	8.3
Environmental Protection	1,228.4	0.6	1.1	11.9	100.0	2.8	0.9	0.1	52.5	11.7	46.4	93.8	1.2
	214.6	0.1	0.2	2.1	100.0	34.7	11.9		47.1	51.1	51.9	99.0	1.0
Health-care and Sanitation	10,349.1	4.8	9.1	100.0	100.0	31.5	20.4	28.0	86.5	4.8	9.0	95.5	4.5
Overall Total	215,771.1	100.0	100.0	100.0	100.0	11.8	4.5	14.2	79.1	3.5	12.5	91.5	8.5

Source: FGV/IBGE/CEF Regionalization of Public Sector Transactions 1985. (Based - accrual or accounting). Includes direct and decentralized civil servic, including Social Welfare funds and excluding state-owned companies. Actual amount: updated to 1991 prices (Deflator - IGP) and using the average foreign exchange rate (US$/Cr$408.73). Net Expenditures: excludes foreign debt service and transfers. Overhead: staff and Social Welfare levies; other purchases of goods and service; medical aid and Social Welfare transfers to the private sector and abroad, debt charges, subsidies. Capital Expenditures: fixed investments, financial investments and amortization of debt. Own Expenses: overall total (after deduction of intra-governmental transfers) less transfers to other levels of Government.

Table 8. Amount and Structure of Outlays on Environment Programs in 1985
Consolidated Central Government[1]

Selected Programs	Outlays - 1985 US$ in mil. 1991 (A)	In % x Outlays Total (B)	Net (C)	Function (D)	Distribution by Economic Category and Function Total (E)	Staff (F)	Other Purchases (G)	Social Welfare (H)	Overhead (I)	Fixed Investments (J)	Capital Expenses (K)	Own Expenses (L)	Inter-Governmental Transfers (M)
Pres. National Renewable Resource	53.1	0.0	0.1	1.1	100.0	52.3	34.1		87.3	6.9	10.0	97.3	2.7
Reforestation	25.4	0.0	0.0	0.5	100.0	0.2	13.6		13.9	3.2	86.1	100.0	
Meteorology & Climatology	3.7	0.0	0.0	0.1	100.0	64.6	31.5		96.0	3.8	4.0	100.0	
Agriculture	4,822.6	2.8	6.3	100.0	100.0	8.8	8.8		58.3	1.0	40.9	99.2	0.8
Art/Archeo. National Assets	5.2	0.0	0.0	0.1	100.0	68.3	30.7	0.6	99.7	0.3	0.3	100.0	
Education and Culture	3,873.6	2.3	5.0	100.0	100.0	54.2	11.9	5.8	71.9	4.3	5.0	76.9	23.1
Administration	41.9	0.0	0.1	0.6	100.0	61.1	20.7	0.0	81.8	0.4	0.4	82.2	17.8
Studies, Survey, Research	31.3	0.0	0.0	0.4	100.0	62.8	17.5	7.1	87.5	12.4	12.4	99.8	0.2
Personnel Training	1.3	0.0	0.0	0.0	100.0	15.3	29.8		45.1	0.0	0.0	45.1	54.9
Sanitary Medical Aid	5,600.7	3.3	7.3	77.3	100.0	30.9	8.9	51.4	91.6	1.8	1.8	93.4	6.6
Control/Errad Transm. Diseases	245.1	0.1	0.3	3.4	100.0	59.9	31.8	0.0	91.7	5.4	5.5	97.2	2.8
Specialized Assistance	753.3	0.4	1.0	10.4	100.0	1.3	84.8	0.0	95.5	0.0	0.2	95.7	4.3
Feeding and Nutrition	8.3	0.0	0.0	0.1	100.0	83.5	15.2	0.0	98.7	1.3	1.3	99.9	0.1
Sanitary Supervision and Inspection	222.4	0.1	0.3	3.1	100.0	1.8	93.1		99.9	0.1	0.1	100.0	
Therapeutic/Prophyl. Products	53.8	0.0	0.1	0.7	100.0	64.0	20.9		84.9		0.0	84.9	15.1
Mother/Child Care	108.3	0.1	0.1	1.5	100.0	16.1	8.2	0.0	25.6	65.7	65.9	91.5	8.5
Environmental Protection	174.8	0.1	0.2	2.4	100.0	27.7	10.4	0.9	38.2	60.4	61.5	99.7	0.3
Health-care and Sanitation	7,241.2	4.2	9.4	100.0	100.0	28.2	20.6	39.8	89.9	4.1	4.1	94.0	6.0
Overall Total	172,032.9	100.0	100.0	100.0	100.0	6.3	3.5	15.3	82.2	1.3	10.0	92.3	7.7

Source: FGV/IBGE/CEF Regionalization of Public Sector Transactions 1985. (Based - accrual or accounting). Includes direct and decentralized civil service, including Social Welfare funds and excluding state-owned companies. Actual amount: updated to 1991 prices (Deflator - IGP) and using the average foreign exchange rate (US$/Cr$406.73). Net Expenditures: excludes foreign debt service and transfers. Overhead: staff and Social Welfare levies; other purchases of goods and services; medical aid and Social Welfare transfers to the private sector and abroad, debt charges, subsidies. Capital Expenditures: fixed investments, financial investments and amortization of debt. Own Expenses: overall total (after deduction of intra-governmental transfers) less transfers to other levels of Government.

Table 9. Amount and Structure of Outlays on Environment Programs in 1985
Consolidated Central Government[1]

Selected Programs	Outlays - 1985 US$ in mil. 1991 A	In % x Outlays Total B	Net C	Function D	Distribution by Economic Category and Function Total E	Staff F	Other Purchases G	Social Welfare H	Overhead I	Fixed Investment J	Capital Expenses K	Own Expenses L	Inter-Governmental Transfers M
Pres. National Renewable Resource	69.2	0.2	0.2	7.9	100.0	51.6	19.8		77.8	11.6	22.2	100.0	
Reforestation	0.6	0.0	0.0	0.1	100.0	96.7	3.3		100.0			100.0	
Meteorology & Climatology	1.1	0.0	0.0	0.1	100.0	62.1	35.9		98.0	2.0	2.0	100.0	
Agriculture	870.7	2.0	2.3	100.0	100.0	35.6	22.7		82.4	7.1	17.3	99.6	0.4
Art/Archelo. National Assets	19.0	0.0	0.1	0.5	100.0	76.5	11.9	0.3	88.7	9.2	11.3	100.0	
Education and Culture	7,107.4	16.2	19.0	183.5		79.4	9.4	1.2	90.1	9.0	9.1	99.2	0.8
Administration	373.0	0.9	1.0	12.0	100.0	68.9	26.7	0.1	95.7	4.2	4.2	99.9	0.1
Studies, Surveys, Research	5.1	0.0	0.0	0.2	100.0	43.0	17.0	0.1	60.1	39.9	39.9	100.0	
Personnel Training	0.5	0.0	0.0	0.0	100.0	88.8	11.2		100.0			100.0	
Sanitary Medical Aid	1,467.4	3.4	3.9	47.2	100.0	58.3	32.3	0.9	91.6	6.8	6.8	98.4	1.6
Control/Errad Transm. Diseases	12.2	0.0	0.0	0.4	100.0	59.4	25.2	0.6	85.1	14.9	14.9	100.0	
Specialized Assistance	31.9	0.1	0.1	1.0	100.0	57.7	30.8		93.4	6.6	6.6	100.0	
Feeding and Nutrition	2.7	0.0	0.0	0.1	100.0		100.0		100.0			100.0	
Sanitary Supervision and Inspection	0.5	0.0	0.0	0.0	100.0	98.4	1.6	0.1	99.9	0.1	0.1	100.0	
Therapeutic/Prophyl. Products	10.9	0.1	0.1	0.3	100.0	16.3	21.5	0.4	68.9	9.0	41.1	100.0	
Mother/Child Care	43.8	0.1	0.1	1.4	100.0	61.8	37.6		99.9	0.1	0.1	100.0	
Environ..ental Protection	1,120.1	2.6	3.0	36.0	100.0	1.5	-0.2	0.0	55.1	6.4	44.5	99.5	0.5
	39.8	0.1	0.1	1.3	100.0	65.6	18.4		86.3	9.9	9.9	96.2	3.8
Health care and Sanitation	3,107.9	7.1	8.3	100.0	100.0	39.0	19.9	0.5	78.8	6.4	20.2	99.0	1.0
Overall Total	43,738.2	100.0	116.7	100.0	100.0	33.4	8.7	9.8	66.5	12.1	21.9	88.5	11.5

Source: IGV/IBGF/CEF Regionalization of Public Sector Transactions 1985. (Based - accrual or accounting). Includes direct and decentralized civil service, including Social Welfare funds and excluding state-owned companies. Actual amount: updated to 1991 prices (D-flator - IGP) and using the average foreign exchange rate (US$/Cr$408.7)). Net Expenditures: excludes foreign debt service and transfers. Overhead: staff and Social Welfare levies; other purchases of goods and services; medical aid and Social W elfare transfers to the private sector and abroad, debt charges, debt charges, subsidies. Capital Expenditures: fixed investment, financial investments and amortization of debt. Own Expenses: overall total (after deduction of intra-governmental transfers) less transfers to other levels of Government.

Table 10. Municipal Outlays (Capitals and Metropolis) of Brazil, on Health-care and Sanitation Programs by Economic Category, in 1985 - in Average 1991 US$

Function/Program	Total Outlays			Distribution by Category of Outlays					
	US$ mil.	% Total	% Function	Staff	Other Purchases	Gov't Transfers	Overhead	Fixed Inv.	Capital Exp.
Overall Total	7,053	100		33	18	8	76	18	24
Health-care & San.	720	10	100	40	20	20	81	19	19
Health-care	486	7	67	58	26	8	93	7	7
Administration	103	1	14	53	32	11	96	4	4
San. Assist./Nutri.	205	3	28	63	25	4	93	7	7
Hospital aid	178	3	25	55	23	11	91	9	9
Sani. Env. Preservation	234	3	33	3	7	44	56	44	44
Administration	1	0	0	68	20	0	89	11	11
Env. Protection	121	2	17	2	3	84	89	11	11
Basic Sanitation	24	0	3	21	19	0	59	41	41
General Sanitation	88	1	12	0	8	0	9	91	91

Source: IBGE, Public Sector Economic Statistics (special tables). Updated by average 1991 prices (Deflator IGP-DI) and converted by the average foreign exchange rate for the year (US$/Cr$408.73). Overhead includes current expenditures, debt service and Government transfers, etc. Capital Expenditures include fixed investments, financial investments and amortizations.

Table 11. Outlays by Rio de Janeiro Metropolitan Region Municipalities on Health-care and Sanitation Programs, by Economic Category, in 1985 - in Average 1991 US$

Function/Program	Total Outlays				Distribution by Category of Outlays					
	US$ mil.	% Total	% Function	% Brazil	Staff	Other Purchases	Gov't Transfers	Overhead	Fixed Inv.	Capital Exp.
Overall Total	1,186	100		17	46	17	11	87	9	13
Health-care & San.	120	10	100	17	50	32	0	82	18	18
Health-care	106	9	88	22	56	35	0	91	9	9
Administration	13	1	11	13	56	40		97	3	3
San. Assist./Nutri.	86	7	71	42	59	35		94	6	6
Hospital aid	7	1	6	4	23	22	2	47	53	53
Sani. Env. Preservation	14	1	12	6	1	12		13	87	87
Administration	5	0	4	4						
Env. Protection	0	0	0	1		1		1	99	99
Basic Sanitation	9	1	7	10	23	12		35	65	65
General Sanitation						19		19	81	81

Source: IBGE, Public Sector Economic Statistics (special tables). Updated by average 1991 prices (Deflator IGP-DI) and converted by the average foreign exchange rate for the year (US$/Cr$408.73). Overhead includes current expenditures, debt services and Government transfers, etc. Capital Expenditures include fixed investments, financial investments and amortizations. Brazil covers consolidation of capital and metropolitan municipalities.

Table 12. National Treasury Expenditures on Environmental Actions - 1991

Function/Program	Annual Amount US$000	Per Capita Expenditure US$/inh.	In Proportion to	
			GDP	Outlays
General Sanitation	6,905,772	46.4	1.67	10
Programs	6,967,123	46.8	1.69	100
Health-care	6,486,304	43.6	1.57	93
Sanitation	440,518	3.0	0.11	6
Environmental Protection	40,300	0.3	0.01	1
Sub-programs	6,776,464	45.5	1.64	100
Science and Technology	248	0.0	0.00	0
Environmental Survey/Amazonia	248	0.0	0.00	0
Pres. Nat. Renewable Resources	1,060	0.0	0.00	0
Protection of Plant/Animal Life	1,060	0.0	0.00	0
Integrated Programs	468	0.0	0.00	0
Soil Cons/Rural Micro-basins	468	0.0	0.00	0
Culture	6,403	0.0	0.00	0
Hist. Art. Archeol. Assets	6,403	0.0	0.00	0
Mineral Resources	1,406	0.0	0.00	0
Pollution Control/Env. Quality	1,406	0.0	0.00	0
Water Resources	7,634	0.1	0.00	0
Drought Prevention/Protection	7,634	0.1	0.00	0
Urban Planning	86,636	0.6	0.02	1
Urban Infrastruc. (Sanitation)	86,636	0.6	0.02	1
Health-care	6,304,132	42.3	1.53	93
Feeding and Nutrition	559,656	3.8	0.14	8
Education	281,750	1.9	0.07	4
Health-care	114,736	0.8	0.03	2
Aid (mil distribution)	163,170	1.1	0.04	2
Medical/Sanitary Assistance	4,766,224	32.0	1.16	70
Civil Servants & Other Prog.	213,987	1.4	0.05	3
Overall	4,552,237	30.6	1.10	67
Control of Trans. Diseases	533,400	3.6	0.13	8
Sanitary Inspection	19,759	0.1	0.00	0
Therapeutic/Prophyl. Products	425,094	2.9	0.10	6
Sanitation	329,191	2.2	0.08	5
Water Supplies General	7,272	0.5	0.02	1
Sanitation	227,739	1.5	0.06	3
Urban Areas and Environments	25,136	0.2	0.01	0
Rural Areas and Environments	12,366	0.1	0.00	0
Drainage Work	36,622	0.2	0.01	1
Emergency Social Programs	116,775	0.8	0.03	2
Others	36,840	0.2	0.01	1
Sewage Systems	29,180	0.2	0.01	0
Environmental Protection	39,285	0.3	0.01	1
Plant and Animal Life Protection	17,796	0.1	0.00	0
Flood Prevention/Protection	21,490	0.1	0.01	0

Source: From data in Central Government Balance Sheets - 1991, Ministry of Education, Finances and Planning/DTN. At average annual prices and foreign exchange rate (US$408.73). In % of Expenditures: function over total outlays, excluding debt service. National Treasury Resources, excluding revenues collected directly by funds and supervised organizations (such as financial applications, fines and sales), as well as FGTS-funded loans. Selected environmental sub-programs with exclusion of administration, planning and financial charges; sum of the sub-programs differs from outlays by programs of functions.

Table 13. Sources of Financing for National Treasury Outlays on Sanitation
and Environmental protection Programs - 1991

Sub-program	Amount Distribution		Distribution by Source			
	US$ 000	%	Ord. Funds	Foreign Cred. Operations	Billings	Others
Sum	488,659	100	48	26	25	0
						0
General Sanitation	227,739	47	33	51	15	0
Urban Planning	95,668	20	78		22	2
Water Supplies	72,213	15	50		48	0
Sewage Systems	29,180	6	21		79	
Flood Prot./Protection	21,490	4	100			
Community Assistance	20,663	4	53		47	
Special Programs	18,856	4	46	52		2
Environmental Survey	1,687	0	22	78		0
	1,153	0	100			
	12	0	100			

Source: From data in Central Government Balance Sheets - 1991. Ministry of Education, Finances and Planning/DTN, excluding health-care program. At average annual prices and foreign exchange rates (US$/Cr$ 408.73). National Treasury Resources, excluding FGTS and decentralized civil service direct revenues.

Table 14. Real Development of Outlays on Health-care and Sanitation
by the State and Capital Municipality of Rio de Janeiro - 1990/91

| Year | Expenditure - US$ mil. 1991 | | | Capital % | Function/Total % | |
	State	Capital	Sum		State	Capital
1980	153	110	263	42	4.6	10.7
1981	144	95	239	40	4.4	10.7
1982	168	114	282	40	4.5	11.0
1983	133	90	223	40	4.7	11.1
1984	145	92	237	39	5.3	12.4
1985	182	96	278	35	5.1	10.7
1986	340	142	482	29	6.8	11.6
1987	428	214	642	33	9.7	16.7
1988	482	142	624	23	10.4	12.1
1989	615	179	794	22	15.2	12.9
1990	550	172	722	24	10.5	11.1
1991*	240	201	441	46	5.3	9.4

Sources: Ministry of Education, Finances and Planning, Treasury, State and Municipal Finances. Includes
budget outlays only for the direct civil service. Values updated by average 1991 prices and converted at
the average foreign exchange rate for this year (US$/Cr$408.73).
* For the State, excludes SUS transfers to the Health-care Fund.

Table 15. Rio de Janeiro State Government Expenditures on Environmental Actions - 1991

Function/Program	Outlays in US$ mil.			% Participation			
	Projects	Activities	Total	Projects	Function	Actions	Total
Agriculture	2,271	34,413	36,684	6	100		1
Pres.Nat.Renewable Res.	1,568	3,065	4,633	34	13	2	0
Protraction Plant/Animal Life	1,588	3,065	4,633	34	13	2	0
Public Prot. and Security	6,008	392,707	398,715	2	100		9
Health-care		464	464		0	0	0
Sanitary/Medical Aid		464	484		0	0	0
Education and Culture	397,964	171,523	569,486	70	100		12
Culture		29,768	29,766		5		1
Hist.Art.Archeol. Assets	4		4	100	0	0	0
Health-care and Sanitation	93,081	147,071	240,152	39	100	98	5
Administration	6,413	104,289	110,702	8	48	45	2
Government Planning Health-		162	162		0	0	0
care		16,564	16,564		7	7	0
Protection Against Damage		449	449		0	0	0
Personnel Training		1,203	1,203		1	0	0
Medical/San. Assistance		9,882	9,882		4	4	0
Control of Transm.Diseases		153	153		0	0	0
Therapeutic/Prophyl.Products		4,877	4,877		2	2	0
Sanitation	84,968	8,366	93,333	91	39	38	2
General Sanitation	84,968	8,366	93,333	91	39	38	2
Environmental Protection	1,700	17,690	19,390	9	8	8	0
Pollution Control	1,700	17,690	19,390	9	8	8	0
Environmental Actions	94,653	150,559	245,252	39		100	5
Overall Total - State	715,369	3,848,969	4,564,338	16			100

Sources: Data from Rio de Janeiro State Budget Implementation - 1991. Amounts converted at the average foreign exchange rate (US$/Cr$408.73). Includes outlays made (accrual) only by the direct civil service.

Table 16. Rio de Janeiro Municipal Government Expenditures on Environmental Actions - 1991

Function/Program	Outlays in US$ mil.			% Participation			Sources of Fin.	
	Projects	Activities	Total	Projects	Function	Total	Ord. Funds	Linked Funds
Administration and Planning	174,676	162,747	337,423	48		16	100	0
Administration	81,943	7,736	89,680	9		4	98	1
General Sanitation		377	377	100	0	0		100
Education and Culture	304,423	41,622	346,045	12		16	98	2
Pres. Nat.Renewable Res.	4,822	147	4,968	3	2	0	100	
Botanical Gardens & Zoo	4,822	147	4,968	3	2	0	100	
Culture	6,537	3,434	9,970	34		0	100	
Hist.Art.Archeol. Assets	52	23	75	31	0	0	100	
Housing and Urban Improve.	235,568	549,412	785,004	70		37	96	2
Sanitation		2,390	2,380	100	1	0	100	
General Sanitation		2,390	2,380	100	1	0	100	
Env. Protection	49	8	56	13	0	0	100	
Pollution Control	49	8	56	13	0	0	100	
Health-care and Sanitation	167,101	34,101	201,201	17	96	9	91	8
Administration	3,898		3,898			0	100	
Health-care	143,269	11,911	155,180	8	76	7	94	6
General Administration	9,544	3	9,547	0	5	0	100	
Sanitary/Medical Aid	130,168	11,909	142,074	8	69	7	93	7
Sanitary Inspection	3,558		3,559		2	0	100	
Sanitation	18,834	22,189	42,123	53	21	2	81	18
General Sanitation	18,834	22,189	42,123	53	21	2	81	18
Environmental Actions	168,125	37,044	205,170	18	100	10	91	8
Overall Total Outlays	1,275,308	861,071	2,136,380	40		100	96	2

Source: Data from the Rio de Janeiro Municipal Balance Sheets - 1991. Includes only direct municipal civil service budget outlays. Environmental actions: included in programs under other functions and excluding administration. Amounts converted at the average foreign exchange rate (US$/Cr$408.73).

Table 17. Sao Paulo Municipal Government Expenditures on Environmental Actions - 1991

Function/Program	Outlays US$ 000	Distrib. Programs		Sources of Financing		% Outlays	
		Projects	Activities	Ordinary Funds	Linked Funds	Actions	Total
Education and Culture	541,453	11	89	20	80		17
Culture	51,246	11	89	100			2
Hist.Art.Archeol. Assets	2,944	19	81	100		1	0
Housing and Urban Improvement	478,949	17	83	100			15
Health-care	4,770		100	100		1	0
Sanitary/Medical Aid	4,770		100	100		1	0
Health-care and Sanitation	632,657	13	87	100		88	17
Health-care	447,624	2	98	100		83	14
Sanitary/Medical Aid	435,056	2	98	100		81	14
Sanitation and Inspection	3,227		100	100		1	0
Sanitation	85,015	67	33	100		16	3
General Sanitation	85,015	67	33	100		16	3
Environmental Protection	19		100	100		0	0
Pollution Control	19		100	100		0	0
Environmental Actions	540,371	13	87	100		100	17
Overall Total Outlays	3,201,928	88	12	100	16		100

Source: Data from the Sao Paulo Municipal Balance Sheets - 1991. Includes only direct municipal civil service budget outlays. Environmental actions: included in programs under other functions and excluding administration. Amount converted at the average foreign exchange rate (US/Cr$408.73).

Table 18. Rio de Janeiro Metropolis Municipal Expenditures on Health-care and Sanitation
Spatial Distribution - 1988/91

Major Municips. in the Rio Metropolis	Population		Function Outlays/1991 US$ 000			
	000 inh.	Distr. %	1988/91 Average	Distr. %	1991	Distr. %
Rio de Janeiro	5,336	58	173,332	83	201,201	78
Nova Iguacu	1,286	14	9,915	5	19,102	7
Sao Goncalo	748	8	5,879	3	8,214	3
Duque de Caixas	665	7	9,032	4	15,091	6
Sao Joao de Meriti	425	5	2,438	1	4,988	2
Niteroi	416	5	3,505	2	4,402	2
Itaborai	161	2	1,754	1	2,000	1
Nilopolis	158	2	1,754	1	2,429	1
Sum/Weighted Average Simple Average	9,195	100	207,599	100	257,428	100

Sources: ABRASF, DTN/SIAFI, Finance Section. Deflator IGP. Converted at the average 1991 foreign exchange rate
(US$/Cr$408.73).

Table 19. Rio de Janeiro Metropolis Municipal Expenditures on Health-care and Sanitation: Real Development - 1988/91

Major Municipalities in the Rio de Janeiro Metropolis	In Constant Values/US$ 00 (at av. 1991 for exch. rate)				Average Growth Rate 88/91% p.a.	In Per Capita Values/US$ 000 (at average 1991 for exch. rate)					Average Growth Rate 88/91% p.a.
	1988	1989	1990	1991		1988	1989	1990	1991	Average	
Rio de Janeiro	141,72	178,552	171,848	201,201	12	27	34	32	38	33	12
Nova Iguacu	3,198	6,733	10,625	19,102	81	3	5	8	15	8	79
Sao Goncalo	4,117	6,228	4,959	8,214	26	6	9	7	11	8	24
Duque de Caixas	5,059	5,895	10,084	15,091	44	8	9	15	23	14	42
Sao Joao de Meriti	722	1,254	2,788	4,988	90	2	3	7	12	6	89
Niteroi	2,584	2,466	4,588	4,402	20	6	6	11	11	8	19
Itaborai	1,221	1,528	2,268	2,000	18	8	10	15	12	11	14
Nilopolis	1,331	1,293	1,923	2,429	22	9	8	12	15	11	22
Sum/Weighted Average	159,939	203,950	209,081	257,428	17	18	23	23	28	23	16
Simple Average					39	9	11	13	17	12	38

Source; ABRASF, DTN/SIAFI, Finance Section. Deflator IGP. Converted at the average 1991 foreign exchange rate (US$/Cr$408.73).

Table 20. Rio de Janeiro Metropolis Municipal Expenditures on Health-care and Sanitation
Relative Importance in Local Budget - 1988/91

Major Municipalities in the Rio de Janeiro Metropolis	Function Participation in Total Budget Outlays					Variation Outlays Function/ Total	Contribution of Function to Variation in Total Outlays			
	1988	1989	1990	1991			88/89	89/90	90/91	88/91
Rio de Janeiro	12	13	11	9	11	0.6	13	11	9	9
Nova Iguacu	11	13	17	29	17	2.6	13	17	32	29
Sao Goncalo	27	22	15	21	21	0.7	22	15	22	21
Duque de Caixas	17	15	19	18	17	1.1	15	19	18	18
Sao Joao de Meriti	5	9	16	24	14	6.0	9	16	26	24
Niteroi	7	5	8	7	7	0.9	5	8	7	7
Itaborai	20	18	18	18	18	0.9	17	18	18	18
Nilopolis	15	12	15	20	16	2.0	12	15	21	20
Sum/Weighted Average	12	12	12	11	12	0.7	13	12	10	11
Simple Average	14	12	15	18	15	1.6	13	15	19	18

Sources: ABRASF, DTN/SIAFI, Finance Section. Deflator IGP. Converted at the average 1991 foreign exchange rate
(US$/Cr$408.73).

Table 21. Municipal Income x Revenues in the Rio de Janeiro Metropolis:
Real Development and Origin of Funds - 1988/91

Major Municipalities in the Rio de Janeiro Metropolis	Annual Growth (Health)	Annual Growth Rate Outlays (% p.a.)			Annual Growth Rate Revenues (% p.a.)				Variation Determinants for Total Revenues (100%)					
									Own Funds			Third Party		
		Total	Overhead	Capital	Total	Taxes	ICMS	FPM	Taxes	Other	Sum	ICMS	Other	Sum
Rio de Janeiro	12	22	9	66	40	36	14	13	38	43	79	15	6	21
Nova Iguacu	79	31	24	66	31	54	25	28	19	17	35	36	29	65
Sao Goncalo	24	37	34	47	34	56	40	-8	32	6	38	37	25	62
Duque de Caxias	42	41	43	31	39	28	59	2	17	4	21	68	11	79
Sao Joao de Meriti	89	15	17	8	19	45	17	3	27	16	43	33	23	57
Niteroi	19	22	10	153	25	38	16	-1	52	13	66	17	17	34
Itaborai	14	21	15	56	22	36	41	19	17	6	23	30	47	77
Nilopolis	22	11	8	42	15	27	47	5	15	27	42	19	40	58
Sum/Weighted Average	16	23	11	65	39	36	19	8	35	39	74	18	8	26
Simple Average	38	25	20	59	28	40	33	7	27	16	43	32	26	57

Sources: ABRASF, DTN/SIAFI, Finance Section. Deflator IGP. Converted at the average 1991 foreign exchange rate (US$/CR$408.73).

7. Summary of Recent Research on Urban-Environmental Issues

Marcio Seroa de Araujo Coriolano

1. Introduction

The Rio de Janeiro case study covers environmental degradation and the vulnerability of high-risk urban situations in metropolitan Rio de Janeiro. This paper outlines various topics currently under study that could help reduce environmental degradation in metropolitan Rio de Janeiro. Due to limited time and access to sources, this paper should be considered preliminary and exploratory, being neither a full record nor a detailed analysis of surveys in the urban and environmental areas.

A loose-knit infrastructure and uncontrolled occupation of hillsides, marshes and river/canal banks increase the urban vulnerability in Greater Rio. This Report highlights scientific and technological output on issues involving human settlements subject to government intervention, water quality in hydrographic basins; soil stability; pollution control and appropriate technologies for upgrading environmental conditions. This covers risk factor diagnosis, appraisal of government action programs, and the development of experimental programs and technology for management and reduction of these factors.

This outline covers the period 1970-92. Major university centers and public or private organizations in the State of Rio de Janeiro that had already consolidated lines of research on the issues selected were identified. Then the methodology involved interviews with specialists and research coordinators, and a thorough review of library materials and other published catalogs in the identified institutions. Also included are some projects carried out elsewhere in Brazil that could be applicable to Rio de Janeiro.

2. Aspects of urban and environmental policy: a chronology of lines of research

The first half of the 1970s saw an across-the-board reorganization of Brazil's urban development policy, backed by Supplementary Law No. 14 (1974) and the Interministerial National Urban Policy Council. The National Housing Bank (BNH) was set up in 1964 to manage the National Housing Financing System, and was restructured in 1974 as an urban development bank. In 1971 the National Sanitation Plan was set up to channel massive investments into water and sewage networks, benefiting state sanitation companies, to the detriment of municipal water and sewage services. In 1973 the Special Environment Bureau (SEMA) was set up; however, lack of interest in environmental matters hampered implementation of any effective policies or allocation of adequate technical and financial resources.

In 1974, the authorities earmarked control of pollution in the Guanabara Bay as high priority, due to excessive discharge of domestic and industrial liquid wastes. Early efforts were backed by the UNDP and WHO through the Guanabara State Environmental Clean-Up Project. The

Development Foundation (FUNDREM), the State Environmental Engineering Board (FEEMA) and the State Rivers and Lakes Superintendency (SERLA) were all set up.

This period also saw a strengthening in the scientific and technological structures slanted to urban and environmental issues at both the government and University levels. This spurt carried on to the end of the 1970s, featuring cheaper construction programs using innovative techniques, as well as urbanization of slums.

Private and public investments began to shrivel during the early 1980s. This process of financial retrenchment imposed greater selectivity on urban programs, resulting in increased local participation, the transfer of costs to communities and lower levels of expenditure on construction, operation and maintenance/overhead. Outstanding in this context was the BNH Build-It-Yourselves self-help program, featuring simplified infrastructure.

In 1985, the National Constructed Environment Technology Association (ANTAC) was set up. As municipal and community experiences multiplied, the first dissemination networks began to appear. This process coincided with increasing environmental awareness within the governmental structure: during this period Law No.6,902 set up ecological stations, and Law no. 6,903 established the National Environment Policy.

The legal requirement of Environmental Impact Reports (RIMAs) encouraged university-level studies, a process boosted further by Decree No. 88,351 (1983) that required supervision of environmental resources, protection of eco-systems, and control of polluting activities. This decree also provided incentives for research into technologies for the rational use and protection of environmental resources.

Urban policy began to unfold from 1987 onwards, despite the deepening economic crisis and the merger of BNH with CEF federal savings and loan organization. Cuts in academic funding led to a search for foreign financing. The "Our Common Future" Report (1987) focused international attention on Brazil, prompting the establishment of the Brazilian Natural Renewable Resources Institute (IBAMA).

The administration that took office in 1990 leaned heavily towards a stronger environmental policy. This occurred in parallel with a weakening in the political and institutional apparatus handling urban issues, a major byproduct of the decentralization stipulated in the 1988 Constitution. Brazil's National Environmental Policy (PNMA) maintains the nation's conservationist stance, while encouraging technological development, land distribution and environmental education, in line with internationally accepted policies.

Rio's 1988 floods highlighted environmental degradation and its underlying causes: rivers flowing into the Guanabara bay need dredging, slope erosion must be stopped, vulnerable areas should be urbanized and environmental education programs need to be implemented. All part of the Rio Restoration Project, these topics are arousing much interest in local research centers, particularly the Guanabara Bay Basic Sanitation and Clean-Up Programs.

3. Outline of some research institutions and topics

Some relevant experiences with appropriate urban infrastructure technologies

Many research centers and universities in Brazil have worked with projects developing alternative basic sanitation (sewage disposal and water supply) technologies. The 1978 BNH Symposium encouraged research that simplified and rationalized small-town and slum-community sanitation systems, lowering installation, operation and maintenance costs. Although many were developed in the Northeast and São Paulo State, their results may be used for Rio de Janeiro.

Outstanding among the research projects cataloged by BNH (1987/88) are studies of aerobic and anaerobic stabilization pond capacities, operation and maintenance (1979, São Paulo Environmental Sanitation Technology Company (CETESB)), producing new performance parameters. In 1982 CETESB formulated criteria for sewage stabilization pond designs, adapted to Brazil's hot, wet climate.

In 1982 the Rio Grande do Norte Water and Sewage Company (CAERN) began development of low-cost technological alternatives for sewage treatment. The results were published in 1984, supplying vital input for the development of simplified sewage systems in other places, including Rio de Janeiro's Baixada lowlands. This project consisted of three experiments: the condominium or block main system featuring a low-cost single collection point; reduced, simplified sewage networks with multi-input cess pits for primary sewage treatment; and small, local sewage treatment stabilization ponds. Outflow was sized for irrigation of parks and nursery gardens.

Between 1980 and 1982 FEEMA developed a set of data processing programs that provided the optimum design solution for sewage networks. Use of these programs ensures health and environmental protection and while cutting installation costs by 20 percent. The efficacy of this approach has been validated by the sewage station prototype built on Ilha do Governador (Governor's Island) and assessed through a pilot network in the Santa Cruz administrative zone.

In 1983 FEEMA implemented its project aimed at Biodetection of Toxic Wastes in Water Supply River Systems. It reviewed criteria for description, analysis and control of water-bodies and developed low-cost bio-tests more sensitive than similar physical and chemical tests, working with a Rio Paraiba do Sul reference water source. In 1984 FEEMA researched seven new types of septic tanks, designed to reduce costs, pollution and household sewage.

Other projects have pinpointed cheaper, simpler solutions for supplying water to outlying urban slums. Particularly noteworthy is the 1981 CETESB study of direct pumping systems, avoiding costly reservoir and mains construction through the use of hydropneumatic tanks. Designed for underwater springs in suitable topography, it can also be adapted for use with above-ground water sources for small communities needing no chemical treatment.

The results of the 1987 survey of an alternative sanitation system installed in Olinda were significant: on 3.5 hectares with 1,350 inhabitants, this micro-drainage system used premolded sisal-reinforced concrete conduits, and surfaced roads with a soil/concrete mixture. Household garbage was collected in carts; bathrooms and cess pits were built or upgraded and a garbage composting plant was installed.

Appropriate dissemination networks

There are two well-known systems for dissemination of alternative experiences in the urban and environmental areas. Between 1986 and 1989 the Municipal Experiences Communication Network (RECEM) collected, documented and disseminated information from a variety of sources. Experiences cataloged under sanitation and slope protection include (a) implementation of an individual link-up system with group metering, for water distribution in slums with community taps; (b) installation of a simplified chlorinator for cisterns (powdered chlorine and clean sand); (c) implementation of a condo-collection. system; (d) slope retention by planting bamboo shoots; (e) electrolytic sewage treatment, cutting costs by 90 percent compared to the activated sludge method.

The Brazilian Municipal Administration Institute (IBAM) set up a similar system in 1986—Information System on Innovative Projects and Experiences (SPE)—which also identified, selected, registered and publicized unconventional or creative experiences, particularly when implemented by municipalities. However, it was not a network, and it often did not catalog projects carried out by research and development institutions. Over 3,000 experiments are cataloged, 400 on the computer, classified into 13 topics, including Environment, Sanitation, Public Health, and Alternative Technologies.

Human settlements in outlying urban areas

There is an ample range of research projects which have been carried out by institutions in Rio de Janeiro that spotlight the processes of slum formation, provision of urban services, unique ways of providing these services, and the take-over of urban areas by low-income sectors of the population. Noteworthy are the 1991-92 IBAM surveys as well as those carried out by the Rio de Janeiro University Research Institute (IUPERJ), financed by BNH. Of prime interest here are research surveys that provided input for government urban development programs, as well as those under way at IBAM. Financed by the Ford Foundation, its Urban Research Center was launched in 1968 to provide input for Brazil's National Urban Development Policy.

Since 1974 IBAM has been studying major distortions in housing use, pinpointing shortages of BNH-financed low-cost mass housing compared to conventional land subdivisions; and analyzing variables such as location, construction and dweller profiles. Studies of housing in outlying suburbs of Rio de Janeiro were extended in 1978, and in 1979 IBAM published a wide-ranging survey of low-cost mass housing projects in the six most heavily-populated areas of Greater Rio, with emphasis on type of construction and residents' life styles. Three 1982 research projects studied the growth process of outlying suburbs.

Surveys of the acceptance of official urban housing schemes were carried out by IUPERJ, with results for BNH programs appearing in 1980. Subsequent surveys focussed on common factors in grassroots protest movements in outlying Rio suburbs. In 1985 IBAM helped develop urban and architectural standards for slum improvement, particularly the Marcilio Dias slum. The CPU also investigated alternative experiments in urban development.

Cash-strapped, research organizations have limited more recent projects. IBAM has recently been offering technical consulting services to train municipal staff to cope with new urban management responsibilities assigned by the 1988 Constitution.

Control of environmental pollution

Set up in 1975, FEEMA is responsible for control of polluting activities, combating disease-transmitting vectors and undertaking environmental studies, which totaled over 400 by 1982. FEEMA's air, water and soil pollution control activities were boosted by the 1977 Polluting Activities Licensing System that registered over 5,000 environmentally-harmful economic activities. Air pollution studies took priority, and research tended to concentrate on: asphalt plants; coal transportation, handling and storage; rock-drilling and blasting; sulfur dioxide and other emissions from the Duque de Caxias oil refinery. Accumulated data allowed broader studies of air contamination in the city of Rio de Janeiro and critical areas throughout the State. An institutional air pollution control model was developed, as well as a master plan for particulate air pollution in the metropolitan region, an air quality data-monitoring system, and an air quality monitoring system.

Soil pollution was also covered by FEEMA studies, particularly the effects of polluted water used to irrigate vegetable farms, with identification of entero-parasites. Water quality control parameters were also developed, based on hydrographic basin characterization studies. Of particular interest are studies of fish processing plant wastewater treatment, mercury-contaminated wastewater from chlorine plants; oil pollution control systems and pollution prevention systems for lagoons and the Guanabara Bay. FEEMA also carried out studies on detection and control of toxic pollutants in drinking water through sampling plans, later extended to test sea water for urban beaches.

National and scientific output shrank between 1983 and 1986, due to the government view of the agency as basically being responsible only for supervision and control. The next studies covered the quality of the State beaches and air pollution. Some lines of research were followed under the Brazil-Germany Technical Cooperation Agreement, for air and noise pollution, and more particularly accidental pollution, emphasizing prevention and control of industrial risks.

In 1987 FEEMA returned to environmental research, with the Paraiba do Sul River Environmental Quality Recuperation Program, featuring a study

of CSN steel mill pollution and a broad-ranging proposal for restoring water quality in the mid-Paraiba region. FEEMA also formulated a Gradual Recuperation Project for the Guanabara Bay eco-system, using earlier data and diagnoses. Water and air pollution control activities were maintained, as well as a series of environmental diagnoses covering municipalities in the Lakes Region.

FEEMA is currently reinforcing physical and territorial studies of the metropolitan region, with particular attention to recuperation of the Guanabara Bay. Funded by the Japan International Cooperation Agency (JICA), a social and environmental diagnosis of the area surrounding the Bay is already under way, identifying activities with marked environmental impact in terms of economic and social processes and practices. Under this cooperation agreement, FEEMA should also prepare and process hydrodynamic models of these activities, through measurement of sea currents, and pollution and sediment studies, as well as a water quality optimization model.

Environmental hydro-chemistry

Various University Research Centers are working on water pollution in metropolitan Rio de Janeiro. Outstanding among them is the Environmental Geo-chemistry Program of the Rio de Janeiro State University Chemistry Institute (UFF); the Rio de Janeiro Pontifical Catholic University Chemistry Department (PUC/RJ); the Eduardo Penna Franca Radio-isotope Laboratory of the Carlos Chagas Filho Biophysics Institute at the Rio de Janeiro Federal University, and the Rio de Janeiro State University Oceanography and Hydrology Department, among others.

Teaching and research activities at UFF and PUC/RJ date back to the early 1970s.

The PUC/RJ Chemistry Department pioneered studies of the Guanabara Bay in 1975, and today has the largest volume of chemical data on the Bay and its waters. Problems studied included pollution by heavy metals, eutrophication and silting. A hundred years of water contamination by metals such as mercury, lead, cadmium, chromium, copper and manganese was studied, highlighting large concentrations (up to 2g/kg) of chromium and copper in the Northwest part of the Bay. These results were used by FEEMA as the benchmark for launching more effective action against polluting industries. Bayer do Brasil, for instance, installed a wastewater treatment station and cut monthly chromium emissions from two tons to twenty kilograms. Zinc and lead producers were also pinpointed. The primary output of the Bay is possible only because organic materials from domestic sewage cancel the algicide effect of copper.

Studies of sewage-induced eutrophication revealed oxygen levels below those needed by aerobic life forms. Internal nutrient flows proved important for maintenance of eutrophic conditions. These and other studies were carried out under the Brazil-Germany Bilateral Agreement. Joint surveys carried out with German researchers to determine copper, cadmium, nickel, cobalt and manganese concentrations in the Rio de Janeiro State coastal waters showed that the Guanabara and Sepetiba Bays export metals and particles. Particle dispersion was also studied for the Ipanema undersea sewage pipe, also shown to be a source of heavy materials.

From 1979 onwards activities slowed as economic crises pared research funding. However, a bilateral cooperation project with the University of Venice studied organic compounds contaminating the Guanabara Bay. Preliminary studies showed a wide variety of compounds in the sediments, including hydrocarbons and plastics.

The UFF environmental geo-chemistry researches are more recent, starting in the early 1980s and concentrating more on shoreline lagoon systems, their nutrients and nutrient cycles, as well as trophication, eutrophication and general functioning.

The government-run Studies and Project Financing Company (FINEP) sponsored studies of transportation and the behavior of heavy metals in the environment, produced both by natural weathering and urban wastes, in Rio de Janeiro State river systems and river, lake and estuary sediments. Mangrove swamps were later included. After 1985, research was extended to cover the water balance, allochthonous sources of biogenic materials and heavy metals, organic materials cycles, sedimentation, trophic and eutrophic studies of lagoons, estuaries and bays, as well as sedimentology and hydrochemical conduct of catchment basins.

Outstanding among projects at this period were surveys of heavy metals in Sepetiba Bay fish, the distribution of nutrients of heavy metals in sediments and surface water in mangrove swamps and coastal marshes, along the Brazilian Southeast, and in various Rio de Janeiro State estuaries.

From 1989 onwards, research has concentrated more on the hydrochemical behavior of river basins and contamination by heavy metals due to human activities: wildcat mining, urbanization and other economic and social processes. Sepetiba Bay has warranted special interest since 1988 through the Sepetiba Bay Management Study, sponsored by the International Federation of Institutes for Advanced Studies (IFIAS), with a multidisciplinary study scheduled for 1992.

The Eduardo Penna Franca Radio-isotope Laboratory has been providing input for Sepetiba Bay studies; during the 1980s it expanded to cover other environmental problems: industrial pollution by heavy metals in both the Guanabara and Sepetiba Bays, as well as the Guandu and Paraiba do Sul river systems that supply much of Greater Rio de Janeiro with its drinking water.

Recent laboratory studies carried out with the UFF concluded a review of human and environmental contamination of the Sepetiba Bay, showing expanding settlement and dwindling natural resources, with heavy sewage pollution. Heavy metals are carried in by the Guandu river and São Francisco Canal, as well as industrial wastes.

Current research projects take varied approaches aimed at understanding the dynamics of heavy metals and their effects of marine organisms, providing input for more effective monitoring of a region with a high potential for tourism, fishing and industry. The institutes interviewed reported problems of interrelationships among various centers working in this field and located in Rio de Janeiro, regarding integration of their activities, as well as very limited funding. UFF complained of a certain isolation which must be hampering investigations, while PUC/RJ recalled that interaction with the competent government agencies is rare.

Environmental geo-technology

A relatively new multidisciplinary subdivision of civil engineering, geo-technical engineering involves studies and solutions for different types of engineering problems associated with soil, rock and fluids in earthy materials. The Geo-mechanical Research Department of the Rio de Janeiro Municipal Geo-technical Department is highly experienced in geo-technical studies and today offers its services to other municipalities. It was set up in 1967, after heavy rains caused citywide landslides that killed over 200 people, in order to identify and study the city's topographical problems and illegal settlements in high-risk areas. It is currently responsible for supervising hillside construction, licensing retention walls and supervising slope stabilization.

The Geo-Risk Project Landslide Susceptibility Map was prepared by the Geo-mechanical Survey Division in accordance with quantitative methods used to establish an instability rating for all Rio de Janeiro hillsides, on a scale of 1:25,000. Four factors—geology, steepness, surface deposits and land use—were initially selected to assess relative landslide potential. Some 1,500 combinations of these factors define four classes of landslide susceptibility: very low, low, moderate, high. These are shown in different colors on a computer-prepared map. Identified by remote sensing on an ongoing basis, high-risk areas are being detailed on a scale of 1:2,000.

The Geo-technical Department is also implementing the Hillside Monitoring System. Developed with the UFRJ Engineering College Electronics Laboratory, this allows long-distance monitoring of difficult-access slopes through electric sensors that measure soil shift, rainfall, pressure, load, flow, and other parameters.

In order to ensure technical and scientific backing for the activities of its Geo-mechanical Research Division, since 1987 the Geo-technical Department has maintained agreements with universities, particularly the Geo-technical Sector of DEC/PUC/RJ. Its Slope Stability Project analyzes rupture mechanisms and factors associated with slope instability, through determination of the characteristics of nonsaturated hydraulic conductivity. It is backed by Canada's International Development Research Centre (IRDC).

4. Final comments and conclusions

With a wide and varied output, many of Rio de Janeiro's university centers and institutions have over twenty years experience in urban environmental studies, carried out by highly specialized staff who participate regularly in international events and interchanges. Most water resources, soil and environmental pollution laboratories are reasonably well equipped, thanks to public and private technical cooperation agreements.

Much hydrochemical experience has been built up regarding contamination and degradation of the major hydrographic basins of Rio de Janeiro State, as well as its lagoon and mangrove swamp systems. Discussions have intensified recently over ecological issues and environmental degradation in more urbanized coastal towns, which have spurred considerable progress is the study of relationships between land use, distribution of urban activities and environmental degradation of renewable natural resources, applicable also to other areas. Geo-technical specialization is well advanced in Rio de Janeiro, due largely to its topographical conditions, soil characteristics, hillside settlements and repeated problems with cloudbursts.

Scientific research and government actions are closely aligned, backed by skilled staff and technical cooperation agreements. Results may well be applicable to other regions also, and risk monitoring services are already being rendered to other municipalities. Pollution control activities in Rio de Janeiro also have a lengthy history, although trimmed somewhat some ten years ago due to staff and funding shortages. Development of these technologies was deeply affected by the relative slackness of national urban and environmental policies formulated during the recession that began in the mid-

1980s, although later encouraged by decentralization.

There are nevertheless a few critical issues that seem to hamper progress and the search for effective solutions:

- Insufficient interchange of experiences.
- Sparse sources of regular financing (the most frequent complaint).
- Inadequate integration between research centers and their main users: government agencies and organized communities.

FINEP has been encouraging and backing research for some 25 years. It is currently deeply involved in the Environmental Sciences Sub-Program (CIAMB), of the Scientific and Technological Development Support Program (PADCT), coordinated by the CNPq, CAPES and FINEP itself. This Sub-Program aims at development of environmental management technology, with methods and techniques for the recuperation of environmental quality, including land use, water resources, and extractivist activities, with emphasis on integrated models.

When interviewed, FINEP was analyzing 25 experimental research and development projects in Rio de Janeiro, submitted by eleven institutions. It has set up an Environmental Program to manage funding for environmental projects, but financing seems insufficient. At least one university center explicitly stated its preference for seeking outside cooperation in order to guarantee regular funding.

Despite frequent academic, technical and public events on environmental issues, the centers lack an interchange of experiences, particularly in geo-chemical surveys. Integration between research centers and government agencies responsible for urban and environmental policies and programs is still only incipient, obviously depending on funds available, although there is much room for discussion of results already achieved.

General recommendations for discussion include the following:

- Expand this outline of institutions and their research to include others such as collection, treatment and disposal of solid wastes, as well as geo-referenced data systems, etc.
- Encourage appraisal of projects aimed at recuperation of the urban environment in the metropolitan region.
- Spur systematized, integrated discussion of academic contributions, public and private agencies, and NGOs (see Box 7.1), in order to resolve environmental degradation and urban vulnerability.
- Support implementation of a unified data base on technological research and development applied to Rio's urban environment.

- Open up discussion with research institutions of policies, programs and projects for intervening in the metropolitan urban environment, ranking priorities and alternatives incorporating technical and scientific advances.
- Assess sources of funding for research activities, their priorities and financing and investment and conditions, in order to discuss relevant aspects such as lines of financing and investment priorities; possible expansion of funding, integration of sources and dovetailing of financial conditions; priority ranking of research projects in view of limited resources.
- Encourage state and municipal governments to restore and foster expanded technical structures and staff training in applied environmental research and development.

Box 7.1: NGO Strategies for Urban Development in the Rio de Janeiro Metropolitan Region: The View of the NGOs

Pedro Braile

With a population expected to top 13 million by the year 2,000, the Rio de Janeiro metropolitan region needs properly-routed, safe, effective, environmentally-friendly, low-fare public transportation, preferably fueled by nonpolluting electric power and natural gas. Rail and subway systems also need investment and improvement. Greater use should be made of solar energy and biogas (methane) produced from garbage.

Although rivers and canals are degraded by residential (organic) and industrial (chemical) wastes, over 80 percent of Rio homes have treated water. However, less than 20 percent of household sewage is treated, and only 30 percent is even collected.

Despite the installation of air pollution control equipment in large FEEMA-monitored companies, they still emit 92,299 tons of sulfur dioxide and 65,580 tons of particles. In Copacabana, Botafogo and Lagoa, vehicles emit some 4,000 tons of sulfur dioxide and particles annually. Containing lead, copper, iron, zinc, manganese and organic matter, these particles damage the respiratory system.

Only the city of Rio de Janeiro has an effective garbage collection system. It handles 5.5 tons of garbage daily, dumped in huge landfills that pollute surrounding areas and water.

Mechanization and urbanization (heavy traffic, industry, civil construction, aircraft) boost noise pollution. In 1980 over 50 percent of the population lived in areas considered excessively noisy over 80 percent of the time.

Urban violence has ballooned; organized crime, clandestine weapon sales, drug traffic, the kidnapping and robbery industries, and extermination groups have forced the ordinary citizen into a defensive cage. NGOs are pushing for increased open policing (as during Rio-92) and Community Civil Defense Centers.

Environmental education and public health campaigns combat the diseases of poverty, using low-cost alternative technologies to provide or upgrade the infrastructure for properly-controlled land settlement. Creative solutions include self-help cooperatives, garbage recycling for profit, water savings, child-to-child dissemination of basic health care information, etc.

Solutions to these complex problems come more from NGOs (Residents' Associations etc) rather than through traditional political organizations, due to better knowledge of local conditions and requirements, and a more immediate interest in preserving and/or enhancing local environmental conditions.

IV. Operational Experience and Technological Issues

8. The Rio Reconstruction Project: The First Two Years

Luiz Roberto Cunha and Marcio Miller Santos

Background

With a population of some 11.2 million in 1990, the Rio de Janeiro metropolitan region consists of 14 municipalities. The February 1988 floods severely affected its central districts, split into Rio de Janeiro itself, the Baixada Fluminense dormitory lowlands (Duque de Caxias, Nilopolis, Nova Iguaçu and São João de Meriti), and the resort hill-town of Petropolis.

The terrain covered by the Rio Reconstruction Project area is diverse: small shoreline plains and lagoons stretch along the foot of the Serra do Mar coastal range; many hill-sides are heavily—and illegally—settled by tight-packed slums, particularly the Maciço da Tijuca massif. Hit badly by the flash-floods, it is the most densely populated area of the Rio de Janeiro metropolitan region. The downtown area closest to the Guanabara Bay houses the port as well as the city's financial and administrative center. It has had drainage since the city was founded in 1565. The second subregion is the surrounding Baixada Fluminense. A reasonably adequate drainage system was installed in these marshy lowlands between 1936 and 1945. The third subregion—Petropolis—lies high in the Serra do Mar coastal range, where the valleys of its broken terrain guide streams into a town-center canal whose limited flow capacity causes periodic flooding. Slopes throughout the entire Rio de Janeiro metropolitan region are thinly covered by soil, due to erosion spurred by irregular settlement that has cleared much of the Atlantic rain-forest that once protected them and is today limited to steep valleys, hilltops and secondary growth such as the Tijuca National Park. Increasing urbanization has blocked natural watersheds, increasing the risk of flooding after heavy rains.

Although the demographic growth rate has slowed since the 1950s, the proportion of the state population living in the Rio de Janeiro metropolitan region rose from 78 percent in 1970 to 81 percent in 1990. The 1990 Household Census records 3.2 million homes, 59 percent of them in the Municipality of Rio de Janeiro and 25 percent in the Baixada lowlands. Of this total, 84.3 percent are supplied with water, leaving 225,000 without water mains; 83.4 percent have their own sanitary installations. There is a generalized lack of separate rainfall and sewage systems, resulting in a (FEEMA) estimated 18.6 m/sec of raw sewage being discharged into the Guanabara Bay, a result of only 30 percent of the total sewage being properly treated. While 73.8 percent of households have garbage collection schemes (resulting in 5,118 tons of garbage a day disposed of in sanitary landfills lacking run-off protection), the remainder burn or dump locally. Only 522 tons were run through recycling stations (State of Rio de Janeiro 1989). In 1992 a composting and recycling plant was inaugurated in Rio de Janeiro, with a daily capacity of 1,200 tons.

Rio is Brazil's major tourist gateway, over 70 percent of its working population are employed in the services sector.

Finance and the civil services are also important to the local economy. Insufficient jobs have spawned a ballooning informal economy over the past few years. Over recent decades, rapid urbanization and the lack of a housing policy has led to intensive occupation of hill-sides and river-banks by low-income sectors.

Since the turn of the century, increasing rural emigration, high land prices and inadequate transportation have forced poor families to settle on hill-sides close to jobs in downtown Rio. IPLAN-RIO estimates that today the city of Rio de Janeiro alone has an estimated 1.1 million people—20 percent of its population—living in *favelas* (slums). Although all municipalities in this study have legislation covering land use and zoning, compliance is loosely enforced; environmental protection areas are particularly vulnerable due to real estate speculation and spreading slums. Outward growth has been marked in the Baixada lowlands and the West Zone, where low-cost, no-infrastructure subdivisions sold on the installment plan have allowed poor families to build their own homes. Starting in the 1930s, this type of activity spurted during the 1950s with improved drainage and increased industrialization, as downtown areas became relatively saturated.

Petropolis grew independently of Rio de Janeiro. Originally the Imperial summer resort, unceasing commercial and industrial growth has clogged most of its narrow valleys, forcing families to live on steep bluffs, where forest clearing encourages land-slides.

Rio's tropical climate (high-altitude tropical for Petropolis) features two main seasons: dry winters and rainy summers, especially in February and March. The effects are multiplied by unorganized land settlement combined with a lack of investment in basic infrastructure—drainage, sewage, garbage, transportation, and housing. Major land-slides occurred in 1759 and 1811 (city center), regularly during the 1940s, with major events occurring in 1966 and 1967 (over 100 and 200 deaths respectively), as well as in 1988.

Macroeconomic policy

The lack of ongoing government policies has hampered the implementation of cogent investment policies for the Rio de Janeiro metropolitan region, a situation exacerbated by its division into capital (Rio de Janeiro) and state (Guanabara). After the 1975 merger of the two, sparse funding and ineffective administration combined with blurred investment priorities to hamstring the implementation of wider-ranging and more effective measures to handle urban and environmental issues, forming hothouse conditions for calamities such as the February 1988 floods.

Like its predecessors, the Integrated Urban and Regional Development Plan on the drawing board in 1987 scheduled investments in water supplies, sewage, drainage, urban cleaning, mass housing, urban transportation and environmental protection, while failing to make adequate provision for the handling of extreme events such as cloudbursts and flash-floods.

The major reason for this lack of planning continuity is financial. Constantly strapped for cash, the State of Rio de Janeiro has long been unable to undertake major investment programs; the year-end 1991 accounts showed a payroll of US$ 51 million and accounts payable of US$ 217.6 million, against a cash balance of only US$6.3 million. This series of deficits has been passed on from one administration to the next, or been financed by issuing government bonds. Worse still, Rio de Janeiro could not fall back on the state financial system, as the State Bank was in receivership and the State Development Bank was bankrupt.

This lack of funding has inevitably slashed investments in infrastructure, making calamities such as the 1988 land-slides almost inevitable. Despite a recessionary economy and sagging tax revenues, much of this shortfall is traceable to excessive debt service and massive payrolls, which blocked access to foreign financing.

As State financing capacities faded away during the 1980s, inflation soared. federal government attempts at stabilization centered on successive price freezes and fruitless endeavors to control the public debt, slashing investments and spurring recession and unemployment. This adversely affected state economies, particularly that of Rio de Janeiro, with its heavy dependence on the services and government sector.

The Rio Reconstruction Project was thus structured in accordance with the limited financing capacity of the States and the specific problems of Rio de Janeiro. In counterpart to World Bank loans, financing from CEF federal savings and loan bank would also provide funds. This system speeded up the operation although reducing its autonomy, while decentralizing public investments.

Responding to the 1988 disaster

Although summer storms are normal in Rio de Janeiro, the February 1988 rains were exceptionally heavy. They affected Petropolis early in the month, followed by the Baixada Fluminense lowlands and the West Zone, and at the end of the month a cloudburst flooded the densely-populated city itself with more rain than normal for an entire quarter. Together with a lack of planned human intervention in the environment, disorganized growth and inadequate investments in basic infrastructure over the past few years led

to tragic consequences. Huge volumes of water rushing down the partly-eroded slopes of the Tijuca massif caused immense land-slides and swept away large amounts of garbage dumped by *favela*-dwellers. The water-borne refuse blocked many major thoroughfares, destroyed drainage systems, and clogged many of the city's main canals. Artificially-drained marshy areas were also affected, largely due to poor maintenance of their drainage systems, illegal river-bank—and even river-bed—construction, and the virtual absence of a sewage network. This also prompted a spurt in contagious diseases, with leptospirosis rising from 15 cases in 1985 to 1,039 in March 1988, with 35 deaths. Petropolis was totally cut off by land-slides blocking access routes, hampering rescue and aid efforts. As 150 schools were damaged and many others were used to shelter homeless families, the school year started late.

The final count: some 300 dead, over 1,000 injured, and thousands left homeless, as well as widespread damage to property and production. Any assessment of the direct damage—destruction of streets and thoroughfares, bridges, canals, schools, health centers, public buildings, water and sewage networks, electric power and telephone lines, flooded stores and factories, transportation systems—must also include some six days of lost production, although weekend flooding did not affect the financial markets. Less intense rains over the following weeks also caused damage, due to broken drainage systems, particularly in the Baixada Fluminense. State government experts and World Bank representatives estimated the economic costs of this calamity at some US$935 million, of which US$435 million covered lost production, US$400 million in physical damage, US$50 million tourism revenues lost, and US$50 million to underwrite immediate clean-up and unblocking measures.

Box 8.1: Environmental Quality Recuperation Project for the Rio de Janeiro Metropolitan Region
Hélia Nacif Xavier

The Projeto Ambiente-Rio Environmental Protection Program was set up in 1991 by Presidential Decree, motivated by the level of sanitary and environmental vulnerability of Rio de Janeiro, the effects of this situation on the Guanabara Bay, the need to rationalize actions and investments already allocated or implemented, the opportunity to upgrade the nation's international image on environmental issues presented by Rio-92.

Financed during Stage 1 by FGTS funds, foreign loans, government budget allocations and counterpart funding from the state and municipalities, this project is scheduled in three stages:
* Stage 1—1991/1992.
* Stage 2—1993/1995.
* Stage 3—1996/2000.

It absorbed the PRONURB urban sanitation program, the PROSANEAR low-income population sanitation program, the PROSEGE emergency job generation program, and the PROBASE basic urban infrastructure program. IBAM produced a series of eight studies between December 1991 and March 1992 on the following:
* Preliminary Model of Computerized Monitoring and Control Program.
* List of Assessment Studies and Preliminary Proposed Criteria.
* Preliminary Proposed Assessment Criteria.
* Preliminary Proposed Project Management Organization.
* Preliminary Proposed Project Management Structure.
* Inventory of Agencies, Projects, and Legislation.
* List of Agencies, Projects, and Legislation.
* Register of Agencies, Projects and Legislation—Handbook.

Recent political and institutional changes have halted this project, and its future is unclear.

While recuperation (see Box 8.1) measures bring things back to normal, urban protection and development programs are vital in reducing the impact of possible future calamities to a level that society can handle. Settlement configuration in the Rio de Janeiro metropolitan region demands urban development and environmental programs to provide protection against cloudbursts. However, while the more developed nations include a cost/benefit analysis in the decision process, Brazil and other developing countries undervalue human life to such an extent that low-visibility projects rate low priority. Worse still, decisions are often postponed for financial reasons. The governments involved thus decided to use this calamity, the prompt support of the World Bank and the possibility of obtaining additional federal

funding, to put into practice some of the studies prepared for the State Integrated Urban and Regional Development Plan to implement a prevention program.

During the rescue phase, the State and Municipalities were helped by the federal government, as well as the population in general and foreign governments and institutions. However, foreign funding was required to cope with the high costs of infrastructure, reconstruction and prevention. Since the director of the World Bank's Brazil Department was in town for other matters, contacts were streamlined. Nine days after the first contact with the World Bank mission, the Rio Reconstruction Project was already detailed. The State took over coordination of the Baixada Fluminense municipalities and Petropolis.

Pre-assessment, assessment and negotiation meetings were held alternately in Washington and Rio, with side-trips to Brasilia. As this was an emergency project, the World Bank Board approved the project on June 24. This project was planned, coordinated and carried out by the GEROE emergency work and recuperation executive group. Since neither the state government nor the various municipalities had sufficient funds to implement all the measures and work needed to repair the flood damage and prevent fresh calamities, the state government and the Rio de Janeiro city council turned to the World Bank. The CEF savings and loan institution—which had already earmarked funding for some sanitation measures in the region—was made the financial intermediary responsible for channeling World Bank funds. Although this financing scheme furthered rapid approval of the project, it also became one of the elements responsible for delays in its implementation.

The project covered:

- Reconstruction and repair of flood-damaged basic infrastructure (state government).
- Implementation of a short-term flood alleviation program (Rio de Janeiro Municipality).
- Institutional measures reducing the consequences of future floods (Baixada/Petropolis municipalities, under state government supervision).

Responsibilities of the state government:

- Road System: work on 40 sites, repaving some 100 kilometers of highways, construction of around 7.5 kilometers of retention walls and reconstruction or repair of 17 bridges.
- Drainage: micro, meso and macro-drainage implemented in rivers and eight river basins, over a surface area of 125,000 hectares, draining some 14.8 cubic meters, building canals and dikes,

as well as a 4.8 kilometer-long outflow pipe.

- Sewage: construction of some 70 kilometers of sewage mains, 17,000 building connections, three pumping stations and two treatment stations, one a stabilization pond.
- Solid Wastes: construction of recycling and composting plants in the Baixada Fluminense municipalities in accordance with the Metropolitan Region Solid Residues Plan.
- Reforestation: seedling-planting over 1,200 hectares along 30 degraded slopes in Rio de Janeiro and Petropolis, usually alongside *favelas*.
- Urbanized Plots of Land: implementation of some 5,000 urbanized plots of land in the Baixada Fluminense lowlands and Rio de Janeiro for resettlement of families living alongside rivers and canals scheduled for dredging. Some 1,600 families who lost their homes in the floods or living on high-risk slopes in Petropolis would also benefit.
- Public Installations: repair and implementation of damage-prevention measures in water supply systems on 22 sites.
- Civil Defense: acquisition of 23 vehicles fitted for emergency fire and flood rescue operations, with heavy-duty pumps and winches.
- Technical Assistance: development of civil defense plans, reforestation schemes and slope retention programs, with improved garbage collection and added emphasis on environmental education (see Box 8.2).

Responsibilities of the Rio de Janeiro Municipality:

- Road System: repaving some 12.5 kilometers of roads, construction of around 3.2 kilometers of retention walls, and re-construction or repair of three bridges.

Box 8.2: Coordination Plan for Environmental Protection and Civil Defense Actions—Rio de Janeiro

Hélia Nacif Xavier

Plan and Area of Study

This plan consists of three subplans: civil defense, reforestation and slope retention, and lays down basic guidelines on land use and strategies for coordinated control of urban sprawl while avoiding environmental degradation in the Rio de Janeiro metropolitan region. It emphasizes the importance of intersectoral and intergovernmental actions, in an area characterized as a large coastal plain subject to flooding around the Guanabara and Sepetiba Bays. It divides this area of 7,518 square kilometers into seven units:

- Greater Rio (municipal Rio, Niteroi, São Gonçalo, Nilopolis, São João de Meriti, much of Nova Iguaçu and Duque de Caxias, all subject to floods, although previously drained.
- Outlying towns (Petropolis, etc.) where lower-income outlying suburbs are at high environmental risk due to flood and or landslides.
- Sparsely-populated outlying suburbs.
- Hills and plains used mainly for grazing.
- Fragmented vacant areas with a few squatters, mainly hillocks and mangrove swamps.
- Strip development along thoroughfares.
- Critical points (quarries, brick-clay mines, sand-diggings, garbage dumps).

General and Specific Objectives

Long- and medium-term objectives are not explicit, but should be directed towards adoption of permanent monitoring and control systems, fostering reforestation, slope retention, civil defense, and land use.

The Institutional Question

This is seen as vital to implementation of the plan, due to the complexity of the approach. The plan should put forward suggestions on maintenance of an integration and coordination scheme involving the effective participation of government agencies and communities, through committees and commissions.

Diagnosis of Trends

This analysis will study past events such as the 1988 disasters and pinpoint actions to reduce the recurrence of such problems, defining legal and other measures to minimize environmental aggression. A demographic forecast, to be prepared by the World Bank, will include the economic outlook and estimated industrial growth, with particular attention to input materials and industrial wastes.

Land Use Guidelines

A 1:1,000,000 map of the area will be prepared, which will highlight the following environmental protection areas:

- The slopes of the coastal range.
- Other permanent environmental protection areas such as mangrove swamps and forests, as well as river banks.
- Formally-constituted environmental protection areas such as federal, state or municipal parks.
- River-head protection areas.
- Vulnerable areas susceptible to erosion and needing reforestation.
- Degraded or deforested hillsides about to become high-risk areas.
- Low, flat areas subject to flooding that need draining.
- Outlying areas and quarries.
- Degraded but recuperable mangrove swamps.

- Drainage: re-construction, repair and recuperation of primary, secondary and tertiary drainage in six rivers, through dredging and canalization.
- Slope retention: removal of rubbish and land-slide prevention measures at 52 sites, with rock removal and/support, opening-up of drainage channels, construction of retention walls and planting of ground cover.
- Urbanized Plots of Land: implementation of some 5,400 urbanized plots earmarked for resettlement of families living in flood-damaged areas, in accordance with a resettlement plan.
- Public buildings: repair and rehabilitation of some 89 municipal schools.
- Technical Assistance: Education and training programs on garbage disposal, safe house construction methods, prevention of resettlement of high-risk and protected forest areas, illegal mining control, project management, and works supervision.

Responsibilities of the remaining municipalities:

- Slope retention: removal of rubbish and land-slide prevention measures at 52 sites, with rock removal and/support, opening-up of drainage channels, construction of retention walls and planting of ground cover.
- Public buildings: repair and rehabilitation of some 29 municipal schools.

Funds were also allocated to a 10 percent contingency Fund. The 12 largest projects (drainage/sewage) account for some 60 percent of funding allocated to Parts A and C. Some 80 minor tasks, later batched for tender purposes, needed less than 1 percent of the total A/C group's budget. This occasionally prevented the executive agency from carrying the work out, i.e., some school repairs and the urban section of the Baixada Fluminense road system.

Some items—drainage and urban plots—were closely linked, the latter being included in the project solely because it was impossible to implement the drainage program without relocating families living on river-banks and even along silted-up river-beds.

Drainage, sewage and garbage were not analyzed in depth during the negotiations phase. An outside consulting firm was hired by the State to carry out technical, institutional, environmental, economic and financial assessments.

Although the financing scheme, featuring large amounts of federal funding to be passed on by the CEF, streamlined approval of the project, it needed to be made properly operational in order to make the project effective. Funds were not always available, and intensive negotiation was needed from the subcontracting stage onwards in order to ensure its availability. As the CEF funds came from the FGTS Length of Service Guarantee Fund and the return on financing granted to States and Municipalities, Brazil's recessionary economy reduced these funds in real terms, as employment and wage levels sagged, and unemployment allowances rose. The recession also pruned tax revenues, while outlays—particularly the Rio de Janeiro State civil service payroll—continued. This resulted in a breach of credit with various creditors, especially the CEF. These problems with funding continued through 1989 and 1990, prompting delays in the project. As the CEF lacked standard contracts, many project components had to be negotiated individually.

Complex and clumsy, the Rio de Janeiro State administrative structure was improved by the establishment of the GEROE coordination group. Its small staff was headed by State Secretaries involved in the project, backed by outside consultants, thus streamlining implementation of the project and ensuring compliance with physical and financial schedules. Interfacing with the municipalities and the World Bank, it also speeded up documentation.

Studies showed that while CEDAE was well equipped to install extensive water and sewage systems, SERLA needed reinforcement for implementing large-scale drainage projects. Petropolis and the Baixada Fluminense municipalities experienced difficulties in complying with project requirements, a situation that was ultimately resolved for the hill-town by setting up a GEROE-type coordinating body. Of the Baixada districts, by early 1991 only Nilopolis had begun work, due to debt problems and a lack of organizational structures.

The World Bank stipulates specific subcontracting norms and supervises jobs closely, refusing to financial outlays not in accordance with its standards. Difficulty in complying with these requirements experienced by the State civil service was due to a 20-year lack of experience with multilateral-organization funding. Differences in interpretation were resolved by the Attorney-General, giving priority to World Bank rules. Practices that clashed included: setting upper and lower limits on bids; drawing tied bids (the Bank recommends fresh bids be submitted); use of the two-envelope system, one with the documentation, the other with the financial bid; participation open only to pre-registered firms. The Bank recommends that consulting firms be selected from a 3-6 name short-list, by quality. Snags related to problems with bidding procedures delayed many tenders and subcontracts, especially international tenders for drainage and retention-wall supervision.

Mandatory resettlement of families living on river-banks or along silted-up river-beds scheduled for dredging was based on urbanized plots of land rather than government housing, due to another set of incompatible rulings involving possible subsidies. However, this did not further the project, as families needed to be moved to new homes, or at least skeleton houses. The lack of housing in which to relocate families hampered full implementation of the drainage project. Community participation and self-help is vital in this type of action, and there are now some 60 residents' associations in the resettlement area.

Since no drainage work could begin before families were rehoused on some 5,000 plots or ready-built mass housing, the dredging and housing time-schedules had to be tight-knit. Back-up activities included upgrading housing, essential public services and land-titles, balanced by efforts to reduce the effects of the project on families not resettled, and checking the distance from new homes to work places. Four low-cost housing complexes were allocated for resettlement, as land ownership and other problems arose over the plots. After two years, only 10 percent of the families had been settled, delaying the dredging and draining project.

Recommendations

Fresh calamities are prevented not only by construction, but also by institutional and educational measures. The Technical Assistance sector of the project includes slope retention, reforestation, civil defense, and an environmental education program. They have been incorporated into the Civil Defense and Environmental Protection Coordinated Action Plan (1990), which has not yet been put out for tender. Community participation is once again essential, as well as continuity in government policies.

It is recommended that:
- Any complex financing scheme should seek to simplify procedures, streamlining approvals and clarifying doubts, dovetailing schedules and allowing tighter overall control.
- Tenders for bids should harmonize World Bank regulations with local

legislation before issuing the call for tender, to avoid doubts and legal issues.
- Implementation of programs of work must be linked to the development and implementation of community measures (resettlement in this case), including behavioral changes.

- Emergency recuperation plans and urban rehabilitation should be handled in separate stages, thus allowing a prompt start on urgent repairs (schools and roads) without being tangled in red tape.
- Prevention measures should include cost/benefit studies, environmental impacts, and institutional capacities.

9. Rio and the World Bank—The Start of a Productive Relationship

Braz Menezes and Thereza Lobo

Addressing the problems of urban degradation and environmental vulnerability on a sustainable basis can only be done within the context of a broader political, socioeconomic and institutional framework. The chapter by Cunha and Miller (this volume) describes the arrival of the World Bank in Rio de Janeiro in 1988 after an absence of nearly 20 years. It also discusses the Bank's catalytic role in initiating activities and actions on a broad front of urban environmental concerns, and makes some recommendations for such operations in the future. This chapter[6] reflects on the "doing by learning" experience, some tangible results under the project to date, and the broadening of the relationship between the municipality of Rio and the Bank, leading up to the negotiation of follow-up projects by both the Bank (rehabilitation and transfer of the Brazilian Urban Train System (CBTU-RJ)), and by the Inter-American Development Bank (IDB) (depollution of Guanabara Bay).

Nearly five years before UNCED, the Bank was invited to Rio de Janeiro to deal with the devastating results of severe and prolonged rains in the metropolitan region of Rio (see Cunha and Miller, this volume). The nature of the damage (landslides, flooding, collapsed structures, and breakdown of basic services) and the geographically wide, disaster-affected area required more than directly-targeted reconstruction. The type of damage demanded a broader view of urban environmental management—one focused on prevention—hence the implementation of a program to target institutional strengthening (improved coordination, instruments, policies, and plans) that would in time lead to an increased and sustainable capacity for dealing with Rio's serious environmental problems. Because of the emergency, the Bank had to make a rapid appraisal, take some calculated risks, and move quickly.[7] The three levels of government were expected to continue regarding the project as a high priority after loan approval. This, however, was not the case.

Several crucial and interrelated groups of problems can be readily identified as having had a serious impact on project performance: the institutional framework; rapidly changing economic and financial reforms by the federal government; intermittent conflict between the different levels of government; and the cyclical rhythm of alternate state and municipal elections every 24 months—elections that are generally followed by a significant replacement of experienced technical and administrative staff, leading to institutional discontinuity.

The deterioration of the institutional framework for urban policy at the federal level had already been under way for some time (see Menezes, this volume). Successive state administrations had also starved local institutions of funds. The only agency with a mandate to overview metropolitan development—FUNDREM—was weak and in decline, awaiting impending changes. Meanwhile, a new constitution that was scheduled to be discussed and ratified later that year (1988) would shift substantial institutional responsibilities and resources to state and municipal governments, and become effective in March 1989. The institutional design for the project therefore had to take into account predictions of future changes, and had to build into the project the elements of an institutional development component for both the state and the municipality of Rio.

Institutional arrangements for the project

Until the Rio Project, the Bank had not previously financed any urban or environmental projects directly with the state or the municipality of Rio. Thus there was no readily available or reliable experience of previous dealings with the multitude of institutions, especially at the level of the state government. Two alternative solutions were agreed on. At the state level, there were often overlapping functions between institutions responsible for urban and environmental services, and little evidence that anything was being done to resolve this issue. Because of the emergency, it was agreed to create a special agency (GEROE) reporting to the governor, to coordinate all activities and actions and establish a modus operandi for resolution of interagency conflicts. GEROE was to remain a small unit, supported by specialist, technical, and management consultants, and wherever possible reliance was to be placed on the private sector for project preparation and execution. At the municipal level, the situation was somewhat different. The agencies appeared to have an adequate technical capacity to execute their respective subcomponents, as the City was left at least this legacy when the national Capital was moved to Brasilia. What was missing however, was an overall systematic structure for preparation and programming of works, allocating resources, coordinating cross-sectoral activities, and monitoring and evaluating performance. A program of technical assistance for strengthening the municipality's agencies was put in place.

In hindsight, perhaps the most significant institutional decision, that was to adversely impact the project performance, was the selection of the Caixa Economica Federal (CEF) as the financial intermediary and cofinancier of the project. The financial situation of both the state and municipality was precarious, and their respective contributions in counterpart funds were minimal. The only source of possible counterpart funding, therefore, was from CEF, which administers the FGTS[8]. Given the emergency nature of the project, both the municipality and the Bank would have preferred to work with a commercial onlending agent. The state was ambivalent about this, but there was no other alternative as CEF was already funding some ongoing sanitation contracts. The federal government designated the CEF to be the Borrower of the Bank loan, with onlending arrangements to the state and the municipality. CEF (traditionally a first line savings bank) had only the previous year (1987) inherited the responsibilities and staff of the erstwhile BNH, which was extinguished as part of an administrative/fiscal reform. The presence of experienced BNH staff reassured the Bank. However, the difficulties encountered in merging the two different corporate cultures, and the increased risk that the other internal difficulties within CEF could not have been predicted at the time (as described in Menezes, this volume).

The impact of macro policies

The project confronted severe difficulty arising from macroeconomic instability and structural adjustment policies, which created additional problems to an already complex situation. Constant changes decreed in "economic packages" modified monetary policies, changed national currency, modified indexes for contract adjustments, and so forth (see Box 9.1). All this presented serious practical problems for CEF. The complexities of operating within a constantly changing macro-financial policy scenario, and at the same time, adapting CEF/BNH's traditional policies on pricing and adjustments of ongoing contracts, constantly paralysed the Rio Flood Reconstruction project, and other projects financed by the Bank[9]. The cumulative cost to the national economy of such delays on all the other national programs also administered by CEF, must be truly astronomical.

Fluctuating political tensions

The complex political tensions fluctuated alternately between the state and municipality in 1988, and have historically characterized Rio de Janeiro. The tensions were temporarily swept under the carpet due to the widespread national public sympathy for Rio's plight following the floods. These provided an opportunity for the state and the municipality to extract concessions and financial support from the federal government, which was at the time introducing tight fiscal controls on state and municipal spending, focused initially on Rio (allegedly as an example).

These tensions were often to erupt into confrontations, directed at each other, or at the federal government, represented by CEF. The economic recession reduced overall payroll deductions, which in turn led the Governing Council (Conselho Curador) of the FGTS to occasionally place a freeze on cash flows through CEF—even for ongoing contractual commitments. Each such problem introduced further delays. It was also generally believed however, that the flow of funds from the CEF was used by the federal government to extract political support for various causes—first by the Sarney Administration, and subsequently by the

Collor Administration. Finally, further delays were brought about by the discontinuity of key officials with the change of the state administration in 1990, and with each change in the presidency of CEF.[10]

Some results: the municipality of Rio

By far the most positive results of the Rio Flood Reconstruction Project are visible in the completion of the program for the municipality of Rio, under the experienced leadership of Rio's outgoing Mayor Marcello Alencar. Urban vulnerability has been reduced through a large number of physical interventions designed to improve and control the environment. These included macrodrainage works in 5 river basins; 420 different contracts for slope stabilization; solid waste collection and disposal; repair of bridges, roads, embankments; and some resettlement and housing. Many of the contracts were let at below original estimated costs and completed on schedule.

Much credit for this success is due to the foresight of the mayor in retaining the full technical team inherited from the previous administration. The team had been trained to prepare good sound projects and administer their execution. This experience was extended to the municipality's vast program (outside the project), which has enabled the mayor to leave the city of Rio, different and much improved from the one he received at the beginning of his administration in 1989.

The city's financial health was restored. The municipality was encouraged (through a Bank covenant) to prepare and implement a plan for its financial recovery[11]. The mayor's financial and technical staff had wanted to prepare such

Box 9.1: Macro-Financial Adjustments, 1986-92
Braz Menezes

1986 The Cruzado Plan changed the name and value of the currency, imposed an exchange rate freeze, instituted a price freeze, imposed and changed the "index" to be applied for monetary correction, and imposed a salary adjustment in the public sector.

1987 Another price freeze, a new wage policy, and an exchange rate devaluation were introduced.

1988 The year of the floods. Extensive debates and discussions on a new stabilization package did not materialize, and another minister came to office. A serious attempt was made to move away from the policy of price and wage freezes, and negotiations were resumed with foreign banks over the external debt. The year ended with an annual inflation rate calculated at 998 percent.

1989 In January, the government announced yet another "Summer Plan," which decreed various measures of fiscal reform, froze prices and wages, extinguished formal indexation for contracts of less than 90 days (but protected savings), permitted correction of public prices and tariffs, devalued the cruzado by 17 percent, and implemented a policy of real interest rates.

1990 In March, with inflation running at 82 percent per month, the Collor Plan was launched, based on strong fiscal and administrative reforms. The money supply was drastically reduced through, among other things, an 18-month freeze of savings withdrawals, the reintroduction of price fixing, the adoption of a floating exchange rate, and extensive trade liberalization policies. The cruzeiro replaced the cruzado as the unit of currency. Inflation dropped sharply and then started to rise. The economic team was replaced.

1991 The new minister adopted more orthodox measures for financial and economic policy through, among other things, carefully containing aggregate demand, maintaining high interest rates, containing wage hikes, and liberalizing tariffs and prices for public services. Other measures included a floating exchange rate and a slow and constant devaluation of the cruzeiro. The year finished with an annual inflation of 480 percent.

1992 Political events in connection with the impeachment of President Collor led to a change of government in October.

Source: GERSA-RI/Caixa Economica Federal.

a plan specifically to take advantage of provisions under the new constitution. But as political will was weak, the Bank was a useful catalyst in that decision. A property recadastration and revaluation were financed under the project. The impact of these interventions has left the city with plenty of cash to carry out its investments and liquidate a substantial portion of past debts. The project also financed a component for environmental education, control of illegal mining, and reforestation. These have been successfully executed. The municipality prepared its master plan in 1991, which for the first time outlines a

significant number of environmental policies and considerations in land use controls and development.

Four years later, the municipality has substantially completed its part of the project, and would have done so earlier, but for the delays of counterpart funds from the CEF. The project has achieved its objectives, urban vulnerability has been reduced, through a series of interventions designed to improve and to control the urban environment. Medium- and long-term objectives in terms of the recovery and the prevention of disasters has led the municipality down the path of conservation. More importantly, perhaps, the mitigation of natural hazards and environmental degradation has become a priority. These works have long been the object of attention of the agencies responsible for civil defense in the city. The main result may be seen in the fact that, although there have been many heavy rains after 1988 in the city, no major disaster has occurred. Also, the works executed under the slope contentions subcomponent generated new technologies that improved the technical capacity of the municipal agencies.

On the negative side, a number of problems delayed execution of the resettlement component. The most important ones are as follows:

• Political pressures in relation to the area to be serviced.

• Changes in the initial objectives—from serviced lots to houses.

• Return of the homeless to the risky areas, since little alternative (low-risk) land is available in the congested development of the municipality, and since affordable urban transport to the periphery is not available.

• Resistance from families to leaving high-risk areas.

• Self-construction without adequate technical assistance, which created new vulnerabilities.

The State of Rio de Janeiro

The new state administration of Governor Leonel Brizola, which took over in March 1991, reaffirmed its interest in continuing the project. Many problems faced at that time were due either to serious delays in the provision of counterpart funds by the CEF or to problems of "administrative irregularities" inherited from the previous state administration (Governor Moreira Franco) in connection with the administration and implementation of a number of macro-

drainage contracts. Although Bank guidelines on procurement were rigorously applied, and many subprojects were satisfactorily completed, the last six months of that administration were characterized by some unfortunate events in the professional management of the contracts entered into in mid-1990 by SERLA (the executing agency). It is not clear to what extent these problems were "aided and abetted" by GEROE and its consultants at the time. The Brizola administration therefore inherited the state's component of the project, paralyzed on two counts: (a) the state had defaulted in its repayments to the CEF, and CEF had turned off its flow of funds; (b) the Bank had effectively intervened to bring all civil works to a complete standstill, to permit the incoming administration to complete a full audit of the irregularities, and at the same time, undertake a number of institutional and organizational steps within SERLA and GEROE, to ensure that such problems would not be repeated in the future.

For its part, the Bank also placed some preconditions for continuing with the project with an eventual objective of restructuring the project so that it can be properly and efficiently completed by December 1994 within the administrative mandate of the current administration. Doing so, would enable the state to benefit substantially from the proposed investments in a follow-up Guanabara Bay depollution project, currently being negotiated with the IDB. Nearly two years later, the state is poised to move ahead and successfully implement a revitalized, well-targeted, and integrated program, provided that the political will can be sustained, and that the state's bureaucratic machinery will allow it to do so.

The state's initial concern was directed towards the reorganization of GEROE. The whole structure of the unit changed. New technical people have assumed responsibilities, supported by selected technical assistance. GEROE's coordination role has been strengthened, with a delegation of responsibility for execution moved directly to specific agencies, legally competent to provide such responses. The use of "Contract Plans" between GEROE and executing agencies has been introduced, with the use of specific and monitorable time-bound financial, physical and operational targets.

A substantial effort has been put on reorganizing SERLA and, similarly, strengthening its institutional capacity. The technical audits were successfully completed and instrumental in redirecting the financial, technical and institutional focus of SERLA. Several executing agencies (CEHAB, IEF, and FEEMA, among others) have also been reorganized to improve their response.

The project focus has been improved. Besides the fundamental works of macro-drainage that are back in progress after a major restructuring, other important actions related to the urban environment are been developed. All of them tackle the most needed aspects of urban vulnerability and environmental degradation. One of them is the resettlement subcomponent. Targeted to homeless families or to those families living along the river edges, the subcomponent now contemplates also the reurbanization of those areas that suffered drainage works. Complementary investment projects have been prepared to strengthen the impact of components under the project. For example, at the beginning of the project there were about US$7 million allocated for solid waste disposal and treatment. In discussion with the IDB-financed Guanabara Bay Depollution Project (see Box 9.2) now includes US$17 million and a new specific subproject was defined for the Baixada Fluminense, one to the poorest areas of the state.

In terms of reforestation, initially the project was restricted to the municipality of Rio and the municipality of Petropolis. The state is now proposing to extend the scope of this component to the Baixada Fluminense, where many river edges have to be reforested. Planting techniques were improved in order to adapt to the preventive actions of slope contention. Environment education is one of the main targets of the subcomponent of Technical Assistance. It is to be executed by FEEMA, the state environmental agency, in collaboration with a number of NGO's and community organizations. The environmental education program is designed to support the social and physical interventions contemplated under the project.

Building institutional technical capacity

One of the main constraints emerging from the Rio Flood Reconstruction experience is the fragility of the institutions: the lack of coordination, either internal to a certain level of government, or among the three levels—federal, state, and municipal. Both the chapter on institutional issues (see de Gões Filho, this volume) and the discussants at the Rio conference highlighted this problem. No matter what issue was discussed—technical, financial or institutional—the common ground would always be underlined as the difficulty of having all, or even some of the institutions involved, or interested in sitting together to discuss and agree on the common problems.

Often one can find overlapping—if not contradictory—functions performed by two or three agencies at the same level of government. The best example is the state water and sewerage company (CEDAE), and the environmental agency (FEEMA). At the municipal level, the situation is not much different.

Box 9.2: Basic Sanitation Program for Guanabara Bay
Hélia Nacif Xavier

Main Aspects

Phase I of the Basic Sanitation Program for the Guanabara Bay Catchment Area will need financing of US$667 million, of which US$217 million will come from local funds and US$ 480 million from IDB, with an expected reduction of 30 percent in pollution. A total clean-up would take ten to fifteen years and cost some US$ 4 billion. This Program is currently being renegotiated with the IDB; talks should be concluded by early 1993 with Bank approval of the Program. The 1991 Descriptive Report gave an overview of Phase I and highlighted important aspects: Sanitation, macro-drainage and resettlement; garbage; supplementary environmental programs; tax revenues and digital mapping.

The Guanabara Bay catchment basin covers an area of 4,000 square kilometers, incorporating 14 municipalities, 12 of which are in the Rio de Janeiro metropolitan region: Belford Roxo, Duque de Caxias, Itaborai, Mage, Guapimirim, Nilopolis, Niteroi, Nova Iguaçu, Rio Bonito, Rio de Janeiro, São Gonçalo, and São João de Meriti. Its topography ranges from the Tijuca massif and the coastal range to sprawling coastal plains with sand-spit vegetation and mangrove swamps. It is traversed by some 35 large rivers, with steep upper reaches and gently-sloping lower reaches, pouring a volume of up to four billion cubic annually into the Guanabara Bay.

The main sources of pollution include two oil refineries; two ports; 6,000 industries; 12 shipyards; 16 oil terminals; raw sewage; treated sewage; oil discharge; and garbage dumps. The major consequences of environmental degradation include reduced commercial fishing (down 90 percent); destruction of mangrove swamps; water unsuitable for bathing; catastrophic, costly floods; outbreaks of waterborne diseases, such as schistosomosis, leptospirosis, infectious hepatitis, typhoid/paratyphoid fever, and gastroenteritis; increased silting (81 cm/100 years—base: 1938-62); and garbage-blocked water courses and dry riverbeds used for housing.

Sanitation

The Guandu River supplies some 80 percent of the water for Rio de Janeiro and the Baixada Fluminense lowlands, considered of good quality. Niteroi and São Gonçalo, in particular, lag badly. Sewage networks cover 30 percent of the Rio de Janeiro area, servicing some 70 percent of the population, with the Atlantic Ocean, and the Guanabara and Sepetiba Bays forming the final recipients. The rivers running through the Baixada Fluminense reflect lack of infrastructure, and often become open sewers. Other municipalities either lack sewage systems completely, or have outdated, inadequate networks.

The Guanabara Bay Clean-Up Program schedules a hike from 15 percent to 33 percent for sewage treatment between 1992 and 1994, and from 33 percent to 65 percent after full implementation of the Program. Improvements in water supplies should benefit 1.75 million people, of whom 1.45 million live in the Baixada Fluminense and the remainder in São Gonçalo.

Macro-Drainage and Resettlement

The Acari, Timbo, and Faria rivers are scheduled for dredging to solve severe flooding problems, largely due to disorganized settlement and loss of riverbank vegetation that has silted up their beds. As the Acari River runs through densely populated areas and cross major thoroughfares, it puts communities at risk, disrupts economic activities, and blocks traffic. Macro-drainage should benefit some 190,000 inhabitants, with little resettlement required. The Faria and Timbo rivers are in a similar situation; macro-drainage should benefit some 240,00 inhabitants, with resettlement of some 1,106 families living on riverbanks in dry riverbeds.

Box 9.2 (continued)

Garbage

Although Rio de Janeiro and Niteroi garbage collection services are generally good, ballooning populations demand better disposal facilities, preceded by selective collection and recycling, with special treatment for hospital refuse. Acid runoff pollutes water tables, rivers and canals. Recycling and composting plants currently being launched or built offer valid solutions for from close-to-saturation current dumps, such as Gramacho, Jacarepagua, Itaguai, Morro do Ceu, and Bangu.

Supplementary Environmental Programs

Supplementary environmental programs include control of industrial pollution; accident prevention and control; control of hospital wastes; supervision of activities producing oily wastes; control of land use; control of toxic industrial wastes; control of urban and hospital refuse; control of ballast water from oil tankers; technological information; monitoring of environmental quality; monitoring water quality/statistical backup; monitoring beach quality; monitoring air quality; monitoring industrial pollution; ecosystem stabilization/destabilization indices; socio-environmental analysis; river maintenance; polluting activities—licensing and supervision standards; polluting activities—liquid wastes system; retrieval and interpretation of old data on water quality; updated data base on water quality; monitoring water course flow rates; environmental education; environmental education programs; community participation and dissemination; implementation of conservation units and ecological parks; institutional reinforcement; computerization of environmental agencies; central FEEMA laboratory; personnel training; and SERLA research and development.

Tax Revenues and Digital Mapping

Digital mapping is designed to boost tax revenues and rates through updating records of municipal expansion, identifying sources of pollution and monitoring land use, covering an area of 1,350 square kilometers.

When the institutional framework is consolidated, it is easy to detect grey areas of overlapping functions, and/or areas of untouched problems. This is especially so in the case of metropolitan regional issues. For example, in spite of considerable efforts and funding under the Rio Floods project, it was almost impossible to get the state and municipality to develop and implement a common strategy for the collection, transportation, treatment and disposal of solid waste. Metropolitan transportation is another similar issue that transverses administrative boundaries. No amount of discussion or legislation is going to put an end to encroachment of Rio's hillsides, or the problems of uncontrolled

settlement on other areas of risk, if alternative safe, affordable, and accessible land is not available. Because of its greater capacity, the municipality of Rio has in the past taken advantage of these institutional constraints, and has advanced towards gaining political and institutional space by developing its own actions, in spite of the behavior of other levels of government. The master plan for the municipality of Rio is a good example.

What is at stake is how to design a more transparent and accountable distribution of functions and to search for possibilities of joint actions, in order to avoid the well-known consequences of the concurrent competencies. Another major point to be considered relates to the priority that should be given to the environment in the decision-making process leading to the development of consistent governmental policies, especially in terms of supporting institutions in the social sectors, e.g., health and education. What is not clear, so far, is how to establish the financing priorities. Afonso's document shows how difficult it is to evaluate who is doing what, and how. This is particularly true at the federal level. A major contribution to the sector would be a clear-cut definition of priorities and the assignment of funds accordingly.

The financing crisis of the Brazilian public sector demonstrates that the urban and/or environment sector cannot be sustained independently, unless it is helped by joint action with the private sector. The Rio case may be particularly interesting for further explanation if one accepts the concept that its natural beauty is a public good (as discussed by Camargo, this volume) and the need to develop new institutional and financial arrangements between the public and the private sector, in order to improve urban resilience to environmental degradation. Whether profit- or socially-oriented, private entities have much to say and do.

Building up the institutional capacity of the public sector, however, is of utmost importance for Rio. A comprehensive institutional development program should be launched at the state level and should cover agencies belonging to the three levels of government working in the Rio metropolitan area. By adopting a strategy based on the demand for services and a supply of private and public institutions that could serve their demand, the sector could advance towards a more rational and adequate performance, which would eventually avoid further environmental degradation and urban vulnerability.

The start of a productive relationship

We believe that the Rio Flood Reconstruction project has been instrumental in stimulating some institutional changes, and has been the start to an often frustrating—but substantially rewarding and productive—relationship between the State and Municipality of Rio de Janeiro and the Bank. Earlier we made reference to "the intermittent conflict between the different levels of government, and the cyclical rhythm of alternate state and municipal elections every 24 months . . ." and to inevitable institutional discontinuity. The excellent performance of the municipality demonstrated better than ever the importance of institutional continuity—of retaining experienced technical and institutional support, and providing the value added component of a political vision and the leadership to make things happen.

On the one hand, the short time frame between alternating state and municipal elections, appears to constrain the thinking of longer-term policies and programs that are required to address the problems of the environment, education, health, housing, and transportation. These are not issues that can be resolved in two-year perspectives. On the other hand, provided there is an open dialogue of such issues and a broad consensus of public opinion, there are always "windows of opportunity" where the political leadership does get together and make those momentous agreements that set the pace and timetable for further progress. One such window was the period between 1991 and 1992 when Governor Brizola and Mayor Alencar together—working closely with the federal government—signed an accord in April 1992, which, when implemented, will mark a major policy change towards improving urban mass transport in the Metropolitan Region of Rio de Janeiro. The removal of the Metro debt burden from the state by the federal government, the transfer of operational responsibility of the Metro to the municipality of Rio, and the transfer of the operational responsibility of CBTU-RJ to the state were important and coherent first steps of this reform. The state and municipal government now propose to move quickly to examine and implement important policy changes including physical and financial modal integration and route rationalization focused on improving access to affordable transportation and reducing costs. Financial and administrative reforms would be introduced to stop inefficiency and reduce wastage in publicly owned services (CBTU-RJ, Metro, CTC, CONERJ). Operating subsidies would be better targeted to the urban poor. An increased role would be defined for the private sector and the regulatory system improved. The mayor elect—Cesar Maia—who assumes office in January 1993, has already indicated his full support for this policy.

The World Bank is also supporting this urban transportation project as an important follow-up to the investments already initiated in the metropolitan Region of Rio de Janeiro. Negotiations were concluded in September 1992, and formal presentation to the Bank's Board of Executive Directors is now only awaiting agreement from the federal government. Further initiatives by the Bank will include seeking financial support for follow-up studies, to be carried out by individuals and NGOs, on issues arising out of this conference. These papers would be placed in the public domain to facilitate raising public awareness of the critical issues. In addition, the Bank has agreed to finance a multisectoral review jointly with the state and municipality of Rio during its next financial year, starting July 1993. The building blocks for institutional change are already on the site, and some assembly has started.

Notes

6. This chapter was written *after* the conference to fill in the gap in the institutional memory from a different perspective. Braz Menezes has been the task manager for the project since 1988. Thereza Lobo coordinated the project for the municipality of Rio in 1988, before transferring to the private sector as a consultant. She now also heads the Center for the Study of Public Policies, based in Rio de Janeiro.

7. The project was identified, prepared, appraised, and approved by the Board in less than 100 days.

8. Fundo de Garantia de Tempo de Serviço (Social Security Fund).

9. Another water sector project (PROSANEAR) also with CEF—approved only five days after the Rio Flood Reconstruction Project—disbursed only 26 percent of the loan amount, compared with the Rio flood project's 64 percent over the same period up to June 1992.

10. By the time a restructured Rio project is completed in December 1994, the project will have witnessed the passing of at least four CEF presidents, two state governors, and three municipal mayors.

11.	At about the time of loan signing in September 1988, the *New York Times* carried an article announcing that the outgoing mayor of Rio had formally declared the city bankrupt.

10. Appropriate Technologies for Urban Services: Metropolitan Region of Rio de Janeiro

Dalia Maimon and Claudison Rodrigues

This chapter examines technologies already in use in the Rio de Janeiro metropolitan region that merit wider application. Technological options for urban services include basic sanitation (water supply, sewage and garbage collection), energy, and transportation. Technologies have been selected based on their potential positive impact to affect both the quality of life and economic systems. Persistent problems affecting the delivery of basic services have been noted.

Brazil's rapid industrial growth produced vast urban sprawls—such as Rio de Janeiro—that lack effective official planning and control, leading to social and environmental degradation and spurring conflicts (see Box 10.1). Air pollution and hot patches (+10∘C) caused by overbuilding cause respiratory diseases, allergies and skin cancer. Industrial and domestic wastes pollute water sources—currently some 500 tons of sewage are dumped daily into the Guanabara Bay. Increasing poverty and ineffective public housing policies lead to the settlement of unsuitable sites such as hillsides, marshes, and protected areas.

With a 1991 population of 9.6 million, the Rio de Janeiro metropolitan region covers an area of almost 6,500 square kilometers, with a demographic density that ranges from 0.1 (Mangaratiba and Maricá) to 12.5 (São João de Meriti), averaging out at 1.5. Only 1.7 percent of its 2.8 million homes are shacks, and only 1 percent of households lack electric power. Most of its 480 *favela* slums (home

to 30 percent of the population) have been upgraded over the past decade. However, many land titles are still unconfirmed, leading to disputes between owners and squatters. Highly vulnerable to floods and landslides, illegal settlements destroy forests and ground cover; lacking urban services, they also pollute water sources with sewage and garbage (see Box 10.2).

Water supplies are satisfactory (serving 94.5 percent of homes), and generally of acceptable quality. Although 56 percent of households are linked to the main sewage system, only 4.6 percent of the total volume produced is treated; the remainder is discharged into rivers and canals, flowing into the Guanabara and Sepetiba Bays.

Garbage collection is available to 73.3 percent of Rio de Janeiro households; the remainder burn or dump. Traps at the mouths of the main rivers accumulate some 270 tons of floating garbage daily. Total garbage for 1990 reached almost three million tons, most of which was dumped in landfills that produce acid runoff.

Transportation is largely (66 percent) by bus, with 15 percent by private automobiles, producing 90 percent of the city's air pollution. Railroads are federally run and the subway system belongs to the State. Uncomfortably overcrowded, slow, poorly-maintained and even hazardous, public transportation is noisy and a major culprit in the emission of black smoke. This leads to increased stress and violence, increased by frequent onboard muggings.

Box 10.1: Emergency Planning in Industrial Installations: An Overview
Aquilino Senra Martinez

Operating on a vastly increased scale thanks to technological advances, industrial installations are also more liable to serious accidents: explosion, fire, and toxic or radioactive leaks. Uncontrolled settlement of surrounding areas intensifies population density; the risks of death or injury thus become more widespread than the possibilities analyzed in the environmental hazard studies initially required for new industrial plants.

Industrial accidents cause human and economic losses both inside and outside the installation; the range of damage depends on the source of the risk, local topography and meteorological conditions. Accident prevention measures should thus cover both internal and external areas. Engineering designs should incorporate safety and security systems that reduce hazards and risks to the minimum, particularly in high technological-risk industries such as chemicals, petrochemicals, oil refineries, power stations steel mills etc.

As it is impossible to achieve zero risk, emergency plans must limit the effects of accidents on workers and the neighboring community, specifying emergency procedures and responsibilities. Poorly-designed or badly implemented emergency plans may exacerbate the consequences of an accident, particularly in case of panic.

Basic criteria for emergency plans should include safety and security analysis of the installation at the detailed engineering stage, as greater security means less risk. Normal operational wear and tear can cause accidents or extend their effects; a Fault Tree charts fault frequency in each component and measures individual risk by algebraic formulae.

Risk probability analyses are required for licensing technological-risk industrial installations. Risk quantification guides the installation of hazard barriers—such as closed-circuit pipelines, release tanks and retention buildings—that prevent hazards spreading to the environment. Transition phases (switch on/off, landing/takeoff, pressurization/depressurization) are potentially the most hazardous. Protection systems should not be blocked off for testing (viz. Chernobyl).

In-house emergency plans must first identify sources of risk and quantify consequences in terms of human and economic losses in the emergency areas. Pre-prepared computer simulations of emergency scenarios provide input for taking decisions during a real emergency. Emergency plans must cover announcement of an operational incident by plant workers, declaration of an internal emergency by the shift supervisor in the control room (who also triggers the alarm system), and implementation of emergency procedures. The competent government agencies should be advised, and are responsible for declaring an outside emergency. An emergency should only be declared when lives and property are at risk, as panic may cause more damage than the actual accident.

After no more than thirty minutes of operating according to an emergency plan the Technical Support Center comes into action and takes over. Its Coordinator is generally the Plant Manager, who is responsible for the following:
- Checking emergency staffers.
- Assessing the extent of the accident, counting the dead and injured.
- Analyzing emergency development scenarios in order to anticipate events.
- Contacting outside emergency services (police, fire brigade, hospitals, etc.).
- Maintaining contact with the Outside Emergency Coordination Group, if any.
- Evacuating workers to convocation points.
- Preparing a brief press release.
- Maintaining communications among internal and external emergency staff.

Box 10.1 (continued)

His technical assistant handles the firefighting, physical protection, medical aid, emergency repairs and transportation, technical support and toxic/radioactive materials monitoring teams. External emergency planning focuses on local residents and their homes. The federal, state and municipal governments have agencies that centralize emergency actions. Normally the Civil Defense Corps, they alert medical, police and firefighting services.

When an emergency goes beyond the limits of municipal authority, an External Emergency Coordination Group is set up, chaired by the Federal Government Civil Defense Secretary and consisting of representatives of the Environment Bureau, the Labor Ministry, the State Government, the City Council and the federal or state agency responsible for licensing the installation, as well as police and fire chiefs, doctors, and those responsible for road and rail services, food supplies and shelter for evacuees. In the case of a nuclear accident, the National Nuclear Power Commission declares a state of emergency if necessary; other types of accident are not allocated a specific spokesman under law. This group works out of an pre-established Emergency Operations Center close to the accident, with access to electric power, information on the accident, meteorological data and an effective telecommunications system. It assesses the seriousness of the situation and its effects, recommends protective measures and keeps other government agencies advised. It also keeps the population informed, controls traffic and access of emergency teams, evacuates local communities and provides housing, food and welfare for the homeless, controls convocation points, medical aid and transportation, identifies recuperation measures, coordinates the return of local communities when safe to do so, and issues regular reports for release to the press.

Specific measures are planned for toxic or radioactive leaks, zoned concentrically at radii of 1-5 kilometers, 5-10 kilometers and 10-15 kilometers. Technological systems can reduce accidents, particularly computerized administration of preventive maintenance and repair, monitoring operations, and handling emergency situations. Data on temperature, pressure, flow rates, etc., are computer validated on-line, and displayed/printed in the control room. This speeds up supervision and avoids confusion due to large numbers of meters and dials. It also pinpoints the causes of an accident immediately, ensuring the correct emergency measures are implemented, reducing operator stress and speeding up a return to normal operations. Output includes bar charts, operational graphs, simulated flow charts, historical data on principal variables, logical decision trees, emergency recuperation measures, and liquid waste dispersion displays. Digital switch-off devices fitted to industrial processes can increase security, although software currently available still needs improvement.

Community participation involves advance information on sources of risk, consequences of accidents, and emergency procedures. Residents' Association representatives should be involved, and schools could play a major role through environmental education and educational plant tours. Simulated emergency drills help fine-tune procedures.

Its nuclear power station makes emergency planning particularly vital in the Angra dos Reis area. Simulated emergencies and drills have highlighted slow evacuation, precarious transportation, inadequate roads and fragile telecommunications systems. Technological advances have increased and lowered the probability of serious industrial accidents, while effective computerization and emergency planning can limit their consequences.

Technological pluralism and appropriate technologies

Inadequate services are partially a result of shrinking government funding, a situation which should spur a pluralistic approach to urban management: integrated, innovative, environment-friendly, low-cost, and featuring community participation. Technological pluralism aimed at eco-development blends economic efficiency, social justice and ecological prudence, linking economic and spatial planning. Adapted to macro-eco-systems, these technologies range from simple to sophisticated, satisfying the needs of local populations, recycling wastes and exploiting renewable resources. A review of technological options available to relevant sectors follows:

Housing

Although the National Housing Bank (BNH) financed 4.5 million units in the twenty years prior to its closure in 1986, only 25 percent were earmarked for people earning 0-5 minimum wages. BNH's functions were transferred to the CEF federal savings and loan organization, with states and municipalities taking over low-cost housing construction. However:
- Housing planning is guided by politics rather than occupants' requirements.
- Funding is insufficient to cope with the demand.
- An appreciable slice of the funding has been earmarked for infrastructure, with construction on a mutual self-help basis.
- This mutual self-help build-it-yourself system is not acceptable to the community, which demands state-built housing, which the residents could then modify according to their individual needs.

- No funds are allocated to new technologies or alternative materials.
- Participatory planning has been avoided, skirting long-drawn-out discussions with communities.

Low-cost housing programs in the Rio de Janeiro metropolitan region include:
- PROMORAR: This federal slum-urbanization program acknowledged slum dwellers' integration into the structure of the city in physical, legal and administrative terms, setting specific norms and standards for buildings and town planning, as well as seeking solutions to land title for squatter communities.
- MARCILIO DIAS PROJECT: An interesting experiment funded by the CEF, FINSOCIAL fund and the Social Action Ministry, this project is working with the Archdiocese and Residents' Associations to eradicate slums along the Red-Line Airport Expressway. Building 100 homes on a self-help basis, it also includes urban infrastructure, schools and community centers.
- PREFABRICATED HOUSING: Cooperation strategies are being defined between France and Brazil to build low-cost prefabricated housing. A 1988 self-help prefabricated double-story housing project linking São Paulo and Rheims is already implemented, and others are under way in Fortaleza.

Water and sewage systems

Water supplies and sewage are centralized in the state-owned CEDAE water and sewage company. Its management style is closely tied to technological solutions demanding massive investments in dams, treatment stations, distribution systems etc. Its current technology—imported some 100 years ago—is completely obsolete. Network controls are slack, much water and energy

---

Box 10.2: Land Occupation Plan for the Area of Influence of the Rio de Janeiro Petrochemical Complex

Hélia Nacif Xavier

Physical and territorial characterization was set up by Federal Decree in 1987 under the 1987-95 National Petrochemicals Plan. In 1989 this complex was assigned a site in Itaguai, selected after preparation of six reports on the area. Various factors, mainly political, have prevented its implementation.

Its area of influence was defined as including the municipalities of Itaguai, Mangaratiba, Nova Iguaçu and Rio de Janeiro, covering 1,144 square kilometers undergoing constant expansion. Uncontrolled subdivisions along new highways lack urban infrastructure and thus aggravate flooding in this marshy area, that remains 47 percent rural, with 27 percent set aside for nature reserves, particularly mangrove swamps and river-head areas. Sand-mining worsens flooding and silts up riverbeds. Almost 9,000 hectares are classified as industrial land. Squatters have also settled in outlying areas around towns such as Santa Cruz, Queimados, and Campo Grande, as well as along the railroad.

This area holds some 8.6 percent of the population of the Rio de Janeiro metropolitan region, with industrialization on the rise since 1980. Industrial Districts have been set up in Santa Cruz, Campo Grande and Palmares by the state government, with sizable investments in low-cost mass housing projects.

---

is wasted, there is little adaptation for irregular residential settlements, and interaction with FEEMA—the state environment agency—tends to be hit-or-miss.

Low-cost alternative technologies to solve these problems are featured in CEDAE's PROFACE slum water supplies and sewage program. Basic implementation criteria include:
- Community demands.
- Downstream tie-ins to CEDAE systems.
- Lack of water/sewage services.
- Completion of work started by CEDAE, other agencies, and/or the communities themselves.
- Appreciable population density.
- Respect for *non aedificandi* areas.

CEDAE. participation may be global, partial, involve only operation and maintenance, or merely supply materials and/or technical assistance for community action programs.

Condo-main sewage systems. are low-cost, decentralized networks with sub-basin treatment to reduce pollution to bodies of water. First used by the Rio Grande do

Norte water and sewage company—CAERN, they channel block sewage into outside networks for nearby treatment. Guidelines include the following:
- Rationalization of investments, with a high cost/benefit ratio and faster installation.
- Development of new technologies tailored to micro-regional requirements.
- Elimination of large mains by decentralized local treatment wherever possible.
- Massification, servicing the entire population.
- Community mobilization and agreement at municipal, neighborhood and block levels.
- Sewage systems pave the way for solving other urban infrastructure problems such as drainage, hardtopping, garbage collection, etc.

Simplified sewage networks. collect and carry sewage to treatment stations at low cost. Highly flexible, they need little excavation and minimal inspection, following the natural lie of the land. They are recommended for the following:

- Hillsides with a population density over 300 inhabitants per hectare or more, particularly if no clear-cut residential blocks are defined.
- Where impermeable soil does not allow liquid wastes to drain into the ground.
- Places where the water table is shallow.

Water irradiation treatment. is being studied by the Brazil's IPEN—Energy and Nuclear Institute and the Hydraulic and Sanitary Engineering Department of the University of São Paulo Polytechnic College. A promising alternative for industrial liquid wastes or pollutant sludge from chemical or physical treatment processes, it can eliminate 99 percent of viruses and bacteria and clarify industrial wastewaters. It may also involve accelerators for treating hospital wastes. Current research irradiates polluted water with a high-power electron accelerator also used to sterilize pharmaceutical products and alter dye and paint textures. Only four such electron accelerators are currently found in Brazil: one at IPEN and three in industry. Similar pilot projects are under way in Germany, Boston, and Florida.

Electrolytic treatment of hospital sewage. was developed by the University of Campinas. Highly efficient, very low-cost, simple and fast, it is tailored for small areas. Being odorless, it could be adapted for urban use; NPK-rich scum and sludge may be used as fertilizer.

Garbage collection and recycling

Garbage collection. In Rio de Janeiro garbage is collected by the COMLURB urban cleaning company. Also oversized, its interaction with the FEEMA state environment bureau is flaccid. Disposal is largely in low-cost sanitary landfills; inclusion of environmental costs not traditionally calculated into the cost/benefit ratio now make this technology completely outdated. COMLURB applied to the IDB

for a US\$ 2.6 million loan to build acid runoff retention ponds round the Caxias landfill; the sour, fatty runoff liquid consumes oxygen in water and is responsible for 8 percent—840,000 liters daily—of Guanabara Bay pollution. Soaring demographics demand innovative solutions for both collection (500 grams/inhabitant/day) and disposal, making greater use of recycling.

Large-scale selective garbage collection. Curitiba introduced Brazil's first large-scale selective garbage collection system. Of 700 tons, at least 130 tons of paper, plastic, glass and cans are recycled. Some 30 tons are collected by the city council; the remainder is handled by 1,000-odd scavengers picking through refuse before the garbage trucks arrive. Saving 60,000 tons of paper saves 1,000 trees daily. One ton of recycled paper preserves 25-30 full-grown trees, saves 2½ barrels of oil and cuts 3.2 meters of sanitary landfill.

Small-scale selective garbage collection. Residents in São Francisco, Niteroi have developed a breakthrough home garbage separation system. Paper, glass, plastics and metals are collected by a mini-tractor donated by the German government, and organic materials are composted for fertilizer. Operational costs are covered, leaving a small monthly profit of US\$ 500.

Inmates of the Magé Penal Colony collect 48 tons of refuse daily, separating it on to conveyor belts, while organic material is composted. Each participant receives a minimum monthly wage.

Rio de Janeiro's street and dump scavengers handle primary recycling informally; janitors often separate building refuse for sale. Some private firms (like the João Fortes construction company) use recycled paper in their offices; large condominiums (Mandala and Alfabarra) separate their garbage.

Large-scale recycling. The Caju Recycling and Composting plant has a capacity of 1,120 tons daily, generating 145 tons of recycled materials and 500 tons of fertilizer. It takes some of the pressure off the Irajá plant, which was built eleven years ago and is now hopelessly outdated. COMLURB recently installed another plant in Jacarepagua, at an initial cost of US$ 12 million, to process 600 tons of refuse daily.

The technique used by the Caju plant is French, and involves electromagnetic, ballistic and pneumatic separators, with an aerobic biostabilizer. Total investments topped US$ 23 million. It is located in the highly-industrialized, extremely polluted North Zone. Selective collection speeds up mechanical separation. Sited and built according to inaccurate wind and air flow data, the composting plant produces fetid smells—and local complaints make headlines—within a radius of five miles. The town of Vouete in France uses special worms to compost its organic wastes—a system that is being studied by other districts.

Small-scale recycling. The primary recycling plant built by Vega Sopave for COMLURB in 1977 handles 20 tons an hour. Its output finds an easy market, and operational costs are well below those of large-scale recycling.

Brazil's National Social and Economic Development Bank (BNDES) had a FINSOCIAL-financed program to implement manual garbage recycling in small towns. This created an average of 100 jobs and covered its own administration costs. If introduced into Brazil's 200 largest towns it would produce savings of US$ 600 million annually.

Corporate recycling. KODAK is developing recycling projects for its São José dos Campos (SP) and Resende (RJ) plants. Film reels are ground up and mixed with new material to make parts. The silver emulsion coating on substandard films is removed, after which they are washed and ground up. With this, the company recovers 60 percent of what was previously wasted, for savings of US$340,000.

O Globo newspaper is implementing an Environmental Education Project for its staff, developed by the Brazilian Nature Conservation Foundation, as well as selective garbage collection. The industrial area alone produces 500 tons monthly of waste paper and cardboard.

Reynolds, Brazil's aluminum can manufacturer, is opening up a market for empty soda pop cans. It intends to recycle 780 million cans annually. Inaugurated in October 1991, this project has to date recycled one million cans. In the USA, 55 billion aluminum cans are recycled, out of 90 billion produced, for electric power savings of 95 percent. Cisper recycles glass—2.8 percent of Brazilian refuse—for operational savings of 15 percent.

Garbage collection in slums. On the Morro de Dona Marta hill, and in Curitiba and Petropolis, garbage collection is carried out by local residents who swap bags of garbage for food or bus vouchers, with amazing results. Community street cleaners complete the system—and were the only staff to keep working through a COMLURB strike.

Auctions of machinery and equipment. Companies reduce costs by auctioning off used parts, spares and extra raw materials. In operation since 1974, these auctions top US$ 100 million; held on company premises, the only cost is the 5 percent auctioneer's fee.

Energy

Energy savings. Appropriate technologies save energy, foster sustainable growth, and reduce air pollution and the greenhouse effect, often using nonconventional, readily available energy sources. The oil crises of the 1970s had reduced effects, as companies were changing their power consumption profile, although not reducing energy demands as whole. Use of these new sources did not consider environmental factors, concentrating on relative prices and scarce foreign exchange. Most of Brazil's energy savings programs are implemented by the federal government and state-owned power utilities, peaking only at supply crises.

In Brazil, energy conservation programs are not specifically supported by the state government, as is the case in São Paulo, where heavy industry has prodded the government and academia into seeking solutions. Some successful experiences with appropriate technologies are outlined below.

Energy Savings in the Industrial Sector have been achieved by rationalization programs that range from simple upgrades of existing processes to the incorporation of energy-saving technology and production goods needing less power.

An Energy Diagnosis was prepared by Eletrobras under its Procel electricity-saving scheme, pinpointing major waste points, possibilities of fine-tuning and company potential for conservation. Over the past four years this program has cut electric power use by 10.5 percent, for savings of US$ 600 million.

Less-polluting energy replacement largely involves replacing gasoline by fuel alcohol. The world's most successful energy substitution scheme, Pro-alcool helps lower air pollution, particularly CO_2, a major cause of the greenhouse effect. However, for each liter of fuel alcohol produced, 12 liters of waste liquids are discharged into water-courses, demanding better use of this liquid for fodder and fertilizer.

Replacement of fuel oil by electricity has reduced consumption of that fossil fuel by 5 percent annually, encouraging replacement of fuel oil boilers by electric

models. However, no assessment was made of the construction of hydroelectric plants.

Lower energy consumption. An increase in mileage from 18.9 kilometers/liter to 28.6 kilometers/liter is estimated for specific gasoline consumption between 1983 and 1995, through improved designs and mechanics, as well as the use of new materials. In parallel to decreased demands for raw materials, the energy needed to manufacture an automobile should drop by 30 percent.

In-house company assessment programs help industries pinpoint, quantify and eliminate wasted energy. A survey under way of the twelve companies that consume 60 percent of the energy produced in Brazil should result in a policy cutting general consumption by 3 percent. A specific program offers guidance on efficient boiler adjustment, thus reducing air pollution. A French program for third parties remunerates energy savings consultants in proportion to savings achieved.

The best prospects for energy savings lie in the commercial sector, where infrastructure is responsible for 60 percent of total energy used (São Paulo); for sales of perishable merchandise this figure may reach 90 percent. Building standards also could be modified to make better use of natural lighting and climatization factors.

Household energy consumption is concentrated (70 percent) in refrigerators and electric showers. Street demonstrations guide São Paulo housewives towards more rational use of domestic appliances, for energy savings of 20 percent.

Transportation

Transportation is the major factor affecting the quality of life of urban populations. The Rio de Janeiro Metropolitan Region must aim simultaneously at three objectives in mass transportation:

increased efficiency, lower energy consumption, and less air and noise pollution. Possible actions range from the relatively simple (decentralization, staggered working hours, cleaner fuels, increased use of bicycles) to the ultra-sophisticated (high-speed trains, VLT surface subway). Measures should be coordinated by and among the competent government agencies: federal (railroad); state (subway); municipal (bus), as well as urban planning bureaus.

The demand for urban transportation could be reduced by geographical decentralization and development of new towns. Telecommunications and electronics facilitate relocation of secondary and tertiary sectors in smaller towns or even rural areas.

Rio de Janeiro banks already have their own working hours (10:00 a.m.-4:30 p.m.). Other sectors, particularly the civil service, should follow suit to reduce peak hour demand for public transportation, as in Curitiba and Uberlandia.

Traffic lights should be synchronized to ensure green-light throughflow on main thoroughfares. Sidewalk detectors advise coordinators of traffic volume, for instant selection of suitable synchronization schedules.

Bus transportation capacity (six times greater than private automobiles) could be quadrupled by integrating express or semi-express bus lanes. particularly for cross-town traffic. Larger vehicles seating 105 passengers with doors on both sides boost bus lane efficiency.

Technological innovations in rail transportation include light conventional rail systems, and two linear induction systems, one using conventional wheels and suspension, the other working on magnetic levitation. A fertile field for cooperation, these systems could be eased smoothly into the urban fabric, along bus lanes.

Rio's subway system was partially completed eleven years ago, with two lines.

Of the total 73.7 kilometers planned, only 22.2 kilometers are in service, due largely to a shortage of funds caused by sporadic investments, and political differences between federal, state and municipal governments embroiled in red tape. A possible solution is expropriation of some stations, for reurbanization by private enterprise.

VLT surface subway systems handle 20,000-40,000 seated passengers per hour, carried by a variety of technologies at lower implementation costs than underground subway systems. Nine Brazilian towns or regions (including Salvador, Santos, Goiania, Fortaleza, Brasilia, Curitiba, Teresina, and the Vale do Paraiba) are currently working on implementation of this system. Monorail systems use little ground area but are extremely expensive.

Outstanding among less polluting means of transportation are alcohol or gasohol-fueled vehicles. However, Brazil's subsidized fuel-alcohol program intensified the use of private automobiles and increased traffic snarls. Although it is quite feasible, alcohol is not used by buses and trucks. Trolley buses produce less air and noise pollution; however, implementation costs are high and routes are inflexible. They run on electric power, generation of which either emits CO_2 or destroys eco-systems through hydroelectric plants.

Turbine buses reduce air pollution by 50 percent in Curitiba, but cost twice as much as 105-seat standard buses.

Concluding Remarks

The major problems of the Rio de Janeiro metropolitan region mirror those of other megacities in developing nations: soaring demographic growth which produces pockets of utter poverty contiguous to tiny affluent sectors; dwindling fiscal and financial resources due to sluggish economic activity; and spreading environmental degradation. All this makes Rio vulnerable both in terms of the environment and ambient hygiene, a situation incompatible with its historical natural vocation of tourist center.

Urban infrastructure is provided unfairly and haphazardly, failing to provide adequate services for much of the city's low-income population. Government agencies at all levels are poorly coordinated and lack the requisite administrative framework to foresee impacts, implement integrated actions, and adapt projects to changing needs. Sectorial in approach, they also exclude social and environmental factors from cost-benefit analyses.

The public agencies most involved in providing daily services, such as CEDAE (water and sewage) and COMLURB (garbage) are oversized and need to fine-tune interfaces with FEEMA (environment). Rio's pressing housing shortage cannot realistically be satisfied by conventional techniques; innovative technologies must reduce construction costs for mass housing. Studies show that urbanization of 480 *favelas* and 486 illegal subdivisions, housing 1.6 million people, would cost no more than 0.3 percent of GDP over five years. The state government is lagging in terms of energy conservation, with actions limited to federal utility companies.

Appropriate corrective technologies implemented in the Rio de Janeiro metropolitan region are often confused with low-cost implementation technologies, being aimed almost exclusively at poorer sectors of the population. State giantism leads to North-South cooperation in projects with high construction costs spurred by civil construction lobbies and illegal kickbacks. Successful implementation of basic services in irregularly-settled areas could form the basis for South-South cooperation. Fuel alcohol could help reduce air pollution in Northern Hemisphere nations.

New structures should thus seek to break through sectoralization to set up new institutional arrangements. This is urgently needed in Brazil's energy conservation and pollution control sector. Private sector implementation of such measures demands a separate study, as well as systematic appraisal of appropriate technologies.

L. I. H. E.
THE BECK LIBRARY
WOOLTON RD., LIVERPOOL, L16 8ND

Bibliography

"A prefeitura assumirá o Metrô com déficit." *O Globo*. Rio de Janeiro, February 20, 1992.

"A saída para o Metrô." *Jornal do Brasil*. Rio de Janeiro, March 17, 1989.

"Federalismo fiscal & reforma institucional: falácias, conquistas e descentralização." Rio de Janeiro, mimeo.

Afonso, José Roberto. 1989. "Evolução das relações intergovernamentais no Brasil entre 1968/88: transferências e endividamento." Master's thesis. Rio de Janeiro: UFRJ, mimeo.

Agência de Desenvolvimento do Rio de Janeiro. 1991. *Desenvolvimento Econômico do Rio de Janeiro, Influência da Ação Institucional do Governo Federal*, Rio de Janeiro, Brazil, mimeo.

Ahmad, Yusuf J., Salah El Serafy, and Ernst Lutz (eds.). 1989. *Environmental Accounting for Sustainable Development*. Washington, D.C.: World Bank.

Almeida Magalhães, J. P., R. Bueno, and J. M. Camargo. 1992. *Rio Século XXI: perspectivas e propostas para a economia fluminense*. Rio de Janeiro: Agência Jornal do Brasil.

Amadeo, E., J. M. Camargo, and G. H. B. Franco. 1991. "The Trade-offs Between Economic Growth and Environmental Protection." Research Paper No. 36. Geneva: UNCED.

Anderson, Mary. 1990. "Analyzing the Costs and Benefits of Natural Disaster Responses in the Context of Development." Paper presented at the Colloquium on the Environment and Natural Disaster Management, June 27-28, 1990. Washington, D.C.: World Bank.

Anderson, Mary, and Everett Mendelsohn. 1992. "Technology Tip-Over Points: When 'Good' Technologies Become 'Bad' Technologies." Background Paper (unpublished), Policy and Research Division, the Environment Department. Washington, D.C.: World Bank, August.

Anderson, Mary, and Peter J. Woodrow. 1989. *Rising from the Ashes*. Boulder, Colo.: Westview Press.

Anderson, Mary, and Peter J. Woodrow. 1988. *An Approach to Integrating Development and Relief Programming: An Analytic Framework*. Cambridge: International Relief/Development Project at Harvard University.

Araujo, Aloisio Barbosa. 1991. O Governo Brasileiro e o BID: cooperação e confronto. Rio de Janeiro: IPEA.

Bamberger, Michael. 1988. *The Role of Community Participation in Development Planning and Project Management*. Washington, D.C.: Economic Development Institute, World Bank.

Banco Nacional da Habitação (BNH), Departamento de Estudos e Pesquisas Aplicadas (DEPEA). 1984. *Pesquisas na Area de Saneamento*. Rio de Janeiro: Banco Nacional da Habitação.

Barros, W. T., C. Amaral, and R. N. D'Orsi. 1991. "Landslide Susceptibility Map of Rio de Janeiro." In Bell (ed.), *Landslides*. Rotterdam: Balkema.

Barros, W. T., C. Amaral, R. N. D'Orsi, A. C. Vieira, and L. H. A. Azevedo. 1990. "Metodologia para a identificação de areas de risco geológico no Municipio do Rio de Janeiro com base na tecnologia do sensoriamento remoto." In *Anais do I Simposio Latino-Americano sobre Risco Geologico Urbano*. São Paulo: ABGE.

Berk, Richard A., and Peter H. Rossi. 1976. "Doing Good or Doing Worse: Evaluation Research Politically

Reexamined." *Social Problems* 23(3), February, pp. 337-49.

Brazil-Comissão Nacional da Política Urbana e das Regiões Metropolitanas. "A execução da política de desenvolvimento urbano." *Planejamento e Desenvolvimento, Rio de Janeiro* 5 (53):27-42.

Brazil. Constituição, 1988. "Constituição da República Federativa do Brasil." Brasília, Brazil, Senado Federal.

Brazil. Constituição. 1988. Lei no. 4.320, de 17/03/1964 (Dispõe sobre normas gerais de direito financeiro). Brasília: *Diário Oficial*.

Brazil-Presidência da República. 1991. Comissão Interministerial para a Preparação da Conferência das Nações Unidas sobre Meio Ambiente e Desenvolvimento. *O Desafio do Desenvolvimento Sustentável*. Brasília: CIMA, p. 204.

Brazil-Secretaria do Meio Ambiente (SEMAM). 1991. "Implantação da Secretaria Técnica do Fundo Nacional do Meio Ambiente (FNMA)." Brasília: SEMAM, datilografado.

Brazil-SEMAM. 1992. *Coletânea da Legislação Federal do Meio Ambiente*. Brasília: Instituto Brasileiro do Meio Ambiente e Recursos Naturais Renováveis, p. 797.

Brazil-Secretaria de Planejamento. 1976. *Região Metropolitana do Grande Rio: serviços de interesse comum*. Brasília: Instituto Planejamento Econômico e Social, p. 247.

Almir Bressan, Jr. 1991. "Principais resultados da política ambiental brasileira." Mimeo, p. 38.

"Brizola teme o fechamento do Metrô." *O Globo*. Rio de Janeiro, February 26, 1991.

Caixa Econômica Federal (CEF), Departamento Central de Pesquisas e Extensão Tecnológica (DEPEA). 1988. *Pesquisas Realizadas—Extrato da V edição—sem Resumos Indicativos*. Rio de Janeiro: CEF.

CEF, Departamento Central de Estudos e Pesquisas Aplicadas (DEPEA). 1987. *Pesquisas Realizadas—V Edição Revista e Atualizada*. Rio de Janeiro: CEF.

CEF, Departamento Central de Pesquisas e Extensão Tecnológica (DEPEA). 1988. *Alternativas Tecnológicas nas Areas de Habitação e Saneamento*. Rio de Janeiro: CEF.

Campos, T. M. P., Euripedes do A. Vargas Junior, and Roberto F. Azevedo. 1991. "Geotecnologia Ambiental: Pesquisas em Andamento no DE/PUC—Rio." In *Desenvolvimento e Meio Ambiente—Seminário*. Rio de Janeiro: PUC/RJ.

Centro de Estudos Fiscais, Fundação Getúlio Vargas (FGV). 1989. "Regionalização das transações do setor público." Texto de Acompanhamento de Políticas Públicas no. 13. Brasília: IPEA, June.

Clark, John R. 1990. "Management of Environment and Natural Disasters in Coastal Zones." Paper presented at the Colloquium on the Environment and Natural Disaster Management, June 27-28. Washington, D.C.: World Bank.

Coase, R. 1960. "The Problem of Social Costs." *The Journal of Law & Economics* 3.

Cohen, Michael. 1990. "Urban Growth and Natural Hazards." Paper presented at the Colloquium on the Environment and Natural Disaster Management, June 27-28, 1990. Washington, D.C.: World Bank.

"Collor diz a Brizola que assumirá o Metrô." *Jornal do Brasil*. Rio de Janeiro, February 1, 1992.

Commission of the European Communities. 1990. *Green Paper on the Urban Environment*. Brussels: Directorate General of Environment, Nuclear Safety and Civil Protection.

Considera, C., and Hildete H. P. Mello. 1986. "Industrialização Fluminense— 1930-1980." *Rio de Janeiro* 3 (August).

Constituição da República Federativa do Brasil, 1988, Brasília, Senado Federal, 1988, p. 292.

Coordenação de Política Social (CPS) do IPEA (coord. Solon Viana). "Conta consolidada dos gastos sociais" (tabulations, various editions). Brasília: IPEA, Mimeo.

Coriolano, Marcio S. de Araujo, and Heberto Lira Ferreira da Silva. 1987. "Proposições de um Programa Habitacional. Rio de Janeiro: Instituto de Estudos Políticos e Sociais. Mimeo.

Cunha, Luiz Roberto A., Marcio Miller Santos, and Jusui F. de Castro Filho. 1989. "Ação integrada de reconstrução e defesa contra inundações: o caso da região metropolitana do Rio de Janeiro." In *Impactos Sociais e Econômicos de Variações Climaticas e Respostas Governamentais no Brasil.* Fortaleza, Brazil: PNUMA/ SECPLAN-CE.

Cuny, Frederick. 1983. *Disasters and Development.* New York: Oxford University Press.

"Dados da Fundação de Desenvolvimento da Administração Pública (FUNDAP) mostram que os gastos anuais do Governo Federal no setor de urbanismo, saneamento e meio ambiente decresceram de US$6,2 bilhões em 1980, para US$4,2 bilhões em 1983 e US$2,2 bilhões em 1986." *Folha de São Paulo*, August 4, 1992.

Daly, H. 1990. "Towards an Environmental Macroeconomics." *Revista de Analisis Econômico* 5(2).

"Destino das obas do Metrô." *Jornal do Brasil*, Rio de Janeiro, December 6, 1989.

Dillinger, William. 1989. "Urban Property Taxation: Lessons from Brazil: Case Study." INU Report No. INU 37, April.

Washington, D.C.: World Bank. Working document.

Ehrlich, Paul, and Anne H. Ehrlich. 1989. "Too many rich folks." *Populi* 16(8): 21-30.

"Estado confessa a dívida do Metrô mas não paga." *Jornal do Brasil*. Rio de Janeiro, February 14, 1990.

Estache, Antonio. 1991. "Municipal Environmental Policy Issues in Brazil." LA1IN draft report, December 1990, revised January 23, 1991. Washington, D.C.: World Bank.

"Estado negocia municipalização do Metrô." *O Globo*. Rio de Janeiro, November 20, 1991.

"Falta de verba leva trens à falência." *Jornal do Brasil*. Rio de Janeiro, September 13, 1992.

Fontes, Angela, and Deborah Levinson. 1992. The Paid Mutual-Help Project— A Successful Experience. Rio de Janeiro: IBAM. Unpublished paper.

Franco, Roberto Messias. 1991. "Configuração político institucional da política ambiental brasileira. P. 38, mimeo.

Fundação Estadual de Engenharia do Meio Ambiente (FEEMA). 1990. *Bibliografia Analítica dos Estudos Desenvolvidos pela FEEMA—Suplemento 3, 1988-1990.* Rio de Janeiro: FEEMA.

FEEMA. 1987. *Bibliografia Analítica dos Estudos Desenvolvidos pela FEEMA— Suplemento 2, 1987.* Rio de Janeiro: FEEMA.

FEEMA. 1986. *Bibliografia Analítica dos Estudos Desenvolvidos pela FEEMA— Suplemento 1, 1983-1986.* Rio de Janeiro: FEEMA.

FEEMA. 1983. *Bibliografia Analítica dos Estudos Desenvolvidos pela FEEMA— 1975-1983.* Rio de Janeiro: FEEMA.

Fundação Instituto Brasileiro de Geografia e Estatística (IBGE). 1992. "Censo Demográfico de 1991—Resultados Preliminares." Mimeo (text 16). Rio de Janeiro: IBGE, February.

Fundação IBGE. 1989. "Sistema de Contas Nacionais Consolidadas Brasil." *Série Relatórios Metodológicos*, vol. 8. Rio de Janeiro: IBGE.

Fundação IBGE. Various issues. "Estatísticas Econômicas do Setor Público." Rio de Janeiro: IBGE.

Fundação Prefeito Faria Lima (CEPAM). 1988. *Acervo RECEM 1*. São Paulo: Fundação Prefeito Faria Lima.

Gondim, Linda. 1992. "Projeto Rio—Laboratório de Experiências Inovadoras." Rio de Janeiro: Instituto Brasileiro de Administração Municipal (IBAM), unpublished paper.

Gondim, Linda. 1992. "The Role of the Private Sector in Sustainable Development in Megacities: The case of Rio de Janeiro, Brazil." Rio de Janeiro: IBAM, unpublished paper.

Gonzaga, Paulo. 1987. "Meio Ambiente políticas públicas: a FEEMA diante da poluição industrial." In J. A. Padua (org.), *Ecologia e Política no Brasil*. Rio de Janeiro: Espaço e Tempo/IUPERJ, pp. 181-211.

Governo do Estado do Rio de Janeiro. 1991. *Programa de Saneamento Básico da Bacia da Baía de Guanabara. Relatório Descritivo para o Banco Interamericano de Desenvolvimento*, vol. 1. Description of the Program and its components. Rio de Janeiro: Governo do Estado do Rio de Janeiro, December.

Governo do Estado do Rio de Janeiro—Grupo Executivo para Recuperação e Obras de Emergência. 1989. "Termo de Referência do Plano para Coordenação de Ações de Proteção Ambiental e de Defesa Civil no Rio de Janeiro, componente A-9 do Programa de Reconstrução e Defesa Contra Inundações de Áreas do Estado do Rio de Janeiro." Rio de Janeiro: Governo do Estado do Rio de Janeiro, unpublished paper.

Governo do Estado do Rio de Janeiro, SEDUR. 1988. "Programa de Reconstrução—Rio: Relatório de Avaliação para o Banco Mundial." Rio de Janeiro: SEDUR, mimeo.

Governo do Estado do Rio de Janeiro, SEF. 1991. "A recuperação financeira do Estado do Rio de Janeiro e o Programa de Investimentos para 1992." Rio de Janeiro.

"Governo Federal vai assumir US$2,2 bilhões da dívida do Metrô." *O Globo*. Rio de Janeiro, February 19, 1992.

Green, J., E. Kohlberg, and J. Laffont. 1975. "Partial Equilibrium Approach to the Free Rider Problem." *Harvard Discussion Paper* no. 436.

Guedes, J., E. Ohana, and C. Mussi. 1991. "Análise da Estrutura Funcional do Gasto Público no Brasil 1985-1990." Brasília: IPEA, December, mimeo.

Guimarães, P., J. Carneiro, and S. MacDowell. 1992. "Gasto na gestão ambiental no Estado de São Paulo: um estudo preliminar." *Revista de Administração Pública* 26(2):155-71. Rio de Janeiro: FGV, April-June.

Guimarães, Roberto P. 1992. "Políticas do meio ambiente para o desenvolvimento sustentável: desafios institucionais e setoriais. *Planejamento e Políticas Públicas* 2(7):57-80, June.

Guimarães, Roberto P. 1984. "Ecopolítica em áreas urbanas: a dimensão política dos indicadores de qualidade ambiental." In Amaury Souza (ed.), *Qualidade de vida urbana*. Rio de Janeiro: Zahar, pp. 21-53.

Hamer, Andrew M. 1985. "Brazil: Issues in Human Settlements Policy." Water Supply and Urban Development Dept., Operations Policy Staff, Discussion Paper No. UDD-75, June. Washington, D.C.: World Bank.

Herculano, Selene. 1992. "Do desenvolvimento (in)suportável à sociedade feliz." In Miriam Goldenberg (org.), *Ecologia, Ciência e Política*. Rio de Janeiro: Revan, pp. 9-48.

Hicks, James F., and David Michael Vetter. 1983. "Identifying the Urban Poor in Brazil." Staff Working Paper No. 565. Washington, D.C.: World Bank.

Instituto Brasileiro de Geografia e Estatística (IBGE). 1992. *Censo Demografico—1991: Resultados Preliminares*. Rio de Janeiro: IBGE.

IBGE. 1992. *Pesquisa Nacional por Amostragem de Domicílios—1990: Tabulações Especiais*. Rio de Janeiro: IBGE.

IBGE. 1992. *Pesquisa Nacional de Saneamento Basico—1989: Tabulações Especiais*. Rio de Janeiro: IBGE.

Instituto dos Economistas do Rio de Janeiro. 1991."Uma Proposta para o Desenvolvimento do Estado do Rio de Janeiro." IERJ, mimeo.

Instituto Brasileiro de Administração Municipal (IBAM). 1992. "Ambiente-Rio—cadastro de entidades, projetos e legislação." Rio de Janeiro: IBAM, unpublished paper.

IBAM. 1992. *Perfil Institucional do Centro de Estudos e Pesquisas Urbanas—CPU/IBAM*. Rio de Janeiro: IBAM, August.

IBAM. 1992. *Perfil Técnico—Institucional do IBAM*. Rio de Janeiro: IBAM, December.

IBAM. 1992. *Relatório de Atividades 1991*. Rio de Janeiro: IBAM.

IBAM. 1992. "Sistema de cadastro de projetos e leis—CPL/manual do usuário." Rio de Janeiro: IBAM, unpublished paper.

IBAM. 1992. "Terceiro relatório sobre as atividades desenvolvidas no Âmbito do projeto ambiente-Rio dentro do convênio assinado em 29.10.91 com o MAS." Rio de Janeiro: IBAM, unpublished paper.

Instituto Universitário de Pesquisas do Rio de Janeiro. 1990. *Rio de Todas as Crises. IUPERJ*, mimeo.

International Monetary Fund (IMF). *Government Finance Statistics Yearbook*. Various volumes. Washington, D.C.: IMF.

Kreimer, Alcira. 1990. "Case Studies on Disaster Management: An Introduction." Paper presented at the World Bank Colloquium on the Environment and Natural Disaster Management, June 27, 1990. Washington, D.C.: World Bank.

Kreimer, Alcira. 1989. "Disaster Sustainability and Development: A Look to the 1990s." Paper presented at the World Bank Colloquium on Disasters, Sustainability and Development, June 9, 1989, Washington, D.C.

Kreimer, Alcira, and Mohan Munasinghe, eds. 1991. "Managing Natural Disasters and the Environment." Washington, D.C.: World Bank.

La Rovere, Emílio. 1992. "A sociedade tecnológica, a democracia e o planejamento." In Miriam Goldenberg (org.), *Ecologia, Ciência e Política*. Rio de Janeiro, Revan, pp. 77-104.

Lacerda, L. D., Wolfgang C. Pfeiffer, and M. Fiszman. 1987. "Heavy Metal Distribution, Availability and Fate in Sepetiba Bay, S.E. Brazil." *The Science of Total Environment* 65:163-73.

Lee, Yoon Joo. 1985. "The Spatial Structure of the Metropolitan Regions of Brazil." World Bank Staff Working Paper No. 722. Washington, D.C.: World Bank.

Levinson, Deborah. 1992. "The Urban Context of the Rio de Janeiro Metropolitan Region." Rio de Janeiro: IBAM, unpublished paper.

"Liberada verba para terminar linha 2 do Metrô." *Jornal do Brasil*. Rio de Janeiro, February 22, 1990.

Ligues apreendidas da coordenagco do projeto reconstrução-rio: os primeiros dois anos.

Lucas, R. 1988. "On the Mechanics of Economic Development" *Journal of Monetary Economics*. 22:3-42.

Magrini, Alessandra. 1990. "A avaliação dos impactos ambientais." In Sérgio Margulis, ed., *Meio Ambiente: aspectos técnicos e econômicos*. Brasília: IPEA/PNUD, pp. 85-108.

Maimon, Dália. 1991. "Política Ambiental no Brasil, in Agricultura e Meio Ambiente" no. 1, year 1. Rio de Janeiro: *Revista do NAMA.UFRJ*.

McCaull, Julian. 1974. *Water Pollution*. New York: Harcourt Brace Jovanovich.

Medici, André, and Francisco Oliveira. 1992. "A Dimensão do Setor Saúde no Brasil." Relatório Interno no. 4/92. Rio de Janeiro: IPEA, August.

"Metrô aguarda recursos para a linha 2." *O Globo*. Rio de Janeiro, February 15, 1992.

"Metrô: CPI quer sociedade com empreiteiras." *O Globo*. Rio de Janeiro, August 2, 1991.

"Metrô, sem verba, pode sair dos trilhos." *O Globo*. Rio de Janeiro, February 26, 1989.

Ministério da Economia—Departamento do Tesouro Nacional. 1992. *Balanços Gerais da União—1991*. 3 volumes. Brasília.

Ministério da Economia—Departamento do Tesouro Nacional. 1992. "Execução Orçamentária dos Estados e Municípios das Capitais 1981-1990." Brasília.

Ministério da Economia—Departamento do Tesouro Nacional. 1991. *Finanças do Brasil—1985-1988*. Volume XXX. Brasília.

Malm, Olaf, Wolfgang C. Pfeiffer, M. Fiszman, and J. M. P. Azcue. 1989.

"Heavy Metal Concentrations and Availability in the Bottom Sediments of the Paraiba do Sul—Guandu River System, RJ, Brazil." *Environmental Technology Letters* 10:675-80.

Ministério do Trabalho e da Administração—Secretaria Nacional do Trabalho. 1992. "Informes Financeiros do FGTS." Brasília: MTA, October, mimeo.

"Moreira confirma atraso no pagamento da obra do Metrô." *O Globo*. Rio de Janeiro, June 4, 1989.

"Mudanças no Metrô." *Jornal do Brasil*. Rio de Janeiro, March 7, 1989.

Nemerow, Nelson L. 1978. *Industrial Water Pollution*. Reading, Mass.: Addison Wesley Publishing Company.

Nogueira Neto, Paulo. 1978. "Problemas brasileiros de meio ambiente e seu monitoramento. In *Brasil—Conselho Nacional de desenvolvimento Científico e Tecnológico*. Meio Ambiente, projetos 02. Brasília, CNPq, pp. 93-96.

"Obras do Metrô estão ameaçadas." *Jornal do Brasil*. Caderno cidade, Rio de Janeiro, February 20, 1989.

"Obras do Metrô podem parar de novo por falta de pagamento." *O Globo*. Rio de Janeiro, June 3, 1989.

Organisation for Economic Co-operation and Development (OECD). 1986. *Water Pollution by Fertilizers and Pesticides*. Paris: OECD.

Olson, M. 1982. *Rise and Decline of Nations: Economic Growth, Stagflation and Social Rigidities*. New Haven, Conn.: Yale University Press.

Pantelic, Jelena. 1990. "Issues in Reconstruction Following Earthquakes: Opportunities for Reducing the Risk of Future Disasters and Enhancing the Development Process." Paper presented at the Colloquium on the Environment and Natural Disaster Management, June 27-28, 1990, World Bank, Washington, D.C.

Parker, Ronald S. 1990. "Aid Coordination: The Case of Flood Recovery in Sudan." Paper presented at the Colloquium on the Environment and Natural Disaster Management, June 27-28, 1990, World Bank, Washington, D.C.

Parker, Ronald S. 1990. "Sustainability." A study undertaken for Foster Parents Plan International, East Greenwich.

Parker, Ronald S. 1989. *Developing Evaluation Criteria for Disaster Relief: A Critical Review of the Literature.* Cambridge: Harvard University's Gutman Library.

Peattie, Lisa. 1990. "Participation: A Case Study of How Invaders Organize, Negotiate and Interact with Government in Lima, Peru." *Urbanization and Environment* 2(1):19-30, April.

Perlman, Janice E. 1988. The Megacities Project. A Research/Action Strategy to Transform Urban Policy from the Bottom Up. New York: Urban Research Center, New York University.

Pfeiffer, Wolfgang C., Olaf Malm, L. D. Lacerda, Claudia Santiago Karez. 1992. "Contaminação ambiental e humana por metais pesados. Uma revisão." In *O Ambiente Inteiro.* Rio de Janeiro: Editora UFRJ.

Pinheiro, Souza de (org.). 1992. "Despoluição da Baía de Guanabara. Projeto inovador de saneamento básico." *Revista CIDE/SECPLAN*, year 1, no. 1. April/June, pp. 22-28. Rio de Janeiro: Governo do Estado do Rio de Janeiro, Secretaria Estadual de Planejamento e Controle e Fundação Centro de Informação e Dados Socioeconômicos.

Pinho Filho, Paulo. 1991. "Baía de Guanabara: a recuperação gradual de um ecosistema degradado." Anais do Seminario Cidade Anos 90: Catastrofe ou Oportunidade? Rio de Janeiro: March 18-19, 1991.

PLANAVE S.A.—*Estudos e Projetos de Engenharia.* 1991.

PLANAVE S.A.—*Estudos e Projetos de Engenharia.* 1990.

PLANAVE S.A.—*Estudos e Projetos de Engenharia.* 1990. Plano de Ocupação Territorial da Área de Influência do Pólo Petro-químico do Rio de Janeiro. Relatório Gerencial. Rio de Janeiro: Governo do Estado do Rio de Janeiro (Convênio entre Secretaria de Estado de Indústria e Comércio (SEIC), Secretaria de Estado de Desenvolvimento Urbano (SEDUR) e Companhia do Pólo Petroquímico do Estado do Rio de Janeiro (COPPERJ).

"Plano diretor do Rio." *Jornal do Brasil.* Rio de Janeiro, January 15, 1991.

Preece, Martha. 1992. "Urbanization and Vulnerability in Brazil: The Current Challenges." In Alcira Kreimer and Mohan Munasinghe, eds., 1992, *Environmental Management and Urban Vulnerability.* World Bank Discussion Paper No. 168. Washington, D.C.: World Bank.

Prefeitura do Rio de Janeiro. 1991. Secretaria de Urbanismo e Meio Ambiente. Plano Diretor da Cidade do Rio de Janeiro.

"Prefeitura quer assumir o Metrô antes do fim do ano." *O Globo.* Rio de Janeiro, April 12, 1992.

"Prefeitura vai investir no Metrô." *O Globo.* Rio de Janeiro, November 19, 1991.

Programa de Geoquímica Ambiental. 1991. *10 Anos de Pesquisa em Meio Ambiente.* Niterói, Brazil: Universidade Federal Fluminense (UFF).

Reps, W. F., and E. Simiu. 1974. *Design, Siting, and Construction of Low-Cost Housing and Community Buildings to Better Withstand Earthquakes and Windstorms.* Washington, D.C.: U.S.

Department of Commerce, National Bureau of Standards.

Ribeiro, Maurício Andrés. 1991. "A crise ambiental urbana brasileira." Belo Horizonte, mimeo, p. 36.

Riebsame, William. 1990. "Climate Hazards, Global Climate Change, and Development." Paper presented at the Colloquium on the Environment and Natural Disaster Management, June 27-28, 1990, World Bank, Washington, D.C.

Rio de Janeiro. Secretaria de Planejamento e Coordenação Geral. 1975. *1° Plano de Desenvolvimento Econômico e Social do Estado do Rio de Janeiro.* Rio de Janeiro, p. 725.

Rio de Janeiro. Secretaria Municipal de Administração. 1991. *Meio Ambiente: legislação; ementário seletivo.* Rio de Janeiro, SDO, p. 89.

Santos, Marcio Miller, and Luiz Fernando Rodrigues de Paula. 1989. "Análise da Política de Saneamento no Brasil." In *A Política Social em Tempo de Crise, Volume III.* Brasília: Ministério da Previdéncia e Assisténcia Social.

Satterthwaite, David. 1989. "Guide to the Literature: Environmental Problems of Third World Cities." *Environment and Urbanization* 1(1):76-83, April.

Schramm, Gunter, and Jeremy J. Warford, eds. 1989. *Environmental Management and Economic Development.* Washington, D.C.: World Bank.

Serra, José, and José R. Afonso. 1991. "Finanças públicas municipais— trajetória & mitos." *Revista Conjuntura Econômica* 45(10-11). Rio de Janeiro: FGV, October-November.

Shah, Anwar. 1990. "The New Fiscal Federalism in Brazil." Working Paper WPS 557. Washington, D.C.: World Bank, December.

Shah, Haresh C. 1990. "Earthquake Risk Management Systems for Developing Countries." Paper presented at the

Colloquium on the Environment and Natural Disaster Management, June 27-28, 1990, World Bank, Washington, D.C.

Silveira, Ricardo, and Stephen Malpezzi, 1991. "Welfare Analysis of Rent Control in Brazil: The Case of Rio de Janeiro." INU Discussion Paper No. INU 83, June. Washington, D.C.: World Bank.

Silveira, Sandra, and Fernando S. P. Sant'Anna. 1990. "Poluição hídrica." In Sérgio Margulis, ed., *Meio Ambiente: Aspectos Técnicos e Econômicos.* Brasília: IPEA/PNUD, pp. 85-108.

Smith, B. J., and R. W. Magee. 1990. "Granite Weathering in an Urban Environment: An Example from Rio de Janeiro." *Singapore Journal of Tropical Geography* 2(2).

Sochaczewski, Antonio Claudio. 1988. "Discurso de transmissão de Cargo."

State of Rio de Janeiro. 1989. *National Basic Sanitation Survey.* Rio de Janeiro.

Tanzi, Vito, et al. 1992. "Brazil: Issues for Fundamental Tax Reform." Washington, D.C.: IMF, Fiscal Affairs Dept., April.

Tollison, R. 1982. "Rent Seeking: A Survey." *Kyklos* 35(4):575-602.

Tullock, G. 1986. "Industrial Organization and Rent Seeking in Dictatorships" *Journal of Institutional and Theoretical Economics* 142:4-15.

Turkish National Committee for the International Decade for Natural Disaster Reduction. 1989. *National Plan of Brazil 1990-2000.* Ankara: Ministry of Public Works and Settlement.

The Urban Edge. 1991. "Rio: Big City, Big Mudslides, Floods." Washington, D.C.: World Bank, September/October.

Valentini, Enise, and Claudio F. Neves. 1989. "The Coastline of Rio de Janeiro from a Coastal Engineering Point of View." Paper presented at the Sixth

Symposium of Coastal and Ocean Management, Charleston, S.C., July 11-14.

Varian, H. 1975. "Distributive Justice, Welfare Economics and the Theory of Fairness." *Philosophy and Public Affairs* 4:223-247.

"Venda de terrenos pagará obras do Metrô." *O Globo*. Rio de Janeiro, March 4, 1989.

Viana, Solon, et al. 1991. "O financiamento da descentralização dos serviços de saúde." Documento de Política no. 3. Brasília: IPEA, April.

Wagener, Angela R. 1992. "Química Ambiental na PUC/RJ." Rio de Janeiro: PUC/RJ, Departamento de Química.

Wertheim, Pirola, and Marcio Miller Santos. 1990. "Resettlement of Population: A Challenge to the Drainage Works in Rio de Janeiro." *Anais do Congresso Metropolis '90*. Melbourne, Australia, October 15-16, 1990.

World Bank. 1992. "Project Performance Audit Report. Brazil: Third Urban Transport Project, Recife Metropolitan Region Development Project, Parana Market Towns Improvement Project, Northeast Urban Flood Reconstruction Project." OED draft report, March 27. Washington, D.C.: World Bank.

World Bank. 1992. "World Bank Approaches to the Environment in Brazil: A Review of Selected Projects." Vol. I, *Overview*; Vol. II, *Pollution Control in São Paulo*; Vol. III, *The Carajas Iron Ore Project*; Vol. IV, *The Middle and Lower San Francisco Valley*; Vol. V, *The POLONORESTE Program*. OED Report No. 10039, April 30. Washington, D.C.: World Bank.

World Bank. 1991. "Brazil: Economic Stabilization with Structural Reforms." LA1CO Report No. 8371-BR, January 31. Washington, D.C.: World Bank.

World Bank. 1991. "Urban Policy and Economic Development: An Agenda for the 1990s." World Bank Policy Paper. Washington, D.C.: World Bank.

World Bank. 1989. "Brazil: Adult Health in Brazil: Adjusting to New Challenges." LA1BR Report No. 7807-BR, November 14. Washington, D.C.: World Bank.

World Bank. 1988. "Brazil: Public Spending on Social Programs: Issues and Options." Report No. 7086-BR, vol. II, May 27. Washington, D.C.: World Bank.

Xavier, Hélia Nacif. 1992. "Questões urbanas e questões ambientais." In *Revista de Administração Municipal*, April/June. Rio de Janeiro: IBAM.

Abbreviations and Acronyms

ANPET	-	Associação Nacional de Pesquisa e Engenharia de Transporte
BID	-	Banco Interamericano de Desenvolvimento
BIRD	-	Banco Internacional para Reconstrução e Desenvolvimento
BNDES	-	Banco Nacional de Desenvolvimento Econômico e Social
BNH	-	Banco Nacional da Habitação [National Housing Bank]
CBTU	-	Companhia Brasileira de Trens Urbanos [Brazilian Urban Rail Company]
CEDAE	-	Companhia Estadual de Águas e Esgotos
CEF	-	Caixa Econômica Federal
CEHAB	-	Companhia Estadual de Habitação
CIDE	-	Centro de Informações e Dados do Rio de Janeiro
CNDU	-	National Urban Development Council
COMLURB	-	Companhia Municipal de Limpeza Urbana
CONERJ	-	Companhia de Navegação do Estado do Rio de Janeiro
CODIN	-	Companhia de Distritos Industriais
COPPERJ	-	Companhia do Pólo Petroquímico do Estado do Rio de Janeiro
CTC	-	Companhia de Transportes Coletivos
DNOS	-	Departamento Nacional de Obras de Saneamento
EBTU	-	Empresa Brasileira de Trens Urbanos [Brazilian Urban Transport Company]
EMPLASA	-	Empresa Metropolitana de Planejamento da Grande São Paulo S.A.
ENVPR	-	Divisão de Pesquisa e Política Ambiental
ETE	-	Estação de Tratamento de Esgoto
FEEMA	-	Fundação Estadual de Engenharia do Meio Ambiente
FGTS	-	Fundo de Garantia do Tempo de Serviço
FUNDREM	-	Fundação para o Desenvolvimento da Região Metropolitana do Rio de Janeiro
GEDEG	-	Grupo Executivo de Despoluição da Baía de Guanabara
GEIPOT	-	Brazilian Transport Planning Agency
GEROE	-	Grupo Executivo para a Recuperação e Obras de Emergência
IBAM	-	Instituto Brasileiro de Administração Municipal
INCRA	-	Instituto Nacional de Colonização e Reforma Agrária
IPLAN-RIO	-	Instituto Municipal de Planejamento do Rio de Janeiro
LBA	-	Legião Brasileira de Assistência
MAS	-	Ministério da Ação Social [Ministry of Social Welfare]
MDU	-	Ministry of Urban Development and the Environment
METRÔ	-	Companhia do Metropolitano do Rio de Janeiro
MINTER	-	Ministry of the Interior
NGO	-	nongovernmental organization
ONG	-	Organização Não Governamental
PESZO	-	Programa Especial de Saneamento da Zona Oeste
PMC	-	Projeto Megacidades

PROBASE	-	Programa de Ação em Infra-Estrutura Urbana Básica
PRODEC	-	Programa de Desenvolvimento Comunitário
PROMORAR	-	Programa de Erradicação das Sub-Moradias nas Favelas
PRO-RIO	-	Programa de Reconstrução e Defesa Contra Inundações de Áreas do Estado do Rio de Janeiro
PROSANEAR	-	Programa de Saneamento para População de Baixa Renda
PROSEGE	-	Programa Social de Emergência e Geração de Empregos
REDUC	-	Refinaria Duque de Caxias
RMRJ	-	Região Metropolitana do Rio de Janeiro
SECPLAN	-	Secretaria de Estado de Planejamento e Controle
SEDUR	-	Secretaria de Estado de Desenvolvimento Urbano e Regional
SERLA	-	Superintendência Estadual de Rios e Lagoas
SEIC	-	Secretaria de Estado de Indústria e Comércio
SMDS	-	Secretaria Municipal de Desenvolvimento Social
SNS	-	Secretaria Nacional de Saneamento
UFRJ	-	Universidade Federal do Rio de Janeiro
UNCED	-	United Nations Conference on the Environment
UNDP	-	United Nations Development Programme
ZEI	-	Zona de Uso Exclusivamente Industrial
ZUPI	-	Zona de Uso Predominantemente Industrial

Distributors of World Bank Publications

ARGENTINA
Carlos Hirsch, SRL
Galeria Guemes
Florida 165, 4th Floor-Ofc. 453/465
1333 Buenos Aires

**AUSTRALIA, PAPUA NEW GUINEA,
FIJI, SOLOMON ISLANDS,
VANUATU, AND WESTERN SAMOA**
D.A. Books & Journals
648 Whitehorse Road
Mitcham 3132
Victoria

AUSTRIA
Gerold and Co.
Graben 31
A-1011 Wien

BANGLADESH
Micro Industries Development
 Assistance Society (MIDAS)
House 5, Road 16
Dhanmondi R/Area
Dhaka 1209

Branch offices:
156, Nur Ahmed Sarak
Chittagong 4000

76, K.D.A. Avenue
Kulna 9100

BELGIUM
Jean De Lannoy
Av. du Roi 202
1060 Brussels

CANADA
Le Diffuseur
C.P. 85, 1501B rue Ampère
Boucherville, Québec
J4B 5E6

CHILE
Invertec IGT S.A.
Americo Vespucio Norte 1165
Santiago

CHINA
China Financial & Economic
 Publishing House
8, Da Fo Si Dong Jie
Beijing

COLOMBIA
Infoenlace Ltda.
Apartado Aereo 34270
Bogota D.E.

COTE D'IVOIRE
Centre d'Edition et de Diffusion
Africaines (CEDA)
04 B.P. 541
Abidjan 04 Plateau

CYPRUS
Cyprus College Bookstore
6, Diogenes Street, Engomi
P.O. Box 2006
Nicosia

DENMARK
SamfundsLitteratur
Rosenoerns Allé 11
DK-1970 Frederiksberg C

DOMINICAN REPUBLIC
Editora Taller, C. por A.
Restauración e Isabel la Católica 309
Apartado de Correos 2190 Z-1
Santo Domingo

EGYPT, ARAB REPUBLIC OF
Al Ahram
Al Galaa Street
Cairo

The Middle East Observer
41, Sherif Street
Cairo

FINLAND
Akateeminen Kirjakauppa
P.O. Box 128
SF-00101 Helsinki 10

FRANCE
World Bank Publications
66, avenue d'Iéna
75116 Paris

GERMANY
UNO-Verlag
Poppelsdorfer Allee 55
D-5300 Bonn 1

HONG KONG, MACAO
Asia 2000 Ltd.
46-48 Wyndham Street
Winning Centre
2nd Floor
Central Hong Kong

INDIA
Allied Publishers Private Ltd.
751 Mount Road
Madras - 600 002

Branch offices:
15 J.N. Heredia Marg
Ballard Estate
Bombay - 400 038

13/14 Asaf Ali Road
New Delhi - 110 002

17 Chittaranjan Avenue
Calcutta - 700 072

Jayadeva Hostel Building
5th Main Road Gandhinagar
Bangalore - 560 009

3-5-1129 Kachiguda Cross Road
Hyderabad - 500 027

Prarthana Flats, 2nd Floor
Near Thakore Baug, Navrangpura
Ahmedabad - 380 009

Patiala House
16-A Ashok Marg
Lucknow - 226 001

Central Bazaar Road
60 Bajaj Nagar
Nagpur 440010

INDONESIA
Pt. Indira Limited
Jl. Sam Ratulangi 37
P.O. Box 181
Jakarta Pusat

IRELAND
Government Supplies Agency
4-5 Harcourt Road
Dublin 2

ISRAEL
Yozmot Literature Ltd.
P.O. Box 56055
Tel Aviv 61560

ITALY
Licosa Commissionaria Sansoni SPA
Via Duca Di Calabria, 1/1
Casella Postale 552
50125 Firenze

JAPAN
Eastern Book Service
Hongo 3-Chome, Bunkyo-ku 113
Tokyo

KENYA
Africa Book Service (E.A.) Ltd.
Quaran House, Mfangano Street
P.O. Box 45245
Nairobi

KOREA, REPUBLIC OF
Pan Korea Book Corporation
P.O. Box 101, Kwangwhamun
Seoul

MALAYSIA
University of Malaya Cooperative
 Bookshop, Limited
P.O. Box 1127, Jalan Pantai Baru
59700 Kuala Lumpur

MEXICO
INFOTEC
Apartado Postal 22-860
14060 Tlalpan, Mexico D.F.

NETHERLANDS
De Lindeboom/InOr-Publikaties
P.O. Box 202
7480 AE Haaksbergen

NEW ZEALAND
EBSCO NZ Ltd.
Private Mail Bag 99914
New Market
Auckland

NIGERIA
University Press Limited
Three Crowns Building Jericho
Private Mail Bag 5095
Ibadan

NORWAY
Narvesen Information Center
Book Department
P.O. Box 6125 Etterstad
N-0602 Oslo 6

PAKISTAN
Mirza Book Agency
65, Shahrah-e-Quaid-e-Azam
P.O. Box No. 729
Lahore 54000

PERU
Editorial Desarrollo SA
Apartado 3824
Lima 1

PHILIPPINES
International Book Center
Suite 1703, Cityland 10
Condominium Tower 1
Ayala Avenue, Corner H.V. dela
 Costa Extension
Makati, Metro Manila

POLAND
International Publishing Service
Ul. Piekna 31/37
00-677 Warzawa

For subscription orders:
IPS Journals
Ul. Okrezna 3
02-916 Warszawa

PORTUGAL
Livraria Portugal
Rua Do Carmo 70-74
1200 Lisbon

SAUDI ARABIA, QATAR
Jarir Book Store
P.O. Box 3196
Riyadh 11471

**SINGAPORE, TAIWAN,
MYANMAR, BRUNEI**
Information Publications
 Private, Ltd.
Golden Wheel Building
41, Kallang Pudding, #04-03
Singapore 1334

SOUTH AFRICA, BOTSWANA
For single titles:
Oxford University Press
 Southern Africa
P.O. Box 1141
Cape Town 8000

For subscription orders:
International Subscription Service
P.O. Box 41095
Craighall
Johannesburg 2024

SPAIN
Mundi-Prensa Libros, S.A.
Castello 37
28001 Madrid

Librería Internacional AEDOS
Consell de Cent, 391
08009 Barcelona

SRI LANKA AND THE MALDIVES
Lake House Bookshop
P.O. Box 244
100, Sir Chittampalam A.
 Gardiner Mawatha
Colombo 2

SWEDEN
For single titles:
Fritzes Fackboksforetaget
Regeringsgatan 12, Box 16356
S-103 27 Stockholm

For subscription orders:
Wennergren-Williams AB
P. O. Box 1305
S-171 25 Solna

SWITZERLAND
For single titles:
Librairie Payot
1, rue de Bourg
CH 1002 Lausanne

For subscription orders:
Librairie Payot
Service des Abonnements
Case postale 3312
CH 1002 Lausanne

TANZANIA
Oxford University Press
P.O. Box 5299
Maktaba Road
Dar es Salaam

THAILAND
Central Department Store
306 Silom Road
Bangkok

**TRINIDAD & TOBAGO, ANTIGUA
BARBUDA, BARBADOS,
DOMINICA, GRENADA, GUYANA,
JAMAICA, MONTSERRAT, ST.
KITTS & NEVIS, ST. LUCIA,
ST. VINCENT & GRENADINES**
Systematics Studies Unit
#9 Watts Street
Curepe
Trinidad, West Indies

TURKEY
Infotel
Narlabahçe Sok. No. 15
Cagaloglu
Istanbul

UNITED KINGDOM
Microinfo Ltd.
P.O. Box 3
Alton, Hampshire GU34 2PG
England

VENEZUELA
Libreria del Este
Aptdo. 60.337
Caracas 1060-A

171392

This book is to be returned on or before
the last date stamped below.

04 JUN 1996   19 MAR 2002

27 APR 2007

-4 OCT 1996
3 1 JAN 1997

23 APR 1997

14|5|97

2 5 MAY 1999

- 1 JUN 2001

KREIMER   171392

L. I. H. E.
THE BECK LIBRARY
WOOLTON RD., LIVERPOOL, L16 8ND